# From Darkness unto LIGHT

## Joseph Smith's Translation and Publication of the Book of Mormon

Michael Hubbard MacKay and Gerrit J. Dirkmaat

Foreword by Richard Lyman Bushman

Published by the Religious Studies Center, Brigham Young University, Provo, Utah, in cooperation with Deseret Book Company, Salt Lake City.
Visit us at rsc.byu.edu.

© 2015 by Brigham Young University. All rights reserved.

Printed in the United States of America by Sheridan Books, Inc.

Deseret Book is a registered trademark of Deseret Book Company.
Visit us at DeseretBook.com.

Any uses of this material beyond those allowed by the exemptions in US copyright law, such as section 107, "Fair Use," and section 108, "Library Copying," require the written permission of the publisher, Religious Studies Center, 185 HGB, Brigham Young University, Provo, Utah 84602. The views expressed herein are the responsibility of the authors and do not necessarily represent the position of Brigham Young University or the Religious Studies Center.

ISBN: 978-0-8425-2888-7
Retail US: $24.99

Cover design by Madison Swapp
Interior design by Madison Swapp

Front cover photo by Gerrit J. Dirkmaat

Library of Congress Cataloging-in-Publication Data

MacKay, Michael Hubbard.
 From darkness unto light : Joseph Smith's translation and publication of the Book of Mormon / Michael Hubbard MacKay and Gerrit J. Dirkmaat ; foreword by Richard Lyman Bushman.
   pages cm
 Includes bibliographical references and index.
 ISBN 978-0-8425-2888-7
 1. Book of Mormon--History. I. Title.
 BX8627.M245 2015
 289.3'22--dc23
                              2014046675

# Contents

| | | |
|---|---|---|
| | Foreword | v |
| | Introduction | ix |
| 1. | Retrieving the Plates | 1 |
| 2. | Escaping Palmyra and Copying Characters from the Gold Plates | 25 |
| 3. | Harris's Trip to the East | 39 |
| 4. | Learning to Translate | 61 |
| 5. | Translation and the Lost Book of Lehi | 79 |
| 6. | Returning to the Translation | 105 |
| 7. | Oliver Cowdery and the Translation of the Book of Mormon | 119 |
| 8. | Witnesses of the Gold Plates | 141 |
| 9. | Negotiating with Printers | 163 |
| 10. | Paying for the Book of Mormon: Doctrine and Covenants Section 19 | 181 |
| 11. | The Publication of the Book of Mormon | 199 |
| 12. | Conclusion | 225 |
| | Appendix: By the Gift and Power of Art | 229 |
| | About the Authors | 245 |
| | Acknowledgments | 246 |
| | Index | 247 |

*Replicas of the gold plates, spectacles, and breastplate. Photo by Gerrit J. Dirkmaat.*

# Foreword

This volume is the first of what could be many potential histories coming out of the Joseph Smith Papers Project. Michael Hubbard MacKay and Gerrit Dirkmaat have been editors of the Documents series, which is just beginning to appear. The results of this research can be partially found in the introductions, headnotes, and footnotes of *The Joseph Smith Papers* volumes, but the findings will be properly valued only when integrated into the narrative of early Church history. Only then will readers grasp what the new discoveries mean. The two authors have done just that for Joseph Smith's early years from the recovery of the plates in September 1827 through the publication of the Book of Mormon in March 1830.

Books like this one will bring Latter-day Saint readers up to date on the results of the latest historical research. While, like all histories, *From Darkness unto Light* is necessarily an interpretation, the authors base their story firmly on the original sources. They get down to what historians consider to be the bedrock of historical construction. Working from original materials, the authors introduce readers to aspects of early Church history that are well known to historians but that are not necessarily common knowledge in the Church. MacKay and Dirkmaat also reveal brand new findings in this work. They speak at length, for example, about Joseph Smith's use of two seer stones in translation. In translating, Joseph probably first used the stones set in spectacles that came with the plates, and then, for most of the translation period, substituted one of the stones he had found. Joseph put the seer stone in a hat to exclude the light and read off the translated text by looking in the stone. All the while, the plates lay wrapped in a cloth on the table. Apparently Joseph did not look at the plates through most of the translation.

This description will startle Latter-day Saints who are familiar with artistic depictions showing Joseph Smith translating with a finger on the plates while he writes down the words as they come to him. The image of Joseph with his face in the hat as he translates is not so well known and is much less decorous, which may shock some readers. But it is essential that the Church at large become aware of what historians have discovered in the sources. Failure to acknowledge these factual accounts, almost all of them in friendly sources, can devastate Latter-day Saints who run across them. Feeling that the Church has covered up the truth, they become disillusioned and even angry. This book is an attempt to repair the misconceptions so that the next generation of Latter-day Saints will be better informed.

For years Mormon scholars simply disregarded critical sources, such as the affidavits concerning the Smith family in E. D. Howe's *Mormonism Unvailed*. They felt the critical writings were too biased to be of any use. But in recent years, automatic exclusion of negative reports is no longer the practice. Everything has to be examined and evaluated. MacKay and Dirkmaat work on the principle that bias must be taken into account in analyzing any historical source. The art of the historian is to extract useful information from original sources whether negative or positive. The notes of *From Darkness unto Light* show the authors ranging through sources all across the spectrum. The result is a much enriched and compelling narrative, one that will hold up under critical scrutiny.

In the book's pages, one can almost hear MacKay and Dirkmaat debating the implications of the evidence they turn up. What does this mean? Are we assuming too much? What about the contradictory evidence? Good documentary editors pursue details that most historians overlook or cannot spare the time to investigate: how much profit E. B. Grandin was going to make on publication of the Book of Mormon, for example. Was he

# FOREWORD

dependent on sales of the book to recover his costs? Did he lose money? The authors find that the price he charged—$3,000 for 5,000 copies—promised him far more than the 12 percent printers customarily hoped for. Grandin's projected profit was 33 percent above his costs. Furthermore, once the expenditure was secured by a mortgage on Martin Harris's farm, Grandin was home free. He sold the mortgage to a wealthy Palmyran, Thomas Rogers, for $2,000—enough to assure him his 12 percent profit—and Rogers in turn resold it soon after for $3,000. Everyone benefited financially, save for Harris, who lost his farm. The book pokes into corners like that where no one has looked before.

Some of the investigations have had lasting effect. The search for Martin Harris's mortgage to E. B. Grandin in August 1829, for example, has affected the dating of section 19 of the Doctrine and Covenants. The revelation, which warns Harris of the dangers of refusing to finance publication of the Book of Mormon, has for a long time been dated March 1830, but the insistence on Harris's support in 1830 made no sense coming seven months after he had already mortgaged his farm in 1829. Careful examination of the various versions of section 19 revealed that the date was placed in parentheses in the original printing, indicating the compilers' uncertainty about its accuracy. Over time the parentheses were omitted, and March 1830 was accepted as fact. Now that mistake has been corrected. The most recent edition of the Doctrine and Covenants changes the date of section 19 to summer 1829 in keeping with the new knowledge about Harris's mortgage.

While *From Darkness unto Light* tells a familiar story, enough new information is injected along the line to hold the attention of the most well-informed readers. Everyone knows about the "Caractors" copied from the plates for the inspection of the East Coast scholars Samuel Mitchill and Charles Anthon. MacKay and Dirkmaat have found evidence of many such copies circulating among the Church members in the early years. They were used to arouse interest and to substantiate the reality of the translation. The characters were copied onto paper used to wrap the text of the Book of Mormon as it went off to the press. They remind us of the fact that Martin Harris and Joseph Smith did not know the characters were Egyptian until after Harris's New York expedition in February 1828. The language of the plates could not have come to light until after translation began in March 1828. Before that time, Harris and Smith were more likely to think the characters were ancient American, some variety of an Indian language. They went to Mitchill because he was the country's expert on Indian dialects and likely to Charles Anthon, best known as a classicist, because he also collected Indian oratory. The authors further suggest that Joseph was not sure at first if he was the one to translate the plates at all. He told Joseph Knight he wanted the plates translated, but at first he may have assumed a learned person would do it. The passage from Isaiah 29 struck him with such force because it declared that an unlearned person was to translate.

Readers of the book will find enlightenment on each page. The narrative gives us access to the new knowledge they developed at the Joseph Smith Papers Project. The *Papers* are establishing a standard of historical truth for the Church based on the thorough research and seasoned judgment of the editors. Everything that goes into the annotation of *The Joseph Smith Papers* has been debated, reviewed, and evaluated. The work of MacKay and Dirkmaat is very much their own and does not have an official stamp of approval, but it represents the breadth of new knowledge soon to be available to Church members and people everywhere as the *Papers* volumes appear.

Richard Lyman Bushman
Provo, Utah

# Introduction

In November 1845, the Apostle Wilford Woodruff reflected thoughtfully on his life in the pages of his journal. He wrote, "I . . . have read the Book of Mormon much during the Last twelve years of my life And my soul delighteth much in its words teaching and Prophesyings And in its Plainness. I rejoice in the goodness and mercy of the God of Israel In Preserving the precious Book of Mormon & bringing it to light in our day & generation. It teaches the honest & humble mind the great things of God that were performed in the land of promise now called America in Ancient days And also the great things of God that are nigh even at the doors." Referring to the book as "this Precious treasure," Woodruff testified of the prophecies contained in it and of Joseph Smith, who had translated the work by the power of God.

Woodruff marveled that so many people had come to embrace the Book of Mormon in such a short time. In only fifteen years, thousands of men and women had, like himself, undergone a powerful religious transformation because of the Book of Mormon and Joseph Smith's teachings. "The commencment of this great work & dispensation," he wrote, "was like a grain of mustard seed even small. The Plates containing the Book of

❖ FROM DARKNESS UNTO LIGHT

Mormon was revealed to Joseph Smith & deliverd unto him By an Angel of God in the month of September 1827 & translated through the Urim & Thum-mim into the English language by Joseph Smith the Prophet Seer & revelator who was raised up out of the loins of Ancient Joseph to esstablish this work in the last days."[1]

Woodruff's personal journey of faith had begun years earlier as he searched for truth among the various competing religious claims made by Christian sects during the Second Great Awakening. When Woodruff heard a Mormon elder, Zera Pulsipher, preach in a public meeting in late December 1833 about Joseph Smith and the Book of Mormon, he "felt the spirit of God to bear witness" that his search for truth had come to an end. He wrote, "I truly felt that it was the first gospel sermon that I had ever herd. I thought it was what I had long been looking for." He was baptized, and his journal captured his thoughts about the Book of Mormon: "I believed it was light out of darkness and truth out of the ground."[2]

The centrality of the Book of Mormon and its prophetic translation to Woodruff's personal testimony only grew with time. Eight years later, he wrote with reverence and awe about a meeting of several of the Apostles during which "Joseph the Seer . . . unfolded unto them many glorious things of the kingdom of God." As part of that meeting Woodruff and others were shown the very seer stone that Joseph had used to translate much of the Book of Mormon, and Woodruff exulted, "I had the privilege of seeing for the first time in my day the URIM & THUMMIM."[3]

Wilford Woodruff's conversion to the Mormon faith came years after Joseph Smith no longer had the gold plates in his possession. Unlike John Whitmer and Hiram Page, Woodruff never got to heft, feel, or examine the plates to know that they were real. Unlike David Whitmer and Oliver Cowdery, Woodruff did not see the angel deliver Joseph the plates or witness the miraculous power by which Joseph Smith rendered the inscrutable hieroglyphics into English so they could be read. He only saw the seer stone used to translate the Book of Mormon years after his conversion. Like so many modern-day Mormons, Woodruff had to take the explanations of the Book of Mormon, the gold plates, and the translation process on faith. But as the above quotes from Woodruff demonstrate, these explanations of the translation process came to be not only a part of his faith but a pillar of it. He believed Joseph was indeed the Lord's seer because of the

## INTRODUCTION

great translation work he had performed using the instruments that God had prepared centuries earlier.

However, Woodruff, again like so many believers in the Book of Mormon today, was very much in the minority with his choice to accept the claims made by Joseph Smith of the record's divine nature and origin. Not everyone greeted the prophetic claims of Joseph Smith and the Book of Mormon with such welcoming arms. In August 1829, a Palmyra newspaperman, Jonathan Hadley, published the earliest known account of the retrieval and translation of the gold plates. A bitter skeptic of a book that was about to be published by the competing publisher in Palmyra, Hadley railed on Smith's claims as the "greatest piece of superstition that has ever come within the sphere of our knowledge." Hadley met the idea that Joseph Smith had found the "Gold Bible" with doubt and disdain. He repeated with incredulity the story he had been told about how Joseph had been "visited by the spirit of the Almighty" and told that a nearby hill contained an "ancient record of a divine nature and origin." He informed his readers that the "leaves of the Bible were plates of gold, about eight inches long, six wide, and one eighth of an inch think, on which were engraved characters or hieroglyphics." Hadley further reported that Smith had translated the plates by the means of spectacles found with them and that the book was "soon to be published" in Palmyra. With derision he added how dubious it was that "a person like this Smith (very illiterate) should have been gifted by inspiration to find and interpret it."[4]

From Hadley's first published derisive account of the translation of the Book of Mormon to Wilford Woodruff's total acceptance of it as a gift of God to a shattered, broken, and sinful world, detractors and embracers of the faith have focused on the Book of Mormon as central to the foundation of the religion. When the anti-Mormon author Eber D. Howe, desperate to discredit a faith that his sister and wife had already joined, hired an excommunicated member in 1833 to provide evidence that would destroy the movement, he focused on the origin of the Book of Mormon. Notwithstanding such opposition, in late 1841 Woodruff recorded Joseph Smith's testimony of the book: "Joseph Said the Book of Mormon was the most correct of any Book on Earth & the key stone of our religion & a man would get nearer to God by abiding by its precepts than any other Book."[5] Thus for believers and opponents alike, the gold plates and the story of their translation have been and continue to be a key rampart on the battlefield of faith.

This book was written to provide interested inquirers a detailed explanation of how Joseph Smith and the scribes who served with him described the process by which the gold plates were translated into English and the difficulties encountered as they sought to publish the completed book. Although both members and academics alike often think of this story as well known, recent insights and discoveries associated with the efforts by the Church History Department to annotate and publish *The Joseph Smith Papers* have provided a fuller, richer understanding of the translation and publication of the Book of Mormon. This book will follow what will often seem like the very familiar story of Joseph Smith's efforts from 1827 to 1830, but it will diverge at times to provide the reader with new and significant details about these formative years of Mormonism. Interested readers will find many exciting and new things in the book.

While working as historians and editors of the Joseph Smith Papers Project, we found that newly discovered sources and a closer examination of existing ones revealed a much more nuanced and profound story about the process of translation than has generally been represented in the past. Many of these new ideas and discoveries have been published in *Documents, Volume 1* of *The Joseph Smith Papers,* but only within the brief introduction to the volume and the annotation of various documents contained in it. The research performed in regards to that volume and other volumes of the Joseph Smith Papers Project was critical to the changes made to the section headings in the 2013 edition of the Doctrine and Covenants of The Church of Jesus Christ of Latter-day Saints. While these changes were generally brief, often involving only a new location or date, the implications of those changes for the historical record are quite significant. At times, the new dating entirely changes the storyline of the translation and publication of the Book of Mormon.

For instance, this book contains a new narrative of the complicated and difficult process Joseph Smith undertook to negotiate with several printers to publish the Book of Mormon. Much of our previous understanding of the steps taken to pay for the printing of Book of Mormon has been altered as a consequence of research that corrected the date of Doctrine and Covenants section 19 from March 1830 to summer 1829. This date change has

INTRODUCTION

far-reaching implications for our understanding of the revelation, Martin Harris, the negotiations with the printers, and the delays associated with printing the Book of Mormon. Though we have presented some of this work in public presentations, this will be the first time that our research has been published in full. Therefore, this book uses that research to tell the whole story behind this foundational event.

Just as these new conclusions surrounding the negotiations were informed by research performed on the Joseph Smith Papers Project, the reexamination of these early documents also revealed a new understanding of how Joseph Smith translated the Book of Mormon. In our work on *Documents, Volume 1*, understanding the Book of Mormon translation was critical to understanding Joseph's early revelations, which were apparently received in the same way the gold plates were translated—via the use of seer stones.

Thus this book expands beyond the scope of the research that we did for the Joseph Smith Papers Project and the Church History Department. This expansion will help readers more fully understand two of the foundational events of Mormonism: Joseph Smith's translation of the gold plates and his publication of the resulting text as the Book of Mormon. Throughout this book, the reader will see the translation process haltingly and unevenly unfold as it did for Joseph Smith from September 1827 to June 1829. This book will show Joseph's struggle to learn to translate and then work through each problem of translation, while looking at the experience of each scribe in his or her own historical setting. It will point readers to the primary sources—the original texts—that inform these conclusions. It will examine and explain these sources in a narrative form that takes seriously the accounts of those that were witnesses to the events.

The actual process by which the Book of Mormon was translated, according to the witnesses of the event and the earliest sources, is generally unknown to members of the Church. Because Joseph Smith only explained that "through the medium of the Urim and Thummim I translated the record by the gift, and power of God," little emphasis has been placed upon the actual process of translation.[6] Although the well-known "History of Joseph Smith" recounts Joseph Smith's explanation of the device found with the plates as being composed of two stones, most artists' renderings depicting these events generally excluded images of the stones entirely, and no

xiii

attempts were made to show the stones being used in the way witnesses described. These artists' paintings powerfully conveyed an image to modern Latter-day Saints of Joseph Smith sitting at a table with the plates in front of him, his finger running over the top of the characters, with Oliver Cowdery dutifully seated across from him taking the dictation down. Thus generations of Mormons have come to imagine the translation process in much the same way reflected in these portrayals, a process by which the miracle of translation occurred by Joseph Smith looking at the plates and speaking a translation to Cowdery without the use of any external tools or the seer stones themselves, despite the testimonies of witnesses that the process occurred very differently. Those witnesses make the use of the stones the central aspect of the translation. They give an account of Joseph Smith placing various seer stones into a hat in order to block out the external light. Then God caused words to appear on the shining stones that translated the reformed Egyptian text into English.

Those who are antagonistic toward the Church and Joseph Smith have used this discrepancy between witnesses of the translation and average members of the Church as a cudgel to beat upon the faith of believers. The very use of these witness statements by antagonistic or disrespectful authors or television programs to create a deprecating image of Joseph Smith has further alienated members from a proper understanding of the translation process. These detractors highlight the apparent ridiculousness of a scene that involves Joseph translating with his head buried in a "magic" hat, knowing that such imagery would offend the sensibilities of twenty-first-century Mormons.

Although the witnesses' explanations of the translation process differ from what is generally understood by Church members, the testimonies of these witnesses affirm that the use of the seer stones—placed as they were in a hat to block out the light so the words of God could be read—was the greatest evidence to them of the miraculous nature of the translation. Detractors make light of the translation process. However, they do so without informing their readers that their very sources for such apparently disdainful evidence stated that because of the use of a seer stone in the translation process, they had a greater testimony of the seership of Joseph Smith.

INTRODUCTION

One way we attempt to deal with the problem of the inaccurate portrayal of the translation process is by adding depictions of the translation to this book. These images were created by Anthony Sweat, assistant professor of Church history and doctrine at Brigham Young University. In addition to skillfully crafted artwork of the events surrounding the translation that more closely align with the testimonies of scribes and witnesses, Sweat has performed detailed and informative research on how images of the translation have been used over time. The appendix of this book contains his exclusive essay, "By the Gift and Power of Art," which will help readers understand where the more well-known images of the translation originated and how their less accurate depictions have come to dominate the LDS imagination when considering the translation of the gold plates.

Our book attempts to capture the first-person point of view of Joseph Smith and those who witnessed the translation and publication of the Book of Mormon. Though we have taken into account the perspectives of detractors and nonbelievers in our analysis, the purpose of our book is to understand the coming forth of the Book of Mormon as a miracle, which can best be understood through the accounts of those closest to the process and by those who believed. To Joseph Smith and his friends and family, the miraculous translation process was a reality. In other words, our approach asks the question "How would Joseph and his family explain to others the translation process?"

Each of the chapters presented in our book offers new material, both in sources and in interpretation. In a mostly narrative format, we examine the primary events in the coming forth of the Book of Mormon from September 1827 to September 1830—only occasionally pausing to note significant changes in the story. This book is intended to bring the reader closer to the most important events in this chronology of events through the eyes of those who experienced them. Its scope does not include larger topics such as the influence of broader religious cultures, nor does it generally attempt to place the coming forth of the Book of Mormon within the context of national trends, politics, or Protestantism, except in those times when it is clear that those broader influences were cognizant to Joseph Smith and his colleagues. This does not mean that we do not contextualize and historicize each account to understand it better, but we do attempt to let those closest to Joseph Smith be heard in their own words, while acknowledging that they had their own biases reflected in their accounts and interpretations.

In many ways, our book is an attempt to recapture the religious value of the translation and publication of the Book of Mormon in the minds of believing members. We are not making claims or an argument about the reality of the plates, nor are we making arguments about the historicity of the plates, which can be found in other publications. Instead, *this book tries to get at the heart of what Joseph Smith and those closest to him believed about the translation and publication of the Book of Mormon.*

Nevertheless, no work of history nor any examination of sources that speak of heavenly manifestations and the visitations of angels can demonstrate the reality of these miraculous events. Miracles are by definition events that cannot be replicated by mortal beings absent of the intervention of God. In this sense, logic and historical method cannot fully prove or disprove the miraculous claims made by Joseph Smith or the scribes who worked with him on the translation. Just as one cannot prove with historical sources or scientific inquiry alone the reality of Jesus Christ's Resurrection or of the efficacy of his Atonement to save men and women from sin and death, faith and belief are the necessary ingredients for one to come to know that Joseph Smith was a prophet of God and that he performed the work of a seer in bringing forth the words of the Book of Mormon from darkness unto light. What historians can demonstrate, however, is how the witnesses to these events explained them, how they understood them, and how they came to believe, as Wilford Woodruff did, that Joseph Smith had been called by God to translate gold plates and publish that translation as the Book of Mormon.

## Notes

1. Wilford Woodruff Journals, 2 November 1845, MS 1352, box 1, folder 1, Church History Library, Salt Lake City; original spelling preserved.
2. Woodruff, Journal, 2 November 1845, MS 1352, box 1, folder 1, Church History Library.
3. Woodruff, Journal, 27 December 1841, MS 1352, box 1, folder 2, Church History Library.
4. "Golden Bible," *Palmyra Freeman*, 11 August 1829.

INTRODUCTION ❖

5. Woodruff, Journal, 28 November 1841, MS 1352, box 1, folder 2, Church History Library.
6. *Times and Seasons* 3, no. 9 (1 March 1842).

xvii

*The plates, breastplate, and spectacles in the Hill Cumorah. Watercolor by Anthony Sweat.*

# 1

# Retrieving the Plates

Joseph Smith declared that he founded The Church of Jesus Christ of Latter-day Saints through "the ministering of Angels" alongside the coming forth of the Book of Mormon. When Joseph looked back upon these events years later, he recorded them in his history, remembering that they all began with his First Vision of Jesus Christ and God the Father in the spring of 1820.[1] In Joseph's mind, it all started that spring when he visited a grove of trees near his home.

## Joseph Smith's First Vision

Joseph became deeply concerned with religion around the boyish age of twelve in late 1816 when the Smiths first arrived in Palmyra. For the first year and a half, the Smiths lived in town, selling oil tablecloths and refreshments from a cart before they began working their own farm. While living in the heart of the township, they witnessed the surge of religion that developed in the area. Four major churches offered religious peace to Palmyra's residents, and with camp revivals scattered across New York State when they first arrived, many people were concerned about their own salvation.

## FROM DARKNESS UNTO LIGHT

The Presbyterians drew the largest crowds in Palmyra, but the Methodists attracted many to their meetings also. Just outside of town, toward Rochester, the Baptists had a well-established meetinghouse. By 1823, the Society of Friends had also built a meetinghouse in Palmyra.[2] With several religious options, the churches eventually divided the Smith household. Lucy Mack Smith and her children Hyrum, Sophronia, and Samuel joined the Western Presbyterian Church in Palmyra, while the other sons held back along with Joseph Sr. In time, Joseph Jr. became "somewhat partial to the Methodist sect," though doubt and confusion filled his mind.[3]

In 1818, they built a small log house on the southern border of Palmyra Township, where Joseph labored with his brothers to help provide for their family. The Smiths uprooted and cleared trees from their land to access the rich New York soil for farming and planting. Yet their daily labor on their farm did not completely consume Joseph's mind nor detract from his interest in religion. In the spring of 1820, Joseph thoughtfully left his parents' cabin to seek solace in a recently cleared grove of trees near his home.[4] Like many revivalists convinced by enthusiastic preaching and Bible study, Joseph turned to God personally in prayer to obtain forgiveness of his sins and to discover whether the Methodist sect was God's true church. As he bowed his head in prayer, he faced resistance from "the power of some actual being from the unseen world," which momentarily inhibited Joseph's ability to call upon God, until a pillar of light descended from heaven and rested upon him.[5]

In giving an account of this vision in 1838, Joseph remembered the personal significance of that event. He explained that two beings descended from heaven, and one said, "This is my beloved Son, Hear him."[6] Notwithstanding the extraordinary nature of this event, Joseph did not immediately share this experience with his family, nor did he highlight it to the membership of The Church of Jesus Christ of Latter-day Saints before the Church newspaper, *Times and Seasons*, published his history in 1842. His vision remained personal rather than public for years, though he did tell a local Methodist clergyman in 1820. The preacher encouraged Joseph's silence by holding the young boy in contempt for his claims. Others caught up in the revivalist sentiments had told similar stories and claimed they saw heavenly beings, which threatened those who desired similar authority or believed that experiences like Joseph's had ceased since New Testament times.[7]

2

# RETRIEVING THE PLATES

*The Sacred Grove, Manchester, New York. Photo by Brent R. Nordgren.*

Joseph followed the counsel given to him by Jesus Christ during the vision by avoiding membership in any of the local churches.[8] He remembered, "I had now got my mind satisfied so far as the sectarian world was concerned, that it was not my duty to join with any [church], . . . but continue as I was until further directed."[9] He returned to life as usual, clearing property and laboring to help provide for his family, but reported that community members of various religions began persecuting him.

## Visit of Moroni

During this period, Joseph engaged in digging for buried treasure. Residents reported that Native Americans and colonial Spanish explorers had deposited treasures in local mounds and buried coffers. Folk practices like using a divining rod or finding lost items with a peep stone were often employed as part of the broader religious and agrarian cultures of the early nineteenth century. Joseph's father, who saw value in these practices, likely introduced Joseph to them, but his local peers, some of whom possessed their own stones, also searched for buried treasure in and around Palmyra with Joseph.[10] Though these practices were common, the educated classes

❖ FROM DARKNESS UNTO LIGHT

and polite society frowned upon them.[11] Joseph's participation in treasure seeking eventually led to him being charged with disorderly conduct because lawmakers viewed the practice with disdain and were willing to levy misdemeanor charges on participants.[12] Though it is unknown whether he was specifically referring to his money-digging activities, Joseph remembered, "I was left to all kinds of temptations, and mingling with all kinds of society." He declared, "I frequently fell into many foolish errors and displayed the weakness of youth and the corruption of human nature."[13] Whatever those errors or weaknesses may have been, it caused Joseph to seek after God's forgiveness.

He reported that on the evening of 21 September 1823 he prayed in the upper room of his parents' small log cabin. While he was calling upon God, a light slowly filled the room and an angel appeared near his bedside. The angel was a man who called himself Moroni and declared that "God had a work for [Joseph] to do."[14] The angel explained that he had deposited an ancient record in a hill near Joseph's home. Joseph remembered that the angel said the record was "written upon gold plates, giving an account of the former inhabitants of this continent and the source from whence they sprang" and that the plates must be translated.[15]

Joseph Smith's silent prayer for forgiveness in 1823 began like his First Vision. Yet as he conversed with the angel in his bedroom that night the message was a call to action rather than one of realization, as the First Vision had been. The angel declared that "God had a work for [Joseph] to do," explaining that he was not just any ordinary person, but that "he should be had for good and evil among all nations kindreds and tongues." The angel delivered the message with absolute clarity by repeating it three times in three separate visions that evening and the next day. The angel also visited Joseph once a year for four consecutive years from 1824 through 1827.

During the initial and subsequent visits to Joseph, Moroni described the plates as a record of an ancient American people from which Moroni had been the last surviving prophet. He told Joseph that he would take possession of the plates if he remained faithful.[16] After years of waiting, Joseph explained that he went to a hill near his home in Manchester, New York, on 22 September 1827 and retrieved the gold plates.[17]

4

## Joseph's Early Attempts to Get the Plates

Joseph Smith explained in his history that during one of his visits from Moroni, he was told where "the plates were deposited, and owing to the distinctness of the vision which I had had concerning it, I knew the place the instant that I arrived there." Joseph found them on the "most elevated" hill in the area, "under a stone of considerable size . . . in a stone box." Joseph explained that the "stone was thick and rounding in the middle on the upper side, and thinner towards the edges, so that the middle part of it was visible above the ground, but the edge all round was covered with earth." He remembered removing the earth around the stone and using a lever to remove the stone lid. Looking inside the stone box, he saw "the plates, the Urim and Thummin and the Breastplate."[18]

Joseph explained that upon seeing the plates for the first time in 1823, he "made three attempts to get them and . . . cried unto the Lord in the agony of [his] soul why [he could] not obtain them." In response, an angel appeared, informed him he had not "kept the commandments of the Lord" and therefore could not obtain them. Along with chastening, the angel provided Joseph with hope: "repent and call on the Lord [and] thou shalt be forgiven and in

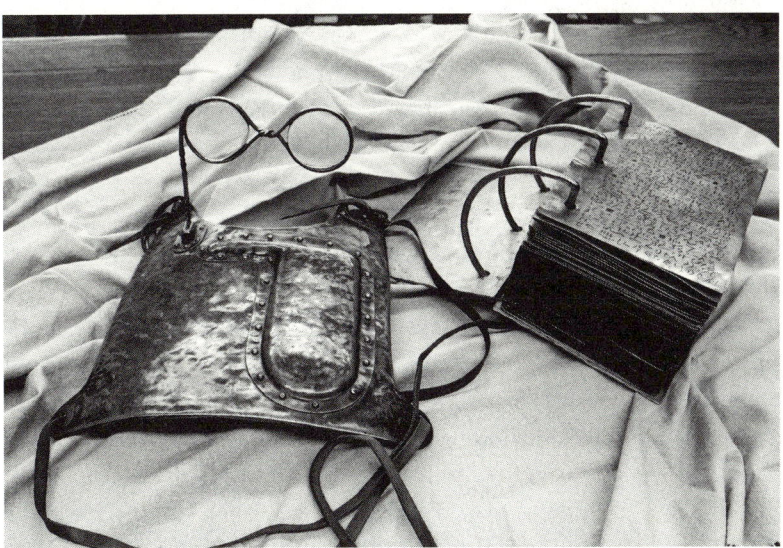

*Replicas of the gold plates, spectacles, and breastplate. Photo by Gerrit J. Dirkmaat.*

5

his own due time thou shalt obtain them." Joseph explained that he had not been able to take the plates at first because he had "been tempted of the advisary and saught the Plates to obtain riches and kept not the commandment that I should have an eye single to the Glory of God." But in the years that followed Joseph had been "chastened and saught diligently to obtain the plates and obtained them not untill I was twenty one years of age."[19]

Joseph kept the visits of the angel secret for the most part. Inevitably, his family and a few close friends found out and anxiously awaited the time when the angel would deliver the plates into Joseph's hands. Joseph Knight Sr., a friend from Colesville, New York, and Josiah Stowell, Joseph's former employer, knew about the visits and traveled to Manchester in late September 1827 to be at the home of Joseph Smith Sr. and Lucy Mack Smith when Joseph Jr. finally retrieved the plates.[20] According to Knight, they made their journey with some trepidation, because although Smith had found the stone box containing the plates in 1823, the angel informed Joseph that if he were not worthy to take the plates in 1827, then he would no longer have the opportunity. According to Knight, if Joseph had done "right according to the will of God," Moroni would finally give him the plates in 1827. This ultimatum kept them in earnest anticipation on the evening of 21 September of that year.[21]

Borrowing Knight's horse and wagon, Smith and his wife, Emma, slipped out of his parents' house in the middle of the night to go to retrieve the plates from the hill after years of anticipation, as commanded by Moroni.[22] Once they arrived at the hill, Emma apparently waited patiently at the bottom while Joseph marched to the top to remove the plates from their hiding place.[23] Not having anything to store the plates in, he pulled them from the ground and stashed them in the woods, rather than taking them home without a covering or a safe place to store them.[24]

Smith explained that "the same heavenly messenger" that delivered the plates also gave him a device that held two stones, which Joseph referred to as "spectacles," and a breastplate to hold the spectacles.[25] According to Lucy Mack Smith, Joseph brought the spectacles home instead of hiding them with the plates, explaining to his mother that "all is right. . . . I have got the key." Lucy remembered that her son handed her the spectacles wrapped only in a silk handkerchief that was thin enough for her to identify the shape and form of the device. She also handled them, demonstrating their physicality as she felt their shape and gazed at the two "smooth stones" bound together in "silver bows" connected with each other like "old fashioned spectacles."²⁶ Joseph selectively showed the spectacles to others within the next two years, but Lucy's account seems to take the experience beyond what one could conjure in the mind's eye and beyond a personal vision.²⁷ With only a transparent handkerchief separating her fingers from the device, she described her experience as physical, and though she never removed the cloth, she remembered seeing through the thin cover.

## Early Efforts to Steal the Plates

Leaving the plates hidden in the woods, Joseph did not initially intend on showing them to anyone, but instead he set out to find a chest or box to keep them in. He later explained that he told his family that "the angel of the Lord says that we must be careful not to proclaim these things or to mention them abroad, for we do not any of us know the weakness of the world, which is so sinful, and that when we get the plates they will want to kill us for the sake of the gold, if they know we have them."²⁸ Joseph Smith's 1838 history declared that "the most strenuous exertions were used to get [the plates] from me."²⁹ He had apparently asked his neighbor Willard Chase, a local carpenter and joiner, twice in September to make a case for him before he retrieved the plates. Chase likely refused because he doubted that Joseph could repay him for the materials and labor.³⁰ Chase remembered Joseph making plans to protect the plates, contemplating the problems that he would face once he had them and knowing that the angel had charged him to keep them hidden. The day Joseph went to the hill to obtain the plates, however, he was still looking for someone to make a box for the plates. Before leaving for the hill, he woke his mother and asked "if [she] had a chest with a lock and key" to store the plates in once he retrieved them, but she had nothing to offer him. Lucy told "him [after he had retrieved the plates] to go to a cabbinet maker who had been making some furniture" for her oldest daughter, Sophronia. Lucy intended to purchase the chest on credit because no one in the family had money to pay for it. She remembered their despondent situation, claiming that they would not be able to pay for the chest, "for there was not a shilling in the house." Instead she negotiated to "pay him for making a chest as [they] did for the other things viz half money [apparently on loan] and half produce."³¹ The next day, Mrs. Wells of Macedon sent for Joseph to work for her digging a well, which Lucy "considered it a provision of Providence to enable us to pay the money we were owing the cabinet maker."³²

Though Joseph tried to keep the plates secret and though only a handful of his friends and family knew about Moroni's visits and Joseph's retrieval of the record, word about the plates slowly got out to local residents in Palmyra. Joseph's inquiry about a chest may have alerted Willard Chase and others to his possession of something valuable, but Moroni had told Joseph not to discuss the plates "abroad." Any of those who knew about the plates and Moroni, including Martin Harris, Lucy Harris, Joseph Knight Sr., Newel Knight, and Josiah Stowell, may have leaked the information to others, possibly even to one of the Smiths.³³

Some of Joseph's neighbors, in particular, felt they were entitled to both see the plates and share in the riches that Joseph could have garnered by their sale. Willard Chase, who knew Joseph personally and had worked with him on occasion, later claimed that the angel told Smith that he could not retrieve the plates until he brought his brother Alvin with him to the hill during one of his annual visits. After Alvin passed away, Chase claimed, the angel commanded Joseph to find another person to assist and that "Joseph believed that one Samuel T. Lawrence [a local resident and fellow money digger] was the man alluded to by the spirit." Chase asserted that Lawrence went with Smith to the hill before 1827 and advised Joseph not to "let these plates be seen for about two years, as it would make a great disturbance in the neighborhood." Chase explained that even though Joseph may have thought Lawrence was to help him retrieve the plates, Joseph instead took his wife, Emma, to the hill in 1827 to obtain them.³⁴

Lawrence may have become embittered after Joseph invited him to the hill to look for the plates, then proceeded to retrieve them without him. Though Chase may have made this connection with Lawrence to perpetuate their claim over the plates, this claim seems possible because the Smiths worried that Lawrence would want to take the plates from Joseph the night he retrieved them. In fact, Joseph Sr. went to Lawrence's house that night in order to stop Lawrence from going to the hill and ambushing Joseph Jr. as he pulled the plates from their hiding place. Knight remembered Joseph directing his father to "stay till near Dark and

RETRIEVING THE PLATES

if he saw any signs of his [Lawrence's] going you [tell] him if I find him there I will trash the stumps with him."³⁵ Lawrence apparently never left his house that night, but these accounts offer the possibility that others knew about the plates and wanted to obtain them for their own profit—some of whom believed they were rightfully their own property, such as Chase and Lawrence.³⁶

After local residents heard that Joseph had found a set of gold plates in Manchester, the possibility of finding treasure attracted numerous others to the hill. Some reportedly went looking for the stone box in which the plates had been entombed. Lorenzo Saunders claimed that he went to the hill only a few days after Joseph retrieved the plates and searched for earth that had been broken in the recent past, but he could not find any. He stated, "There was a large hole where the money diggers had dug a year or two before, but no fresh dirt."³⁷ In an earlier interview, however, he explained that they did not search the whole hill, but only the place "where [Joseph] claimed to g[e]t the plates," allowing for the possibility that Saunders was looking in the wrong spot.³⁸ Even Martin Harris remembered that he went to the hill looking for the stone box. Unlike Saunders, Harris reported that he found the box and he "broke one corner off of the box." He apparently stated, "Some time that box will be found and you will see the corner broken off, then you will know I have told you the truth."³⁹ This Harris account, given near the end of his life, was filled with treasure-digging folklore, such as a claim that he uncovered the box just before it moved deeper into the earth. Without the context of local folklore, David Whitmer explained that others had seen the stone box on the hill. Though he initially thought that the story of the gold plates was only a rumor, he spoke with several young money diggers in Palmyra who claimed to have known where the stone box was located. They told Whitmer that they had seen the "place in the hill that he took them out of."⁴⁰

Compelling stories and news about the plates enveloped local Palmyra residents who had heard about the stone box on the hill. David Whitmer would later state, "I had conversations with several young men who said that Joseph Smith had certainly golden plates." He supposedly asked, "How do you know that Joe Smith has the plates?" after which they replied, "We saw the place in the hill that he took them out of just as he described it to us before he obtained them."⁴¹ Whitmer explained that he was convinced

9

because the money diggers "were so positive" that they had seen the hole and stone box that Smith had taken the plates from. Whitmer remembered, "The community in which he lived was live with excitement in regard to Smith's finding a great treasure, and they informed him that they knew that Smith had the plates, as they had seen the place that he had taken them from, on the hill Cumorah."[42] Local residents expressed confidence in their belief that Joseph had retrieved a set of plates from the hill because the stone box they were taken from was apparently left exposed for decades. In 1893, Edward Stevenson explained after a trip to Palmyra that a local farmer showed him where the stone box once was and that large flat stones had been removed from the hole, "rolled down, and lay near the bottom of the hill."[43] These physical artifacts laid there for years, and the early money diggers seemed to have witnessed the stone box, as it was when Joseph pulled the plates from the stone tomb.

Ironically, while the detractors of Joseph Smith spent the remainder of his life claiming that he had never found any gold plates, had any visitations from angels, or received any visions, Joseph's initial problems with his enemies in 1827 were precisely because they were certain that he had in fact obtained some golden treasure from the hill, and therefore they wanted to take it from him, forcibly if they had no other choice. Those who were most acquainted with Joseph Smith in Palmyra did not doubt he had received the plates but instead took steps to obtain them for themselves or at the very least find remnants of the buried treasure possibly still lying in the hill.

Those who were most anxious to take the plates from Joseph were those who had previously worked with him to find buried treasure in the local area.[44] Joseph, who was hired in 1825 by Josiah Stowell (a friend of the family) to help find buried ore, never hid the fact that he had been involved with the local treasure seekers.[45] Historians have argued that Joseph's association with treasure digging and the use of seer stones prepared him for his larger mission as a prophet and seer.[46] Martin Harris later remembered Joseph's transition away from treasure seeking when "the angel told him he must quit the company of the money diggers, That there were wicked men among them."[47] Even though Joseph removed himself from their company, people like Samuel Lawrence viewed their previous interaction with Joseph as a kind of claim for sharing in the gold plates with him. Yet they had

## RETRIEVING THE PLATES

sorely mistaken Joseph's sacred task of translating the gold plates for his previous secular pursuits.

Referencing the desire of many to share in the treasure, Lucy Smith stated, "It now seemed that satan had stirred up the hearts of those who had in any way got a hint of the matter to search into it and make every possible move towards preventing the work."[48] She explained that Chase gathered approximately a dozen men to find Joseph's initial hiding place for the gold plates. In fact, so desperate were they to uncover the hiding place "they had sent for a conjuror to come 60 miles to divine the place where the record was deposited by magic art."[49] This same story was told over twenty-five years later by Brigham Young, who added that the "conjuror" was "a fortune-teller, a necromancer, an astrologer, a soothsayer, and possessed as much talent as any man that walked on the American soil, and was one of the wickedest men I ever saw."[50] After Chase's conspirators had gathered and began working with Lawrence, Joseph Sr. went to Lawrence's house and through the door heard them scheming about how they would find the plates. Their language was revealing enough that Lawrence's wife, who had seen Joseph Sr. listening in on them, called out to him, "Sam, Sam, . . . you are cutting your own throat." But the conjuror screamed aloud enough for Joseph Sr. to hear, "I am not afraid of any body we will have the plates in spite of Joe Smith or all the Devils in Hell."[51]

Joseph Sr. panicked. He knew Joseph Jr. was in Macedon working for Mrs. Wells, so he quickly returned to his house to ensure that the plates were secure. Not knowing where the plates were, he asked Emma where Joseph had hidden them. Emma did not know where the plates were. Exacerbating their concern that Lawrence would steal the plates, Lucy recalled that Joseph had hidden the plates in a log near the hill where he had retrieved them. Fortunately, Joseph had not left them completely exposed. He had apparently hollowed out the inside of a fallen tree, secreted the plates inside of the log, and then covered the opening with pieces of fallen bark and leaves as a camouflage.[52] This may have provided even more security than reburying the plates would have, because Chase and his group were looking for freshly moved dirt and holes in the ground. Aware of the possible threat, Emma found a horse with Joseph

11

Sr.'s help and rode to Macedon to alert Joseph Jr. of Chase's and Lawrence's plans to find the plates.[53]

Miles away, Joseph was calmly working to earn money to purchase a chest in which to store the plates. Lucy wrote that even before Emma arrived, Joseph was miraculously aware that she was coming. He told her that he knew that the plates were safe. He knew because he had taken the spectacles that he had retrieved along with the plates with him to Macedon. Gazing into them, Smith learned that Emma was on her way to alert him of the threat, but he also saw in the spectacles a vision of the place where he had hidden the plates and knew that Chase had not discovered them. Joseph reassured Emma that "the record was perfectly safe for the present." Nevertheless, he returned with Emma to Manchester. When they arrived, Joseph Sr. was pacing "in great anxiety of mind," but his son assured him that there was no danger of Chase's search party finding the plates. As a precaution, however, they told Hyrum to find a temporary chest to lock the plates in so that Joseph could retrieve them from the birch log and bring them home.[54]

## Bringing the Plates Home

The day after Joseph returned from Macedon, he went to retrieve the plates as both Joseph Smith Sr. and Joseph Knight Sr. scouted the area for signs of the men working with Chase and Lawrence. Joseph traveled three miles to the hill, removed the plates from the log, and then wrapped them in a linen frock. David Whitmer, who later saw the plates, explained that "they appeared to be of gold, about six by nine inches in size, about as thick as parchment, a great many in number, and bound together like the leaves of a book by massive rings passed through the back edges."[55] The plates weighed around fifty pounds, making it difficult for Joseph to walk back to his parents' house with them, let alone run with them if he encountered trouble.[56] He hauled the plates down to the main road leading to Palmyra but quickly realized that anyone who happened to be traveling along that route would see him. Therefore, he left the established road and instead struggled through the woods and underbrush to avoid potential pursuers. Despite his best efforts, however, he was approached by a man "who demanded the plates, and struck him with a club on his side, which was all black and blue."⁵⁷ Lucy explained that the man actually hit Joseph with the stock of his rifle, after which Joseph turned and knocked the man to the ground and ran off as fast as he could, a difficult prospect considering the injury he had sustained and the weight of the plates he was carrying. Lucy went on to explain that after running for a half mile, another unknown man assaulted Joseph. Again escaping, he was attacked by a third person. This time, in trying to defend himself, Joseph struck the marauder so forcefully with his fist that he dislocated his thumb. The force of this blow sent his attacker reeling, and Joseph eventually made it home bruised, wounded, exhausted, and frightened. Katherine Smith, Joseph's sister, later told her relatives that Joseph "came in nearly exhausted, carrying the package of gold plates . . . clasped to his side with his left hand and arm, and his right hand was badly bruised."⁵⁸ Joseph then handed the plates, wrapped in linen, through the house window to Josiah Stowell.⁵⁹

Stowell, who claimed that he was the "first person that took the Plates out of [Joseph Smith's] hands the morning [he] brought them in,"⁶⁰ would have been the first person other than Joseph to feel and heft the plates. As he took the plates from Joseph, he likely felt the contour of the plates, but it was what he saw that made his experience with the plates unique. In the summer of 1830, after Joseph Smith was charged with disorderly conduct, Stowell was called by the defense and sworn in as a witness. He testified under oath that he saw the plates the day Joseph first brought them home. As Joseph passed them through the window, Stowell caught a glimpse of the plates as a portion of the linen was pulled back. Stowell gave the court the dimensions of the plates and explained that they consisted of gold leaves with characters written on each sheet. The printed transcript of the trial read: "witness saw a corner of it; it resembled a stone of a greenish caste." Because Stowell also mentioned in his statement that the record was made of plates of gold, it is difficult to know what he meant by this description.⁶¹ He may have seen the band that sealed two-thirds of the plates together, which may have been made of copper that had oxidized over the years and turned green. Alternatively, he may have seen the breastplate, which could have also been made of copper and appeared green from oxidation.⁶² In any case, the point Stowell made to the court was that the plates were real and that he had seen and felt them.

❖ FROM DARKNESS UNTO LIGHT

When Hyrum learned Joseph had returned with the plates, he immediately brought Joseph the chest he had earlier requested, and Joseph locked the plates inside.[63] The plates were finally safe and in the possession of Joseph's family and friends. Lucy wrote, "When the chest came Joseph locked up the record and threw himself on the bed." Then, "after resting himself a little . . . he went out & related his adventure to his father and Mr. Knight."[64] His father tenderly set his son's dislocated thumb while Joseph recounted the traumatic ordeal.[65] Lucy explained that Joseph also "related to our guests the whole history of the record which interested them very much."[66]

## Hiding and Revealing the Plates

Joseph Knight Sr. recalled that once Joseph had safely hidden the plates, Joseph was more interested in the "glasses," or the device that was later referred to as the Urim and Thummim, than he was with the plates. He declared to Knight, "I can see anything; they are Marvelus." Though Joseph would later use the spectacles for translating the plates, in this period Joseph used them to protect the plates. Lucy wrote that Joseph "could at any time ascertain the approach of danger either to himself or the record and for this cause he kept these

Replica of the hearth in the Smith frame home. Photo by Brent R. Nordgren.

14

things constantly."[67] Through the spectacles, the angel communicated to him that men were still plotting to find and abscond with the plates.

On one occasion, while working in the fields with his father, Joseph hastily returned to the house, apparently warned by the spectacles that a group of hostile men was coming to the house. In preparation for their visit, Joseph and his family dug a hole underneath the hearth large enough to hold the box containing the plates and the breastplate. They then replaced the stone to stop the men from finding the box.[68] Almost immediately after they buried the plates under the hearth, a large group of men approached the house. Thinking quickly, Joseph and his younger brother ran to the door screaming loudly, startling the men, who then dispersed.

While Joseph was able to prevent his enemies from finding the plates, several of his friends and family touched, hefted, and held the plates or the box where they were stored. Several individuals witnessed them underneath the linen covering and even felt the size and mass of the plates. One man revealed that he heard the covered plates rattle and "jink" inside their box.[69] Joseph's sister Katherine had a similar experience. When she was dusting and cleaning, she remembered seeing "a package on the table containing the gold plates," which she picked up to judge the weight. She remembered that they were "heavy like gold." Even more revealing, she "rippled her fingers up the edge of the plates and felt that they were separate metal plates and heard the tinkle of sound that they made."[70] Though Katherine never saw the gold leaves themselves, she saw their shape and witnessed them by both hearing and touch.

Most of Joseph's family claimed that they too had similar experiences. William Smith, for example, who was just a teenager at the time, later wrote that he had "hefted the plates as they lay on the table wrapped in an old frock or jacket in which Joseph had brought them home." Like his sister Katherine, he stated, "he had thumbed them through the cloth and ascertained that they were thin sheets of some kind of metal."[71] Friends too, like Alvah Beaman, also lifted and felt the plates (Beaman also helped hide them under the hearth and replace the bricks).[72] Martin Harris later said that he "hefted the plates many times, and should think they weighed forty or fifty pounds."[73] In fact, most of Joseph's closest friends and family testified to touching, hefting, or seeing the plates.

❖ FROM DARKNESS UNTO LIGHT

While some tried to steal the plates, less hostile visitors simply desired to view them and even negotiated with Joseph in an attempt to get him to share the profits the plates would generate. Joseph Knight Sr. remembered that numerous locals came to the Smiths' house hoping to catch a glimpse of the plates or even flip through the pages.[74] Some offered money and property to see the plates, but Smith steadfastly insisted that he would not show them to just anyone. This apparently angered the visitors, and as a result, "they persecuted and abused [the Smiths]."[75] Samuel Lawrence came to Joseph's house demanding that the plates were at least partially his because he had gone to the hill in search of treasure with Joseph.[76] Possibly knowing that Joseph would not negotiate, Lawrence brought with him a local rodsman, who attempted to use a divining rod to find the plates. Lawrence and the rodsman walked into the west room of the home, where the hearth was located. There, the rodsman pointed his rod directly toward the plates and stated that they were "under that harth." After Lawrence and the rodsman left the house without the plates, Joseph decided that he needed to move the plates again to avoid their discovery if Lawrence and the rodsman returned.[77]

To protect the plates, Joseph removed them from the chest and placed them in his father's small cooper's shop out near the barn, across the road in front of their house. He hid the empty box as a decoy underneath the floor panels in the shop and placed the plates in a large pile of flax in the small loft in the shop. One morning shortly thereafter, Joseph went to the cooper shop and saw the floorboards torn up and the decoy box smashed underneath the floor. Somehow, the intruders had completely missed the plates hidden in the loft. Joseph later obtained another box in which to keep the plates. Martin Harris stated that the new box was "an old Ontario glass-box" that had been cut to fit the length and size of the plates.[78]

Despite the best efforts of his enemies and potential looters, Joseph was able to protect and conceal the plates. While he refused to display the plates for money, his friends and family had multiple interactions with the plates and later testified to their physical reality. Once Joseph had finally obtained the plates and protected them from these early assailants, he set about trying to fulfill the command of the angel to bring forth to the world the messages inscribed on them.

## Notes

1. Karen Lynn Davidson, David J. Whittaker, Mark Ashurst-McGee, and Richard L. Jensen, eds., *Histories, Volume 1: 1832–1844*, vol. 1 of the Histories series of *The Joseph Smith Papers*, ed. Dean C. Jessee, Ronald K. Esplin, and Richard Lyman Bushman (Salt Lake City: Church Historian's Press, 2012), 10; see also D&C 13:1; 20:10, 35; 84:26; 107:20. For the date of the First Vision, see Joseph Smith, "Church History," *Times and Seasons*, March 1, 1842, 707. For sources and analysis of the First Vision, see Dean C. Jessee, "The Early Accounts of Joseph Smith's First Vision," *BYU Studies* 9, no. 3 (1969): 275–94; John W. Welch, ed., *Opening the Heavens: Accounts of Divine Manifestations, 1820–1844* (Provo, UT: BYU Press, 2005), 1–76; Steven C. Harper, *Joseph Smith's First Vision: A Guide to the Historical Accounts* (Salt Lake City: Deseret Book, 2012). See also www.josephsmithpapers.org for images of Joseph Smith's history.
2. Richard Bushman develops the context for the First Vision with detail. His narrative draws from various local accounts and places the events in broader context. See Richard Bushman, *Joseph Smith and the Beginnings of Mormonism* (Urbana, IL: University of Illinois Press, 1984), 42–56.
3. Joseph Smith, History, vol. A-1, 1–2. (When we cite Joseph Smith's 1839–circa 1841 history, labeled as vol. A-1 and partially printed in *JSP*, H1, known as vol. 1 of the Manuscript History of the Church, we will cite the original manuscript found at josephsmithpapers.org. At times we will also cite the *JSP*, H1 volume if the annotation is relevant or if it is helpful to compare the versions that are printed side by side.) "It commenced with the Methodist, but soon became general among all the sects in that region of country, indeed the whol district of Country seemed affected by it and great multitudes united themselves to the different religious parties, which created no small stir and division among the people."
4. *New York Spectator*, 23 September 1843. In this interview, Joseph revealed that he went to a place in the woods where he had been clearing trees and stumps. He also explained that he had left his axe stuck in a stump earlier.
5. Joseph Smith, History, vol. A-1, 2.
6. History Drafts, 1838–circa 1841, in *JSP*, H1:214.
7. History Drafts, 1838–circa 1841, in *JSP*, H1:216; Oliver Cowdery, "Letter III," *Latter Day Saints' Messenger and Advocate*, December 1834, 42; Oliver Cowdery, "Letter IV," *Messenger and Advocate*, February 1835, 78.

8. "I was answered that I must join none of them, for they were all wrong, and the Personage who addressed me said that all their Creeds were an abomination in his sight, that those professors were all corrupt." History Drafts, 1838–circa 1841, in *JSP*, H1:214.
9. History Drafts, 1838–circa 1841, in *JSP*, H1:219.
10. There are a handful of authors that have described the landscape of both religious and folk magic practices in the early nineteenth century that can inform this topic. See David H. Hall, *Worlds of Wonder, Days of Judgment: Popular Religious Belief in Early New England* (Cambridge, MA: Harvard University Press, 1989); Jon Butler, *Awash in a Sea of Faith: Christianizing the American People* (Cambridge, MA: Harvard University Press, 1990); Stephen A. Marini, *Radical Sects of Revolutionary New England* (Cambridge, MA: Harvard University Press, 1982); Ann Taves, *Fits, Trances, & Visions: Experiencing Religion and Explaining Experience from Wesley to James* (Princeton, NJ: Princeton University Press, 1999). Neighbors also interested in scrying were specifically Sally and Willard Chase, who lived next to the Smiths and close in age to Joseph. Samuel Lawrence was another resident who was interested in treasure seeking that Joseph was acquainted with during this period. For Joseph Smith Sr.'s involvement, see Ronald W. Walker, "The Persisting Idea of American Treasure Hunting," *BYU Studies* 24, no. 4 (1984): 429–59; and Richard Lloyd Anderson, "The Mature Joseph Smith and Treasure Searching," *BYU Studies* 24, no. 4 (1984): 489–560.
11. Ronald W. Walker, "Joseph Smith: The Palmyra Seer," *BYU Studies* 24, no. 4 (Fall 1984): 461–72; Alan Taylor, "The Early Republic's Supernatural Economy: Treasure Seeking in the American Northeast, 1780–1830," *American Quarterly* 38 (Spring 1986): 6–33; Keith Thomas, *Religion and the Decline of Magic: Studies in Popular Beliefs in Sixteenth- and Seventeenth-Century England* (New York: Oxford University Press, 1971).
12. William D. Purple, "Joseph Smith, The Originator of Mormonism," *Chenango Union* 30, no. 33 (2 May 1877); Charles Marshall, "The Original Prophet," *Fraser's Magazine*, February 1873, 225–35; Daniel S. Tuttle, "Mormons," *Schaff-Herzog Encyclopaedia, a Religious Encyclopaedia or Dictionary of Biblical, Historical, Doctrinal, and Practical Theology* (New York: Funk & Wagnalls, 1883), 2:1556–57; A. W. Benton, "Mormonites," *Evangelical Magazine and Gospel Advocate*, 9 April 1831, 2; Oliver Cowdery, "Letter VIII" (to W. W. Phelps), *Messenger and Advocate*, October 1835, 201.
13. History Drafts, 1838–circa 1841, in *JSP*, H1:220.

14. Both Joseph Smith and Oliver Cowdery identified the angel as "Moroni." An early draft of Joseph Smith's 1838 history ("Draft 2"), written in the hand of scribe James Mulholland, identifies the angel as "Nephi." But in the same manuscript, the word "Nephi" is struck out and replaced with "Moroni" by an unidentified hand, and the original attribution is noted as a "clerical error." This error was perpetuated in several published versions of the history. This is discussed in History Drafts, 1838–circa 1841, in *JSP*, H1:223n56, 495.
15. History, 1834–1836, in *JSP*, H1:59; History Drafts, 1838–circa 1841, in *JSP*, H1:223.
16. See Joseph Smith, History, vol. A-1, 5–6; *Messenger and Advocate*, February and July 1835; William Smith, *William Smith on Mormonism* (Lamoni, IA: Herald Steam Book and Job Office, 1883), 8–9. Smith wrote of the angel's first visit: "He had on a loose robe of most exquisite whiteness. It was a whiteness beyond anything earthly I had ever seen; not do I believe that any earthly thing could be made to appear so exceedingly white and brilliant. His hands were naked, and his arms also, a little above the wrist; so, also, were his feet naked, as were his legs, a little above the ankles. His head and neck were also bare. I could discover that he had no other clothing on but this robe, as it was open, so that I could see into his bosom. Not only was his robe exceedingly white, but his whole person was glorious beyond description, and his countenance truly like lightning."
17. Joseph Smith, History, vol. A-1, 7–8; Oliver Cowdery explained that the angel Moroni did not first appear to him until possibly the early hours of 22 September 1827. *Messenger and Advocate,* 5 January 1835, 79.
18. Joseph Smith, History, vol. A-1, 5–7.
19. Smith in his 1838 history stated: "I made an attempt to take them out but was forbidden by the messenger and was again informed that the time for bringing them forth had not yet arrived, neither would until four years from that time, but he told me that I should come to that place precisely in one year from that time." Smith, History, Vol A-1, 9. Original spelling has been preserved throughout the chapter.
20. *New England Christian Herald*, 7 November 1832. See also Dean C. Jessee, ed., "Joseph Knight's Recollection of Early Mormon History," *BYU Studies* 17, no. 1 (Autumn 1976): 32–33 (throughout the rest of the book, the original document of this source will be cited); Tiffany, "Mormonism," August 1859, 164; Lucy Mack Smith, History, 1844–1845, Book 5, MS 7. (To encourage reference to the original manuscript we cite the original of Lucy Mack Smith's family history. Readers can access transcripts and digital copies of the manuscript at JosephSmithPapers.org.)

21. "[Joseph Smith Jr.] had talked with me and told me the Conversation he had with the personage which told him if he would Do right according to the will of God he mite obtain [the plates] the 22nt Day of Septemer Next and if not he never would have them." Joseph Knight Sr., History, 2, Church History Library, Salt Lake City. Original spelling preserved throughout book.
22. History, circa Summer 1832, in *JSP*, H1:14; Smith, History, vol. A-1, 9; Katharine Smith Salisbury to "Dear Sisters," 10 March 1886, *Saints' Herald*, 1 May 1886, 260; "Mormon Leaders at Their Mecca," *New York Herald*, 25 June 1893, 12; Sidney Rigdon was recorded to have stated in 1836 that when Smith originally met with the angel, he went "directly for a mattock and shovel, and went to work at the place. After getting down about waist deep Joe came to a nice square stone box.... After clearing out all the earth from around it.... Joe tugged and tugged and tugged [his exact words] but move it wouldn't." John Murdock, "Sidney Rigdon, A Report of a Lecture He Delivered Forty Years Ago Meadville—Rigdon's Account of Joe Smith's Revelation," *Pittsburgh Telegraph*, 24 August 1876.
23. Smith's history described the cement box in this way: "The box in which they lay was formed by laying stones together in some kind of cement, in the bottom of the box were laid two stones crossways of the box, an on these stones lay the plates and the other things with them." Smith, History, vol. A-1, 7.
24. Lucy Mack Smith wrote, "He had deposited [the plates] in a cavity in a birch log 3 miles distant and covered it with the bark of the same." Lucy Mack Smith, History, book 5, MS 6–15; book 6, MS 2. Joseph Smith, History, vol. A-1, 8.
25. Smith, History, vol. A-1, 7–8.
26. Lucy Mack Smith, History, book 5, MS 4–5.
27. Lucy Mack Smith, History, book 5, MS 8–9. Lucy also witnessed the breastplate, which was the third of three items known to have been brought home by Joseph from the hill. She is the only person who left an account about witnessing the breastplate. Like the spectacles, they were wrapped in a thin handkerchief, "so thin that I could see the glistening metal, and ascertain its proportions without any difficulty." Lucy explained that the breastplate was concave on one side and convex on the other side, large enough to start at the neck and reach the middle of a man's stomach. She also explained that it had heavy belt-like straps connected at each corner to fasten the plate to someone's chest.
28. Lucy Mack Smith, History, 1844–45, book 3, MS 12.
29. Smith's history states: "I soon found out the reason why I had received such strict charges to keep them safe and why it was that the messenger had said that when

I had done what was required at my hand, he would call for them, for no sooner was it known that I had them than the most strenuous exertions were used to get them from me." Smith went on to explain: "Every stratagem that could be resorted invented was resorted to for that purpose. The persecution became more bitter and severe than before, and multitudes were on the alert continualy to get them from me if possible but by the wisdom of God they remained safe in my hands untill I had accomplished by them what was required at my hand, when according to arrangement the messenger called for them, I delivered them up to him and he has them in his charge untill this day, being the Second day of May, One thousand Eight hundred and thirty eight." Smith, History, vol. A-1, 9; see also Smith, Journal, 30 April–4 May 1838, in *JSP*, J1:264.

30. E. D. Howe, *Mormonism Unvailed* (Painsville, OH: 1834), 240–48.
31. Lavina Fielding Smith, *Lucy's Book* (Salt Lake City: Signature Books, 2001), 379. See Lucy Mack Smith, History, book 6.
32. Lucy Mack Smith, History, book 5, MS [8]. "Wells <request> a <this> woman whom not <had never seen> one of the family had ever seen or heard of before although She sent purposely for Joseph we considered it a provision of Providence to enable us to pay the money we were owing the cab inet maker." Knight wrote, "I was there several Days. I will say there [was] a man near By By the name Samuel Lawrance. He was a Seear [Seer] and he had Bin to the hill and knew about the things in the hill and he was trying to obtain them." Knight Sr., History, 2.
33. Lucy's history states, "On the 20th of Sept Mr Knight came with his friend to see how we were engaging matters with Mr Stodard and company they remained with us until the 22." Lucy Mack Smith, History, book 5, MS 7. See Knight Sr., History, 2. Smith's history states, "At length the time arrived for obtaining the plates, the Urim and Thummin and the breastplate, In <On> the twenty second day of September, One thousand Eight hundred and twenty seven, having went as usual at the end of another year to the place where they were deposited, the same heavenly messenger delivered them up to me with this charge that I should be responsible for them. That if I should let them go carelessly or <through> any neglect of mine I should be cut off, but that if I would use all my endeavours to preserve them untill <he> [the messenger] called should call for them, they should be protected." Smith, History, vol. A-1, 9.
34. See Howe, *Mormonism Unvailed*, 240–48. Lorenzo Saunders, another local resident associated with Chase, also gave a similar account about Lawrence's involvement with Smith. Lorenzo Saunders, interviewed by William H. Kelley,

17 September 1884, 10, in E. L. Kelley Papers, Community of Christ Library-Archives (CCLA), Independence, Missouri; reproduced in Dan Vogel, *Early Mormon Documents* (Salt Lake City: Signature Books, 1996–2003), 1:125–35. Saunders was likely dependent upon Chase's printed testimony in *Mormonism Unvailed*, but he likely also spoke with Chase.

35. See Knight Sr., History, 2. Joseph's history states, "I soon found out the reason why I had received such strict charges to keep them safe, and why it was that the messenger had said that when I had done what was required at my hand, he would call for them. For no sooner was it known that I had them, than the most strenuous exertions were used to get them from me. Every stratagem that could be invented was resorted to for that purpose. The persecution became more bitter and severe than before, and multitudes were on the alert continually to get them from me if possible." Smith, History, vol. A-1, 8.

36. If Chase's account is correct, which claimed that Samuel Lawrence went to the hill with Joseph Smith, the spectacles were revealed to him. Lawrence's relationship to Joseph, however, is unknown, and this may have been a story intended to build upon Lawrence's abilities with a seer stone and to justify his right to share in the profits garnered from the gold plates. See Lucy Mack Smith, History, 1845, MS 65; Howe, *Mormonism Unvailed*, 240–48; William H. Kelley, 17 September 1884, CCLA, 10.

37. Lorenzo Saunders to Thomas Gregg, 28 January 1885, in Charles A. Shook, *The True Origin of the Book of Mormon* (Cincinnati: Standard Pub. Co., 1914), 135.

38. Interview, November 12, 1884, E. L. Kelley Papers, CCLA.

39. Ole A. Jensen, "Testimony of Martin Harris," copy in Church History Library.

40. "Mormonism," *Kansas City Daily Journal*, 5 June 1881, [1].

41. "Mormonism," *Kansas City Daily Journal*, 5 June 1881.

42. "The Last Man," *Chicago Times*, 17 October 1881.

43. Edward Stevenson, *Reminiscences of Joseph, the Prophet* (Salt Lake City: the author, 1893), 12.

44. Richard L. Bushman, *Joseph Smith and the Beginnings of Mormonism* (Urbana: University of Illinois Press, 1984), 64–76; Ronald W. Walker, "The Persisting Idea of American Treasure Hunting," *BYU Studies* 24, no. 4 (1984): 429–59; and Richard Lloyd Anderson, "The Mature Joseph Smith and Treasure Searching," *BYU Studies* 24, no. 4 (1984): 489–560.

45. When Joseph was asked if he was a money digger in 1838, he replied, "Yes, but it was never a very profitable job to him, as he only got fourteen dolars a month for it." *Elders' Journal*, July 1838, 42–44; *JSP*, D1:345–52.

46. Richard L. Bushman, *Joseph Smith: Rough Stone Rolling* (New York: Knopf, 2005), 48–52, and Mark Ashurst-McGee, "Moroni as Angel and as Treasure Guardian," *FARMS Review* 18, no. 1 (2006): 34–100.
47. "Mormonism," *New England Christian Herald*, 7 November 1832, 22–23.
48. Lucy Mack Smith, History, 1845, MS 65. Lucy wrote, "My husband soon learned that ten or twelve men were clubbed together, with one Willard Chase, a methodist class leader, at their head; and what was still more ridiculous, they had sent sixty or seventy miles for a certain conjuror, to come and divine the place where the plates were secreted."
49. Lucy Mack Smith, History, 1845, MS 65; Howe, *Mormonism Unvailed*, 245–46.
50. Brigham Young, in *Journal of Discourses* (London: Latter-day Saints' Book Depot, 1881), 2:180–81. Young went on to say: "To those who love swearing, it was musical to hear him, but not so to me, for I would leave his presence. He would call Joseph everything that was bad, and say 'I believe he will get the treasure after all.' He did get it and the war commenced directly. When Joseph obtained the treasure, the priests, the deacons, and religionists of every grade, went hand in hand with the fortune-teller, and with every wicked person, to get it out of his hands, and, to accomplish this, a part of them came out and persecuted him."
51. Anderson, *Lucy's Book*, 382.
52. See also Harris's statement that they were hidden in a hollowed-out oak tree. Joel Tiffany, "Mormonism," *Tiffany's Monthly*, August 1859, 165.
53. Lucy wrote, "Emma was soon on her way to her husband she informed of the situation of affairs at home and he went immediately to Mrs. Wells and told here that he must return home to attend to some important business." Lucy Mack Smith, History, book 5, MS 11 and 12.
54. Lucy Mack Smith, History, book 5, MS 11–13.
55. Thomas Gregg, *The Prophet of Palmyra* (New York: J. B. Alden, 1890), 29.
56. See "A Witness to the Book of Mormon," *Iowa State Register*, August 28, 1870; Smith, *On Mormonism*, 12.
57. Tiffany, "Mormonism," August 1859, 167.
58. Herbert S. Salisbury, "Things the Prophet's Sister Told Me," 2 July 1945, Church History Library.
59. Tiffany, "Mormonism," August 1859, 167; Martha Campbell to Joseph Smith, 19 December 1843.
60. Martha Campbell to Joseph Smith, 19 December 1843.
61. *New England Christian Herald*, 7 November 1832.

62. The Book of Mormon later included descriptions of brass breastplates. See Mosiah 8:10.
63. Lucy Mack Smith, History, 1845, book 5, 13.
64. See Lucy Mack Smith, History, book 5, MS 13–14.
65. Benjamin Saunders, a local resident, witnessed the severity of Joseph's wounds just days after the event. Benjamin Saunders interview, "Miscellany," circa September 1884, 19–30, Kelly Papers, CCLA.
66. Lucy Mack Smith, History, book 5, MS 14.
67. Lucy Mack Smith History, book 6, 1.
68. See Sally Parker to John Kemption, 26 August 1838, Family History Library; "A Journal of Mary A. Noble," 2–3, Church History Library.
69. Tiffany, "Mormonism," August 1859, 167.
70. "The Prophet's Sister Testifies She Lifted the B of M Plates," *Messenger* (Berkeley, CA), October 1954.
71. Martha Campbell to Joseph Smith, 19 December 1843, 1, Misc. Correspondence, JSP, Church History Library; Vogel, *Early Mormon Documents*, 1:505 and 508.
72. Knight Sr., History, 3. "About this time Came this Samuel Lawrance and one Beeman a grate Rodsman and wanted to talk with him. And he went into the west Room and they Proposed to go shares with him and tried every way to Bargain with him But Could not. Then Beeman took out his Rods and hild [held] them up and they pointed Dow[n] to the harth whare they ware hid. "There," says Beeman, "it is under that harth." So they had to garde the house until some time in November. He obtaind fifty Dollars in money and hired a man to move him and his wife to Pensylvany to hir Fathers, his wife Being onwell and wanted to go to her Fathers. He Bout [bought] a piece of Land of hir Father with a house and Barn on it. Here the People Began to tease him to see the Book and to offer him money and property and they Crouded so harde that he had to hide it in the Mountin."
73. Tiffany, "Mormonism," August 1859, 167.
74. See Knight Sr., History, 3, and *Journal of Discourses*, 2:180–81.
75. Howe, *Mormonism Unvailed*, 240–48.
76. Chase claimed that Joseph had previously deceived Lawrence, convincing the latter to pay his way to Harmony, Pennsylvania by claiming that Joseph knew about a silver mine that never materialized. Howe, *Mormonism Unvailed*, 240–48.
77. See Lucy Mack Smith, History, 1845, MS 65; Howe, *Mormonism Unvailed*, 240–48; William H. Kelley, 17 September 1884, CCLA, 10.
78. Tiffany, "Mormonism," August 1859, 167.

# 2

# Escaping Palmyra and Copying Characters from the Gold Plates

Just weeks after Joseph Smith retrieved the gold plates, rumors about them spread like wildfire in and around Palmyra. Most viewed the reports of the gold plates with skepticism, if not ridicule. Many, however, were deeply interested in finally making sense of the stories that had circulated. Some even hoped to see or hold the plates in order to judge their value or share in the profits they might generate. This interest quickly turned to harassment that lasted for weeks before Joseph and Emma Smith moved to Harmony, Pennsylvania, in December 1827.

Lucy Mack Smith recorded much of what happened during this period in her 1844–45 history. Her recollection for this period focuses on Martin and Lucy Harris, particularly the latter. It presents Lucy Harris as a person to whom God gave an undeniable witness of the plates, yet who dismissed the witness with little regard for its value. The problem with Lucy Smith's account is that she was not fond of Lucy Harris and seems to paint her in the worst light possible, making it difficult to understand Lucy Harris's real intentions. This same problem of negative bias is also apparent in the way Lucy Smith treats other figures in later chapters of her history. Nonetheless, statements from Martin Harris confirm some of the details in Lucy

❖ FROM DARKNESS UNTO LIGHT

Portrait of Martin Harris. *Painting by Lewis A. Ramsey.*

Smith's history, and though we only have a negative view of Lucy Harris, Lucy Smith's history develops Joseph Smith's relationship with Martin Harris well during this period.

Embracing an accurate view of the Harris family is extraordinarily important to the coming forth of the Book of Mormon. They became keenly interested in what Joseph Smith had unearthed that fall, which led to years of involvement in translating and publishing the Book of Mormon.[1] Martin Harris's brother Preserved had gone to the village and heard the rumors and stories of the plates, likely from some of the money diggers with whom Joseph had previously worked.[2] Martin, who was in a position to help Joseph translate and find funding to print the Book of Mormon, knew the Smith family well and knew about Joseph's visionary background.[3]

When Martin heard about the plates, presumably from his brother, he thought nothing of the matter, considering the stories to be just some of the many tales current among the various hired hands who had searched the hills and caves of Palmyra and Manchester for buried treasure. He thought that Joseph Smith and his fellow treasure seekers had likely uncovered an "old brass Kettle" rather than a set of ancient plates.[4] Likely in early October, not long after he had heard about Joseph's discovery, Martin visited Palmyra village and was asked by one intrigued resident what he thought about the rumors. According to Martin's recollection, he was initially open to the idea that Joseph Smith had in fact retrieved gold plates from the local hill. Unknown to Martin at the time, Joseph had apparently already seen Martin in the spectacles and knew that God had chosen him to help bring forth the Book of Mormon.[5] Possibly after hearing about Martin's interest in the plates, Joseph Smith sent his mother, Lucy Mack Smith, to visit with Martin to find out if he would help Joseph translate the plates.

After traveling from the border of Manchester up through the town of Palmyra and across the Erie Canal, Lucy Smith arrived on the doorstep of Martin Harris's house. Lucy Harris, Martin's wife, answered the door. Joseph's mother explained the purpose of her visit and recounted the details of the discovery of the plates "in order to satisfy" Lucy Harris's curiosity.[6] While Latter-day Saint literature often portrays Lucy Harris as an inveterate enemy of Joseph Smith and his claims to divine revelation, Lucy Mack Smith remembered that Lucy Harris was initially excited about the plates and eagerly discussed them with her visitor (admittedly, this may have been a way for Lucy Smith to emphasize Lucy Harris's dismissal of the plates later). Lucy Smith remembered that Harris "did not wait for me to get through with my story" before responding by offering money to assist Joseph in his efforts to translate. Lucy Smith wrote, "She commenced urging me to receive a considerable amount of money which she had at her own command a kind of private purse which her husband permitted her to keep." Lucy Harris's sister also offered money during the same visit for the project, but Lucy Smith refused both offers, unwilling to commit herself to anything without Joseph's approval. Lucy Harris persisted, however, and was "determined to assist in the business for she knew that he [Joseph] would want money and she could spare $200." Despite the considerable offer, Lucy Smith again demurred and asked instead if Lucy Harris would kindly take her, as she had asked earlier, to visit with her husband, Martin.[7]

At last, Lucy Harris guided Lucy Smith through the house to the fireplace, where Martin Harris was setting the bricks for a new hearth. When Lucy Smith approached the fireplace, Martin declared that he wanted to speak to Joseph and also explained that he would be leaving Palmyra for twelve months. He was desperately working to prepare his farm for his

Lucy Mack Smith. *Sketch by Fred Piercy.* © *Church History Museum.*

long absence, intending to have a hired hand care for his property while he was gone. Martin told Lucy Smith, "I [have] not time to spare," but "[you] might talk with my wife [while you wait]" because, as he explained, he would not be finished until that evening.[8] Once Harris completed his work, he finally met with Lucy Smith. Martin remembered her telling him that Joseph had brought "home the plates . . . and . . . that Joseph had sent her" to recruit his support. Harris explained that he had already planned to go to the Smiths' Manchester home to meet with Joseph after hearing the rumors about the plates, but that he could not go at that time. Harris asked his son "to harness [his] horse and take her [Lucy Smith] home."[9] Joseph's mother recalled that Lucy Harris insisted, "I am coming to see him too and I will be there Tuesday afternoon and stop overnight accordingly."[10]

Lucy Harris lived up to her promise and traveled to the Smiths' Manchester home with her daughter to speak with Joseph, hoping to see the plates before she or her husband offered any support for the translation project. Lucy Smith remembered that as soon as Lucy Harris arrived and sat down with Joseph, "she began to importune my son as to the truth of what he said." She questioned whether Joseph had the plates, and she demanded to see them, believing that she could bargain with Joseph by offering him money to publish the translation of the plates. Joseph explained that the angel who had entrusted the plates into his care forbade him to exhibit the plates to anyone "except those whom the Lord will appoint to testify of them." After discussing the plates with Joseph again that evening, Lucy Harris made one final plea before she retired to bed, stating, "Now Joseph, . . . I will tell [you] what I will do. If I can get a witness that you do speak the truth I will believe it and I want to do something about the translation and I mean to help you any way."[11]

Lucy Mack Smith remembered Lucy Harris having a "remarkable dream" that evening. When she awoke the next morning, she declared that a "personage had appeared to her the night before and said to her that in as much as she had disputed the servant of the Lord and said that his word was not to be believed and asked him many improper questions that she had done that which was not right in the sight of God." However, after the chastisement from the personage, she was shown the plates in her dream and in the morning she was able to describe the record in detail to her daughter and the Smith family. After discussing the dream and pondering its meaning, Joseph handed Lucy Harris and her daughter the wooden box containing the plates.[12] The physicality of the item and sheer weight of the plates served as the evidence that Lucy Harris needed to begin believing that the plates were real. The sound of the plates inside the box may have been partially convincing to the Harrises if the plates shifted inside the box while they held them. Martin Harris remembered that his "daughter said, they were about as much as she could lift. . . . [His] wife said they were very heavy."[13] Even though she knew that Joseph possessed what seemed to be a set of plates, Lucy Harris's experiences slowly faded from her mind, and she eventually discounted her evening at the Smiths' as evidence that the plates existed.

His wife's experience sparked Martin's interest again. Possibly within days of Lucy Smith's visit to his home, he traveled to the Smith home to speak with Joseph Smith and to inquire about seeing the gold plates. Harris was surprised to find that Joseph had already planned to include him in the forthcoming effort to translate the plates.[14] As Harris later explained, Joseph had seen him in his seer stone after an angel had told Joseph that he would identify "the man that would assist him." Martin, like his daughter and wife, lifted the box with the plates inside. As some object shifted back and forth in the box, Martin concluded that the object was a set of plates and that their weight indicated that they could have been made of gold. Like a child investigating a wrapped gift, Harris surmised the contents. He knew that Joseph "had not credit enough to buy so much lead," let alone gold or some other expensive metal. Harris realized that Joseph Smith neither had the means to fabricate nor purchase metal plates. In fact, so destitute were the Smiths, the family had struggled to supply Joseph even with a wooden box. Harris calculated that the plates must have weighed around sixty pounds, which made him believe that, given the size of the box, the plates must have been "lead or gold."[15]

Harris approached the situation very skeptically that day. He prepared a plan to interrogate each member of the Smith family separately to uncover any inconsistencies in the stories they told. When he arrived, Joseph was apparently working for Peter Ingersoll as a laborer, which provided Harris a perfect opportunity to talk with the rest of the family without Joseph's influence. Harris remembered interrogating Emma and other members of the Smith family to try to catch them in a lie. Once

Joseph returned, Martin Harris carefully listened as Joseph told the story of the angel and the retrieval of the plates. Joseph also told Martin that God had chosen him to assist in the translation. Knowing that Joseph's version of the story was in line with the versions his family members had recounted, Martin declared, "If it is the Lord's, you can have all the money necessary to bring it before the world."[16]

One of the more interesting points about these few months between September and November 1827 is how Lucy Mack Smith and Martin Harris remembered these events later. In each of their accounts, they focused on the initial skepticism of Lucy and Martin Harris but quickly turned to the Harrises' reaction to both spiritual and physical evidence of the plates. Each of them apparently had a vision, and both of them interrogated the Smith family, felt the weight of the plates, and likely heard them move about in the box. Lucy Mack Smith and Martin Harris remembered these early events as proof for why they believed and why others should believe.

## Moving to Harmony

While Martin and Lucy Harris were now convinced, not all Palmyra residents reacted so positively. Joseph had worked with many of the laborers in the village digging wells, searching for buried items, and hoping that they would find something in their work that would free them from their daily labors. Moroni had warned Joseph about those who would use the plates to obtain riches and forbade him from showing the plates to any of them. This exclusion provoked those who wanted to profit from the plates. Many were apparently planning to force Joseph to show them the plates, but Harris heard the rumors and warned Joseph before it was too late.[17] As Harris later remembered, "The excitement in the village upon the subject had become such that some had threatened to mob Joseph, and also to tar and feather him." They further declared, "He should never leave until he had shown [them] the plates."[18]

With the growing threats from angry residents, Joseph needed a way to leave Palmyra quickly to live with Emma's family in Harmony, Pennsylvania. Though he did not own a farm, he likely had other things tying him to Palmyra—namely, numerous accounts on credit to pay for his living expenses. Most shopkeepers worked on credit instead of exchanging bills

*Joseph and Emma Smith's home in Harmony, Pennsylvania. Photo by George Edward Anderson. Courtesy of Church History Library.*

or notes, binding individuals to their local market. As they acquired goods from the shops on credit, they later replenished the shop inventory with their own stock of goods produced on their farms or from their trade. If Joseph had attempted to leave before satisfying his debts, a disgruntled creditor could have demanded a warrant for his arrest. In a local tavern, Martin presented Joseph with fifty dollars so Joseph could settle his debts and do the work of the Lord. Harris declared his intention publicly to "give the money to the Lord and called upon all present to witness to the fact that he gave it freely and did not demand any compensation or return."[19]

His debts settled, Joseph "was ready to set out for Penn[sylvania]." A large group of antagonists, however, met to persuade a local physician, Dr. Alexander McIntyre, to help them "follow Joe Smith and take his Gold Bible away from him." Having served as the Smiths' physician for some years, McIntyre refused and told the group that "they must be a pack of devilish fools."[20] Having been rejected by a prominent citizen of Palmyra, the disappointed mob subsequently disbanded.

Still fearing for the safety of the plates, Joseph went to great lengths to hide them. Emma's brother Alva had come up from Harmony with his wagon to help Joseph and Emma move, and Joseph carefully concealed the plates for the several days' journey to Harmony in the wagon. Evidence

31

❖ FROM DARKNESS UNTO LIGHT

suggests that the plates had been transferred between at least three boxes before the group left for Harmony. Martin helped Joseph put the box containing the plates into a barrel, which was filled with beans and then was nailed shut.[21] The efforts they made to hide the plates were soon rewarded. Not long after they left Palmyra, a man claiming to have a search warrant stopped them to search their wagon for the plates. After a thorough search, in which he may have even sifted through the barrel of beans, he did not find the plates and likely returned to the village to report that Smith did not have the plates. Soon after the first search was finished, a second man approached the wagon and conducted a search for the plates, again to no avail.[22] Orson Pratt later highlighted this story in a popular Latter-day Saint pamphlet, *An Interesting Account of Several Remarkable Visions* (1840), which describes many of the miracles and angelic visitations from the founding period of the Church. Pratt included this story as just one example of how the Lord protected the plates.

On their way to Harmony, the Smiths stopped in Harpursville, near Colesville, New York, to see Emma's sister Elizabeth Hale Wasson. According to one late account, while they were there Elizabeth's husband helped Joseph by giving him a trunk where he could store the plates.[23] While Joseph had been forced with previous boxes to nail the box shut to prevent people from looking at them, with this new box (possibly the fourth box in which Joseph had stored the plates), the plates were much more accessible, because it had a lock on the lid. It was also the last box used to store and protect the plates that is mentioned in the historical record. Once Joseph settled in his home in Harmony in late November or early December 1827, he only occasionally went to any length to hide the plates. Emma later recalled, "They lay under our bed for a few months but I never felt the liberty to look at them."[24] For her part, Emma explained, "The plates often lay on the table without any attempt at concealment, wrapped in a small linen table cloth."[25] Emma's son Joseph Smith III also remembered, "My mother told me that she saw the plates in the sack, for they lay on a small table in their living room in their cabin on her father's farm, and she would lift and move them when she swept and dusted the room and furniture. She even thumbed the leaves as one does the leaves of a book, and they rustled with a metallic sound."[26]

When they arrived in Harmony, Joseph and Emma may have lived in her father's house for a short time, but they soon moved onto the Hales' adjoining property in 1828, which Emma's brother Jesse had owned previously after receiving the property from their father.[27] Emma was in her first trimester of pregnancy, and the opportunity to move back to Harmony offered them safety from the growing opposition in Palmyra. The property also gave Joseph the opportunity to start a new life as a farmer.[28] The fourteen-acre farm included a frame home, a barn, and other improvements, which Joseph formally purchased from Isaac Hale on 6 April 1829.[29]

His arrival in Harmony did not come without problems, most of which were related to Emma's family. Joseph had first met Emma while he boarded at the Hales' house in the fall of 1825. Joseph and Emma went against Isaac Hale's wishes when they eloped in January 1827. By August 1827, Joseph had apparently tried to make amends with his new father-in-law, who subsequently offered to help Joseph and Emma get started in their new life. Joseph had opted instead at that time to move to his parents' house in Palmyra, awaiting the time when Moroni would finally allow him to take possession of the gold plates. Belatedly taking Isaac Hale up on his generous offer, Joseph began to live the life of a poor farmer. In fact, Isaac Hale insisted that the price of his arrangement was that Joseph would stop accepting work as a laborer digging for buried silver or gold.[30] Hale was quickly disappointed to find that Joseph claimed he had brought with him from Palmyra a set of gold plates that had been buried in a hill. Hale received these claims with doubt and derision. To make matters worse, Joseph was still under the angelic injunction to show the plates to no one and could not therefore easily allay his father-in-law's concerns. Attempting to convince Hale that the plates existed without showing him the actual plates, Joseph picked up the trunk in which he had deposited the plates and handed it to Hale. Hale remembered vividly the exercise: "I was allowed to feel the weight of the box and they gave me to understand, that the book of plates was then in the box—into which, however, I was not allowed to look." As he had done months earlier with the Harrises, Joseph used this approach to avoid the consequences of showing the plates to others while also offering at least some physical evidence that the plates existed. The experience, however, did not make a believer of Isaac Hale the way it had Martin Harris. Given Hale's willingness to forgive Joseph and Emma and give them favorable terms on his land, he expected Joseph to show him the plates out of respect. Infuriated with what he perceived as Joseph's recalcitrance, Hale demanded that nothing be stored in his house if he could not see it.[31]

Hale's experience illustrates the reluctance certain individuals had when they heard that Joseph Smith had a set of ancient gold plates. Joseph's insistence on keeping the plates out of sight expressed his devotion to the translation and his promise to Moroni, but it also increased curiosity and doubt in the minds of skeptics. The weight of the plates and the fact that he likely heard the sound of metal moving in the trunk was evidence of something to Isaac Hale, but he wanted to hold the plates and inspect their inscriptions before he believed that the plates were not just a cheaply forged fabrication locked inside a trunk. Perhaps it was in part to try to satisfy Hale's doubts that Joseph soon produced paper copies of the characters on the plates.

## Characters on the Plates

Once Joseph and Emma were living in Jesse Hale's former home, their separate living quarters on the property gave them enough autonomy to begin working on the plates. Still driven by Moroni's commandment to translate the plates, Joseph began by doing what Isaac Hale had wanted to do—inspecting them and examining the characters inscribed on their pages. Joseph only had a rudimentary knowledge of written English and had never studied even Greek and Latin like university graduates would have done, let alone lesser-known ancient languages. Joseph had absolutely no ability to decipher any language other than English. He had told Joseph Knight Sr. soon after he had retrieved the plates from the hill that he "want[ed] them translated." Once in Harmony, as Knight wrote, Joseph "began to be anxious to git them translated" and "with hist wife Drew of[f] the Caricters exactly like the ancient and [later] sent Martin Harris to see if he Could git them Translated."[32]

Latter-day Saint historians have been well aware of these accounts, yet Joseph's early attempts to find a translator of the transcribed characters has been almost completely lost to Latter-day Saint history.[33] Without showing them the plates, Joseph had others help him duplicate some of the characters. Emma Smith, for instance, aided Joseph to make copies of the characters, but she never saw the plates herself. It is possible that Joseph was making copies of the characters by placing a paper over the plates and rubbing a piece of charcoal over the inscribed characters. Joseph may have created rubbings of dozens of the plates, then handed them over to Emma to trace or copy the characters onto another piece of paper. Emma would have done her best to replicate the rubbing (if that was how Joseph actually made the copies), but she did not copy characters directly from the plates.

Aside from his wife, Joseph apparently had others help him make copies of the characters from the pages. Late interviews of Harmony residents indicate that Reuben Hale, Emma's brother, may have also helped create copies of the characters. One local historian reported that Reuben "assisted Joe Smith to fix up some characters such as Smith pretended were engraven on his book of plates."[34] Though the historian's report was skeptical toward their authenticity, it pointed towards an additional person who may have helped Joseph make copies.[35] If Joseph produced only one sheet of copied characters, as the history has traditionally been told, why would Joseph have employed two scribes in this period? Furthermore, if there was only one sample, and Joseph had already made the copy himself directly from the plates, why have any scribe at all? Yet there are records indicating not only that Joseph Smith used Emma and Reuben Hale as scribes, but also that he had Martin Harris create other copies of some characters, presumably after Emma and Reuben had assisted.[36]

Smith had the plates in his possession for over four months before Harris took copies of the characters to New York City in February 1828, allowing for the possibility that Joseph had, during that time, studied the characters and made numerous copies.[37] The copies of these characters allowed Joseph Smith and his followers to provide physical evidence to doubters that the plates did exist.[38] Safely living in Harmony, Pennsylvania, over one hundred miles from those who tried to take the plates from him in Palmyra, Joseph began a new era of working with the gold plates.

## Notes

1. See Richard L. Anderson, "Martin Harris, the Honorable New York Farmer," *Improvement Era*, February 1969, 18–21.
2. Tiffany, "Mormonism," August 1859, 167–68. Harris stated, "The first time I heard of the matter, my brother Presarved Harris, who had been in the village of

Palmyra, asked me if I had heard about Joseph Smith Jr., having a golden bible." See Bushman, *Joseph Smith: Rough Stone Rolling*, 48–52; Mark Ashurst-McGee, "Moroni as Angel and as Treasure Guardian," *FARMS Review* 18, no. 1 (2006): 34–100; D. Michael Quinn, *Early Mormonism and the Magic World View*, rev. ed. (Salt Lake City: Signature Books, 1998), 30–65; Ronald W. Walker, "Joseph Smith: The Palmyra Seer," *BYU Studies* 24, no. 4 (Fall 1984): 461–72; and Alan Taylor, "The Early Republic's Supernatural Economy: Treasure Seeking in the American Northeast, 1780–1830," *American Quarterly* 38 (Spring 1986): 6–33.

3. Tiffany, "Mormonism," August 1859, 163. Harris explained that he saw Joseph use the seer stone in the years before 1827.
4. Tiffany, "Mormonism," August 1859, 167. Joseph had by some accounts retrieved one of his seer stones buried underground, stored in a brass kettle. Brigham Young explained that Joseph's seer stone was "obtained . . . in an Iron kettle 15 feet under ground. He saw it while looking in another seers stone which a person had. He went right to the spot & dug & found it." Scott G. Kenney, ed., *Wilford Woodruff's Journal, 1833–1898 Typescript* (Midvale, UT: Signature Books, 1983–1991), 5:382–83; see also Howe, *Mormonism Unvailed*, 257–58; *Wayne Sentinel,* 27 December 1825, 2.
5. Tiffany, "Mormonism," August 1859, 18.
6. Lucy Mack Smith, History, 1845, book 6. Compare Tiffany, "Mormonism," August 1859, 168.
7. Lucy Mack Smith, History, 1845, book 6, [4–7].
8. Tiffany, "Mormonism," August 1859, 168.
9. Tiffany, "Mormonism," August 1859, 168.
10. Lucy Mack Smith, History, 1845, book 6, [4].
11. Lucy Mack Smith, History, 1845, book 6, [5].
12. Lucy Mack Smith, History, 1845, book 6, [5–7].
13. Tiffany, "Mormonism," August 1859, 168.
14. Tiffany, "Mormonism," August 1859, 168. Joseph apparently stated, "Well, I say [see] you standing before me as plainly as I do now" in the seer stone.
15. Tiffany, "Mormonism," August 1859, 168. Harris stated, "Wile at Mr. Smith's I hefted the plates, and I knew from the heft that they were lead or gold, and I knew that Joseph had not credit enough to buy so much lead."
16. Tiffany, "Mormonism," August 1859, 168–70.
17. Tiffany, "Mormonism," August 1859, 170.
18. Tiffany, "Mormonism," August 1859, 170.

19. Lucy Mack Smith, History, 1845, book 6–7.
20. Lucy Mack Smith, History, 1845, book 6–8.
21. Lucy Smith wrote that the plates were "severely nailed up in a box and the box put into a strong cask made for the purpose the cask was then filled with beans and headed up as soon as it was ascertained." Lucy Mack Smith, History, 1845, book 6–7. See also Howe, *Mormonism Unvailed*, 13–15, 18; Rhamanthus M. Stocker, *Centennial History of Susquehanna County, Pennsylvania* (Philadelphia: R. T. Peck, 1887), 554–55; Orson Pratt, *A[n] Interesting Account of Several Remarkable Visions*, 1840, in *JSP*, H2:13–14.
22. Pratt, *A[n] Interesting Account*, 401.
23. "The early Mormons," *Binghamton Republican*, 29 July 1880.
24. Emma Smith Bidamon Interview by Nels Madson and Parley P. Pratt, Church History Library, SLC, 1877.
25. Joseph Smith III, "Last Testimony of Sister Emma," *Saints' Herald*, 1 October 1879, 289–90.
26. Joseph Smith III to Mrs. E. Horton, 7 March 1900, CCLA, in Dan Vogel, *Early Mormon Documents*, 1:546–47.
27. See Harmony Assessment Records, 1828–1831, court records, Susquehanna County Courthouse, Montrose, Pennsylvania, 10, 11, 13, and 14.
28. Joseph Smith, History, 1834–1836, in *JSP*, H1:9; Joseph Smith III, "Last Testimony of Sister Emma," *Saints' Herald*, 1 October 1879, 289; "Mormonism," *Susquehanna Register* (Montrose, PA), 1 May 1834, [1].
29. Agreement with Isaac Hale, 6 April 1829, in *JSP*, D1:29; For the Harmony tax records, see Vogel, *Early Mormon Documents*, 4:421–31. The frame home was twenty-five by twenty feet and included a large cellar with windows, fenced in by a well-built stone wall. It also included a well in the front yard and a spring flowing from the hill behind the house. It is also likely that the property included plowed fields and a few orchards. The north end of the property had maple trees and sugar bushes for maple sugar. It was at the northern end of his property that Joseph likely kept the gold plates hidden away from the "abodes of men" once he removed them from the house.
30. When Joseph faced charges of being a disorderly character in July 1830, Joseph's use of a seer stone was discussed, with the court concluding that he had not searched for buried treasure for at the very least two years. Josiah Stowell believed that Joseph had not been actively involved in money digging since 1826. "Mormonism," *New England Christian Herald*, 7 November 1832, 22–23.

❖ FROM DARKNESS UNTO LIGHT

31. Howe, *Mormonism Unvailed*, 257–58.
32. Knight Sr., History, 3.
33. Michael Hubbard MacKay, Gerrit J. Dirkmaat, and Robin Scott Jensen, "The 'Caractors' Document: New Light on an Early Transcription of the Book of Mormon Characters," *Mormon Historical Studies* 14, no. 1 (Spring 2014): 131–52; Michael Hubbard MacKay, "Git Them Translated," in *Approaching Antiquity: Joseph Smith's Study of the Ancient World* (forthcoming, paper presented at the 2013 Church History Symposium, Provo, UT, March 7, 2013).
34. Blackman apparently interviewed a local resident, who stated that Reuben "assisted Joe Smith to fix up some characters such as Smith pretended were engraven on his book of plates." Blackman, *History of Susquehanna County, Pennsylvania*, 104; Knight Sr., History, 3.
35. Clearly, possibilities abound, because little is known about the origin of these documents. Joseph may have made rubbings and had scribes create handwritten copies, or he may have copied them and used scribal assistance to make better copies or multiple copies, but ultimately nothing is known about the creation of the documents.
36. Joseph Smith, History, circa Summer 1832, in *JSP*, H1:15.
37. See MacKay, Dirkmaat, and Jensen, "The 'Caractors' Document," 131–40.
38. Martin showed the characters he had copied from the plates to individuals throughout his lifetime. See John A. Clark, *Gleanings by the Way* (Philadelphia: W. J. & J. K. Simon, 1842), 217, 222–31. G. W. Stoddard, who was a farmer in Wayne County, New York, claimed Harris was a Universalist and a Methodist. See Howe, *Mormonism Unvailed*, 260–61; Orsamus Turner, *History of the Pioneer Settlement of Phelp's and Gorham's Purchase and Morris' Reserve* (Rochester, NY: Erastus Darrow, 1851), 215; and Henry G. Tinsley, "Origin of Mormonism," *San Francisco Chronicle*, 14 May 1893, 12. For accounts of others who claimed to see the characters from Harris, see Clark, "Gleanings By the Way"; *Episcopal Recorder*, 5 September 1840, 94; and Orsamus Turner's recollection in Turner, *History of the Pioneer Settlement*, 215.

# 3

# Harris's Trip to the East

In February 1828, Martin Harris hurried from Palmyra, New York, to Harmony, Pennsylvania, to tell Joseph Smith that he had seen the Lord in a vision and had been told "that he must go to New York City with some of the characters."[1] This initiates the well-known story of Martin Harris when he visited Charles Anthon in New York City. Using what most Latter-day Saints know about this visit as a launching pad, there is far more to this story than historians have yet to tease out of the existing documents. Demonstrating the possibilities of further light on the subject, a handful of letters written by Charles Anthon have recently been uncovered from the archives of Columbia University. These letters possibly indicate why Harris was sent to him. This and other details have begun to emerge, developing the story far more than we have been able to understand in the past.

Although Joseph and Martin had not spoken with each other for more than three months, by February 1828 this vision brought the men together once again and initiated this foundational event. Joseph's history explained briefly that soon after Harris arrived at Joseph's house, they "proceeded to coppy some of them [the characters] and [Harris] took his Journy to the

❖ FROM DARKNESS UNTO LIGHT

Eastern Cittys and to the Learned."[2] Though they did not know at the time, the Book of Mormon would reveal that this event had been the fulfillment of a prophecy found in the Book of Isaiah. It also became the central story surrounding the characters copied from the gold plates. Yet Joseph Smith never realized this until Martin Harris returned. This well-known story, told even today by Latter-day Saints, will be cast here in light of what their original purpose had been, which will help develop how this trip was relevant to the translation of the gold plates.

This episode began once Harris left Harmony with the ancient characters in hand, eager to begin his journey eastward to find scholars who could shed light upon the meaning of the language of the plates. On his weeklong journey back to Palmyra, before he began traveling eastward, he carefully contemplated what resources he had at his fingertips that could aid him in his quest. One of the closer institutes that may have offered Harris some direction or books to compare the characters with was twenty miles south of Palmyra in Canandaigua. Depending on Harris's route back home, he could have stopped there before leaving to New York City. The Canandaigua Academy, a private school for boys established in 1791, potentially had the resources to help Harris find scholars in the east and even books that may have helped him superficially analyze the characters. Unfortunately, the school paled in comparison to some of the institutes in Philadelphia and New York City, which employed some of the brightest academics in the world working as part of their faculties.

Although Harris's vision had commanded him to go to New York City, he began his trip by gathering information from a former Palmyra resident. A local printer, Pomeroy Tucker, remembered that Harris went looking for scholars who could offer an "interpretation and bibliological scrutiny" of the characters drawn off the gold plates.[3] While Harris's exact plan and whom he intended to visit in New York City is unknown, it is known that he apparently planned to visit the statesman Luther Bradish in Albany, New York. Bradish had lived in Palmyra before he became a successful politician and was an understandable contact for Harris to approach first.[4]

The trip to Albany was nearly 250 miles away on the Erie Canal, but the canal conveniently wound its way between Harris's property and the village of Palmyra, carrying boats back and forth between Lake Erie and Albany.[5] About halfway to Albany, Harris stopped in Utica, where he may

40

have shown the characters to individuals there and even gathered information at the state clerk's office about obtaining a copyright for the translation of the plates once the Book of Mormon was finished.[6] A copyright for the Book of Mormon would be submitted to that office on June 10, 1829, just before the translation was finished. Harris eventually arrived in Albany, where he approached Bradish for information.[7] It is possible that Harris contacted him by letter before he arrived, but regardless of Harris's planning, Bradish likely welcomed Harris because of their common roots in Palmyra.[8]

Harris may have been hoping Bradish could identify the characters, but he likely saw him as a friend that could provide useful information, rather than a specialist, believing that Bradish could help him find scholars to translate the characters. New York citizens had recently elected Bradish to the state assembly, and he was a well-known politician in the state of New York. A rising star in New York politics, by 1839 he would become lieutenant governor of the state. Bradish was not a linguist or a scholar, but he had keen enthusiasm for antiquities and was therefore aware of most contemporary archeological discoveries.[9] He had enough experience with languages and classical studies, given his education, that he may have been able to analyze the characters and direct Harris to individuals who could offer detailed analyses.[10]

*Luther Bradish, Franklin County Historical Society.*

## Scholars of Ancient America

All university graduates studied languages, focusing primarily upon Greek and Latin. Unfortunately, Bradish did not know ancient languages well enough to identify an unknown language with accuracy, which would have

❖ FROM DARKNESS UNTO LIGHT

made it difficult to know who to send Harris to for further analysis of the characters. He did not recognize them himself, and Martin Harris did not know what language was inscribed upon the plates. In the process of translating the plates in 1829, Joseph Smith later discovered that the language inscribed upon the gold plates was "reformed Egyptian." Joseph learned through the translation that an ancient prophet, Mormon, had abridged several records in his possession to create gold plates. Mormon wrote that "we have written this record according to our knowledge, in the characters which are called among us the reformed Egyptian."[11] Regardless of what it said in the Book of Mormon, when Harris left on his journey in 1828, Joseph had not yet translated those words from the plates; therefore, neither of them knew the language that the unfamiliar characters represented.[12]

Even the angel Moroni, Joseph's primary source for knowledge about the plates, apparently did not explain to Joseph that the record was written in reformed Egyptian. None of the records describing Moroni's visit claim that he told Joseph about the language. Reflecting back on Moroni's visits, Joseph remembered him quoting scripture and explaining the details of his prophetic calling, but nowhere in his history did he say that the angel told him what language was written on the plates. Joseph remembered, "the Lord ... revealed unto me that in the Town of Manchester Ontario County N.Y. there was plates of gold upon which there was engravings which was engraven by Maroni & his fathers the servants of the living God in ancient days."[13] His later accounts also left out any reference to the language on the plates. Rather, he explained that Moroni said, "there was a book deposited written upon gold plates, giving an account of the former *inhabitants of this continent* and the source from whence they sprang."[14] Therefore, before Joseph sent Harris to New York City with the characters, he was told that ancient *American* prophets were responsible for the characters on the plates and that the content described the inhabitants of the ancient Americas, leaving him with very little reason to conclude that the plates were written in any form of Egyptian.

After it later became known that the plates were inscribed with "reformed Egyptian," all those who reflected back upon Harris's visit to New York City told the story as if they already knew the characters were "reformed Egyptian." In reality, in February 1828 they had yet to find out about the language.[15] Instead, Joseph sent Harris to New York with the characters with very little

> Charel Anthon was not the first person Martin Harris showed the characters from the plates to.

HARRIS'S TRIP TO THE EAST ❖

information other than the knowledge that the characters were taken from an ancient American source.[16] This is far different from the traditional story told by Latter-day Saints, but it helps make sense of why he visited certain individuals well before he went to Charles Anthon.

William Smith, who was a young teenager at the time, remembered that Joseph did not know how to read the plates when he first brought them home, but once Harris returned from New York City they had a better idea of what language the ancient prophets used. According to William Smith,

*Charles Anthon, ca. 1855–65, Matthew B. Brady studio. Library of Congress.*

43

## FROM DARKNESS UNTO LIGHT

it was not until "the Professor [in New York City] Pronounced the characters to be ancient Hebrew corrupted, and the language to be degenerate Hebrew with a mixture of Egyptian" that Joseph had any idea of the nature of the characters.[17]

It seems unlikely that Harris was looking for an Egyptian scholar. Even if he had been initially looking for a scholar who could decipher Egyptian, he would not have found one in the United States. Although European scholars had begun to use the Rosetta Stone a few years earlier to better understand Egyptian, none of them were in America.[18] Bradish, in particular, did not study Egyptian and could not have identified the characters as Egyptian, at least with any confidence, making it highly unlikely that Bradish would have sent Harris to an Egyptian scholar. It was not until 1822 that the Frenchman Jean Francois Champollion was able to make steps toward deciphering Egyptian hieroglyphs.[19] His work was not widely printed in the United States, and imprints that were published before 1828 were not translated into English, making a search for a scholar of Egyptian hieroglyphs a search for someone who knew the European literature, not for someone who had focused his or her studies on Egyptian.

Bradish instead compared the characters with a language that he was somewhat familiar with. Bradish compared the characters to samples of Middle Eastern writing that he had in his possession. He juxtaposed the characters against those on "a Pass that had been given . . . when traveling through the Turkish dominions; and he thought the characters resembled those of that Pass."[20] His passport-like certificate from the Ottoman Empire was written in Turkish and included a Turkish seal that he likely used to compare against the characters.[21] Likely having little confidence in his comparison, he ultimately sent Harris to New York City to have the characters assessed by scholars of ancient American history.

## Professor Samuel Mitchill, Rutgers College

According to at least one account, after Harris went to Albany and spoke with Bradish, he continued on to Philadelphia.[23] The American Philosophical Society in Philadelphia, under the leadership of Thomas Jefferson in the late eighteenth century and Peter Stephen Du Ponceau by 1828, encouraged research about Native Americans and helped support

> Martin Harris may have visited Samuel Rafinesque and Caleb Atwater, (experts on Ancient American people) in philadelphia

scholarship about their origins, culture, and history.[24] The society was well known, and the work done by its members was frequently published in their journal, *Transactions*.

Likely knowing that Philadelphia was a hotbed for Native American studies, Bradish or someone along the way sent Harris there in hopes that he could find a scholar to translate the characters, believing them to be a language of an ancient American people. Harris could have potentially visited both Samuel Rafinesque and Caleb Atwater, leading naturalists and Native American enthusiasts with the Society.[25] Rafinesque had actively studied North American Indians and their languages since 1819. His interest in Native Americans and their languages may have caused Harris to search him out; he had worked on deciphering Native American languages, had studied many of the pictographs found in the ancient world, and had begun to develop a translation of the Mayan glyphs.[26] Some of Caleb Atwater's academic work focused on Native American languages as well. In particular, he attempted to uncover the origins of the North American Indians.[27] Numerous scholars, like Rafinesque and Atwater, had similarly tried to uncover the ancient origins of the Native Americans, some of whom even believed that they originated from the lost ten tribes of Israel, similar to the seafaring Israelites described in the Book of Mormon.

It is unknown how much Joseph Smith and Martin Harris knew about the debates over the origins of the Native Americans, but various people had offered religious and anthropological theories since the first European explorers arrived in the Americas.[28] Some early theories claimed that the Indians were of Asian origin or even that they were a race derived from the lost city of Atlantis, while most others viewed their origins in Christian terms—for example, claiming they were descendants of Noah or that they were pre-Adamites.[29] Many early Americans, including influential leaders like William Penn and Roger Williams, embraced theories that the Indians were part of the lost ten tribes of Israel.[30] James Adair, a naturalist who spent forty years among the Indians, gave teeth to the argument about the ten tribes by comparing the language, customs, and cultures of Native Americans to Jewish cultures and customs.[31] Reverend Ethan Smith backed away from Adair's approach, but further popularized the theory that the Indians were descendants of the ten lost tribes in his 1825 book entitled *View of the Hebrews*.[32]

❖ FROM DARKNESS UNTO LIGHT

Tabular View of the Compared Atlantic Alphabets & Glyphs of Africa and America. *By Samuel Rafinesque,* Atlantic Journal, *1832.*

More-academic naturalists, like Alexander von Humboldt, provided a very different argument for where the Native Americans came from by systematic analysis of the ruins, hieroglyphics, and personal observations of the tribes. Humboldt argued fervently, with great success, that Native Americans originated from northeastern Asia and had traveled across the Bering Strait before populating the Americas.[33] Humboldt believed that there was originally one common language and that all races derived according to the commonalities found within the languages of other societies. His method and theory were championed by a handful of scholars in Philadelphia at the American Philosophical Society, and Pierre Du Ponceau, the society's leader, was a major proponent of this kind of linguistic research and of Humboldt's conclusions. There certainly was no better place to find a translator for an ancient American document than under the umbrella of the society.

Joseph Smith had apparently been cognizant, even before he retrieved the plates, of the fact that they offered an answer to where the Native Americans originated, which could have sparked the interest of scholars and enthusiasts. In 1835, Oliver Cowdery wrote that one of the reasons Joseph was not able to take possession of the plates for four years was because, at times, he had contemplated the possibility that the translated text from the plates could have generated money and pulled him and his family from the bonds of poverty. Explaining Joseph's retrieval of the plates, Cowdery wrote: "A history of the inhabitants who peopled this continent, previous to its being discovered to Europeans by Columbus, must be interesting to every man; and as it would develop the important fact, that the present race

46

were descendants of Abraham." He went on to explain, "Surely, thought [Joseph] every man will seize with eagerness, this knowledge, and this incalculable income will be mine. Enough to raise the expectations of any one of like inexperience, placed in similar circumstances."[34] According to Cowdery, while the angel initially forbade him from taking the plates, by 1827 Joseph had purged his mind from such thoughts of avarice and had wholly embraced the sacred nature of his prophetic calling. The origins of the Native Americans likely interested Joseph and Martin because of the nature of the gold plates, but the scholars working on those theories were also using the study of Native American glyphs and language to trace the origins, which offered Harris an even greater potential to find someone to translate the gold-plate characters. Although Harris likely did not know it at the time he went to visit the scholars, the Book of Mormon in fact suggests that pre-Abrahamic peoples[35] were the first to travel to America, followed by a group led by the son of Zedekiah,[36] and finally by a small group of the tribe of Manasseh, led by the prophet Lehi.[37] However, the common ground between Harris and the scholars was his possession of what he claimed were ancient American writings and the scholars' interest in translation.

If Harris went to Philadelphia and met with members of the American Philosophical Society, it would have been natural for them to send him to one of the prominent members of the society, Samuel L. Mitchill. He was one of the leading scholars on Native Americans in the New York area, the teacher of Rafinesque, and an avid linguist. After Harris went to Philadelphia he made his way back up to New York. While Bradish may have directed Harris to the American Philosophical Society in general, he might even have sent Harris to Samuel Mitchill in particular.[38]

Mitchill had conducted over thirty years of research and experienced a lifetime of political and academic work in and around New York by the time Harris approached him in early 1828.[39] In particular, he had participated in the 1788 treaty in New York with Native Americans in which they ceded the Western District of New York, and as a US senator he was chair of the Indian Affairs Committee. He had gained an abiding interest in all Native American languages, even learning the Mohawk language early in his career. His studies also built upon Humboldt's theory of the origin of the Native Americans but further claimed that two other races in addition to the Asians had populated ancient America. He believed that Polynesians and Scandinavians also settled the Americas but that the Asian populations subjugated and eventually destroyed the other two races in a final battle in upstate western New York.[40] Harris had apparently been convinced that he "had better go to the celebrated Dr. Mitchill and show them to him. He is very learned in these ancient languages and I have no doubt he will be able to give you some satisfaction."[41]

In 1828, Mitchill was serving as the vice president of Rutgers Medical College in New York City. The short-lived college had been formed through the partnership of New York's Queen's College and New Brunswick's Rutgers College to take advantage of New York City's larger population. Mitchill's position there also allowed him to stay in New York City and benefit from the institutes that had been built in the thriving metropolis.[42]

Despite his prestigious position, individuals hoping to have ancient documents translated had come to Mitchill even before Harris approached him. His previous work made him a well-known expert on the translation of ancient and modern languages.[43] For example, Abraham Edwards of Detroit approached him in 1823 with a manuscript that included foreign characters written on its pages.[44] It was apparently discovered by Edwards "under one of his buildings" and was "a manuscript volume, of between 3 and 4 hundred pages."[45]

Mitchill's method for determining the unknown text in Edwards's Detroit manuscript provides an insight into the similar efforts he likely made to decipher the characters Harris presented to him from the gold plates. When a sample of the Detroit manuscript was sent to Mitchill, he gathered with a few of his colleagues and compared it with samples of writing he had in his possession. They also turned to Noel Antoine Pluche's book that includes samples of French paleography. In one volume of Pluche's book there are numerous samples in varying hands that they used to compare with the characters in the manuscript. They also took the manuscript to the American Bible Society Library (ABS) that had been established in 1817. The ABS's first project was also to translate the Delaware Indian/English parallel text of the Bible. Just before Mitchill visited the ABS, they had moved to their first permanent home in lower Manhattan, where they housed numerous documents "with types [of] various languages in the collection."[46] Mitchill wrote, "When we were almost on the

*[Handwritten note: After meeting with Dr. Mitchel, Martin Harris Frolics the charters to Charles Anthon]*

HARRIS'S TRIP TO THE EAST ❖

point of despair, a large bible, printed about 300 years ago, was produced, and we were enabled to form some idea of the abbreviations and contractions in the text, which threw light upon the MS. Of Detroit."[47]

Just as he had done with the Detroit manuscript, Mitchill carefully examined the characters taken from the gold plates given to him by Martin Harris. He "looked at his engravings—made a learned dissertation on them—compared them with the hieroglyphics discovered by Champollion in Europe, and set them down as a language of a people formerly in existence in the East, but now no more."[48] Yet, regardless of his efforts, Mitchill was unable to determine with certainty the linguistic origin of the characters.[49] Instead, he "confessed he had been unable to understand" them and sent Harris with a note "requesting [Charles Anthon] to decipher, if possible, [the characters]."[50]

## Charles Anthon, Adjunct Professor, Columbia College

After meeting with Samuel Mitchill, Harris made his way to Mitchill's former institution, Columbia College, to show the characters to Charles Anthon. It is here that the Latter-day Saints usually pick up the story, but it is also here that the documentary record begins to reinterpret Charles Anthon's role in Harris's trip to the east. Anthon was educated as a lawyer but began teaching Greek and Latin at Columbia College in 1820. He won acclaim for his publication of an updated edition of *Lempriere's Classical Dictionary* in 1825 but was still just an "adjunct professor" in 1828. While he would eventually became a professor in the Department of Latin Languages at Columbia, by 1832 he was still only the rector of the children's grammar school at Columbia.[51] Unlike Samuel Mitchill, Anthon had done no significant academic work on ancient America or Native American languages.

Still, Anthon was very interested in Native American stories because of a financial enterprise he and an English colleague had undertaken. Washington Irving had recently authored a memoir, "Philip of Pokanoket," about a Wampanoag chief who had generously aided the early English colonists, warming many to the idea of Native American stories. To capitalize on this new interest, in the summer of 1828 Anthon began corresponding

49

❖ FROM DARKNESS UNTO LIGHT

*Portrait of Samuel L. Mitchill.*

with Edmund Henry Barker of Thetford, England, about collecting and printing "specimens of Indian eloquence."[52]

Barker wrote to Anthon: "when you have collected a good stock of materials, arrange them, put a preface to them, print the book contract with an American publisher, take one half of the profits & give the other to me—send over the sheets as they come from the press—I will reprint the book here, make some additions, & give to you half the profits. It is a noble subject."[53] By September of that year Barker was encouraged by Anthon's progress collecting Native American stories, but prompted him to gather the samples more quickly regardless of their "genuiness & authenticity."[54] By the middle of December, Anthon was still looking for Indian stories and speeches, for which Barker wrote, "I hope that the collection of Indian Speeches is advancing to maturity."[55] His search, no doubt, included consulting the prestigious Mitchill, who knew more about New York's Native American populations than anyone else did.

In the midst of Anthon's ongoing efforts to collect tales and speeches, Harris arrived at the college with his account of the gold plates containing stories of American Indians and copies of the characters inscribed on the plates in hand. Anthon, of course, was eager to examine the paper for Harris, and he most likely had hopes that he had found another story for his publication. Knowing that Barker was putting pressure on him, Anthon must have been excited to examine Harris's document. Like Washington Irving's essay, Harris's tale would have been exciting to Americans and Europeans because it was a story about ancient Americans who believed in Christ and who had created a sacred record on gold plates that had only recently been uncovered. Harris's visit fit right within Barker and Anthon's plan to collect essays about Native Americans.

50

Nevertheless, years later, Anthon concealed his own financial interest in examining the characters and instead claimed that the paper was a hoax and that someone had combined characters from different languages to deceive him. He derided Harris's document as a compilation derived from an alteration of "Greek and Hebrew letters, crosses and flourishes, [and] Roman letters inverted or placed sideways." He claimed it was "decked with various strange marks, and evidently copied after the Mexican Calendar given by Humboldt, but copied in such a way as not to betray the source."[56] Once the Book of Mormon was published and Charles Anthon's name became attached to Joseph Smith's story of the retrieval and translation of the plates, a defensive Anthon felt that he needed to protect his reputation. He wrote a letter to E. D. Howe in 1834 as Howe prepared his book *Mormonism Unvailed*, an exposé criticizing the origins of the Church. He again downplayed his involvement by writing to two pastors in 1841 and 1844 to explain what happened when Harris had visited him.[57]

Harris, on the other hand, told a completely different story, which James Mulholland later recorded in Joseph Smith's history. He explained that after Anthon examined the characters, Anthon told him "that they were Egyptian, Chaldeak, Assyriac, and Arabac, and he said that they were true characters." Seeking a scholar's witness that the characters were legitimate, Harris apparently asked Anthon for a certificate of authenticity. Harris recalled that "He gave me a certificate certifying to the people of Palmyra that they were true characters." Anthon's certificate had the potential to offer clout to Joseph Smith's translation of the plates and could have been printed along with the Book of Mormon, but it was soon lost. Harris explained that as he was leaving Anthon's office, Anthon "called me back and asked me how the young man found out that there were gold plates in the place where he found them. I answered that an Angel of God had revealed it unto him. He then said to me, let me see that certificate, I accordingly took it out of my pocket and gave it [to] him." Anthon took the certificate and "tore it to pieces, saying that there was no such thing now as ministring of angels, and that if I would bring the plates to him, he would translate them. I informed him that part of the plates were sealed, and that I was forbidden to bring them, he replied 'I cannot read a sealed book.'"[58]

❖ FROM DARKNESS UNTO LIGHT

Although Harris had first visited the more prominent (and likely more academic) Mitchill, Anthon later became the scholar primarily associated with examining the characters from the plates. His final words to Harris as he sent him on his way, demanding to have the book brought to him, later made Anthon the most relevant person whom Harris had visited in the minds of early Mormons. The earliest newspaper accounts stated that Anthon was only a tangential part of the story,[59] but sometime after Joseph Smith translated a passage in the Book of Mormon in June 1829, Anthon's interaction with Martin Harris became very important. The passage came from the Book of Isaiah in the Old Testament and stated:

> It shall come to pass that the Lord God shall say unto him to whom he shall deliver the book: Take these words which are not sealed and deliver them to another, that he may show them unto the learned, saying: Read this, I pray thee. And the learned shall say: Bring hither the book, and I will read them.
> And the man shall say: I cannot bring the book, for it is sealed.
> Then shall the learned say: I cannot read it.[60]

Only a short time after Smith translated this passage from the Book of Mormon, early believers began explaining that this prophecy had been fulfilled through Harris's experience with Anthon. Early Mormons saw Anthon as the "learned" who declared that he could not read a sealed book. Joseph's 1832 history clearly made this association, stating that Harris "took his Journy to the Eastern Cittys and to the Learned saying read this I pray thee and the learned said I cannot but if he would bring the plates they would read it but the Lord had forbid it and he returned to me and gave them to me to translate and I said cannot for I am not learned but the Lord had prepared spectacles for to read the Book."[61] More specifically, Smith's 1838 history explained that Anthon had actually spoken the words of the prophecy verbatim by saying, "I cannot read a sealed book."[62] Thus Harris's trip to Philadelphia and his interaction with Samuel Mitchill faded over time as they became more and more irrelevant in comparison to his visit with Anthon.

Like Mitchill's forgotten role in Harris's trip to New York City, once Harris returned and Joseph began translating the gold plates, the purpose for the trip also began to fade in the minds of those who were involved.

By 1838, Harris's visit was heralded as proof of the ancient origin of the characters, but according to the earliest sources, the primary reason for his journey to the East with the characters was to "get them translated."⁶³

## Notes

1. History, circa summer 1832, in *JSP*, H1:6.
2. Joseph Smith, History, 1832, 6. Original spelling has been preserved throughout the chapter.
3. Pomeroy Tucker, *Origin, Rise, and Progress of Mormonism* (New York: Appleton, 1867), 42.
4. Richard Bennett argues that there were so few residents in Palmyra in the early nineteenth century that when the Harris and Bradish families lived in Palmyra they would have certainly known each other. He also shows that Nathan Harris (Martin's father) and Joseph Bradish were elected as "pathmasters" in Palmyra in 1796 together and that they were replaced by Martin Harris and Calvin Bradish in 1811. Richard Bennett, "'Read This I Pray Thee': Martin Harris and the Three Wise Men of the East," *Journal of Mormon History* 36, no. 1 (Winter 2010): 186.
5. See 1832 profile of the Erie Canal, www.Davidrumsey.com.
6. See W. W. Phelps to E. D. Howe, 15 January 1831, in *Mormonism Unvailed*, 273.
7. John H. Gilbert, a typesetter in Palmyra, explained that "On his way [to New York City] he stopped at Albany and called on Lt Gov Bradish." John H. Gilbert, "Memorandum, made by John H. Gilbert Esq, Sept 8ᵗʰ, 1892, Palmyra, N.Y.," Palmyra King's Daughters Free Library, in Palmyra, NY.
8. Martin Harris was acquainted with Bradish's family. Both families were early settlers of Palmyra when the population there was minimal, and there are records of Nathan Harris and John Bradish, their fathers, working together on the Palmyra roads. Martin and Calvin Bradish also worked together in 1811. See Bennett, "'Read This I Pray Thee,'" 185–87.
9. See Bennett, "'Read This I Pray Thee,'" 180–85.
10. See Stanley B. Kimball, "The Anthon Transcript: People, Primary Sources, and Problems," *BYU Studies* 10, no. 3 (Spring 1970): 325–52. For earlier work by Kimball, see "I Cannot Read a Sealed Book," *Improvement Era*, February 1957, 80–82, 104, 106; and "Charles Anthon and the Egyptian Language," *Improvement Era*, October 1960, 708–10, 765. For additional studies, see Edward H. Ashment, "The Book of Mormon and the Anthon Transcript: An Interim

Report," *Sunstone* 5, no. 3 (May–June 1990): 29–31; Daniel Bachman, "Sealed in a Book: Preliminary Observations on the Newly Found 'Anthon Transcript,'" *BYU Studies* 20, no. 4 (Summer 1980); David E. Sloan, "The Anthon Transcripts and the Translation of the Book of Mormon: Studying It Out in the Mind of Joseph Smith," *Journal of Book of Mormon Studies* 5, no. 2; Sidney Sperry, "Some Problems Arising from Martin Harris's Visit to Professor Charles Anthon," in *Answers to Book of Mormon Questions* (Salt Lake City: Bookcraft, 1967), 53–61; and Richard B. Stout, "A Singular Discovery: The Curious Manuscript, Mitchill and Mormonism," *Evangel*, 2001–2002, in six parts.

11. Mormon 9:32.
12. At least one scholar suggested to Harris, after he had visited New York City and elsewhere, that the characters he presented to him were possibly Egyptian, but Joseph was given no assurance that he knew the language of the plates until later, when his divinely guided translation revealed it to him. The Book of Mormon is the earliest known account that identified the language, assuming that the lost book of Lehi did not identify the language—meaning that Mormon's statement about the language was not known for sure until over a year after Harris went to New York in May 1829. See below.
13. Smith, History, 1832, 4.
14. Smith, History, vol. A-1, 6; emphasis added.
15. All of the current literature assumes that Joseph knew that the characters were in reformed Egyptian before he sent Martin Harris to New York City. See Kimball, "The Anthon Transcript." See also note 10 above. For Richard Bennett's article, see "'Read This I Pray Thee.'"
16. Upon reflection, both Joseph and Lucy Smith remembered that Moroni's visits between 1823 and 1827 included only general details about the peoples described within the pages of the plates. Joseph's famous Wentworth letter explained in 1842 that the angel Moroni "informed [him] concerning the aboriginal inhabitants of this country, and shown who they were, and from whence they came; a brief sketch of their origin, progress, civilization, laws, governments. . . . I was told where there was deposited some plates on which were engraven an abridgement of the records of the ancient prophets that had existed on this continent." Lucy Smith also remembered that after meeting with Moroni, Joseph would "describe the ancient inhabitants of this continent their dress their maner of traveling the animals which they rode etc.," but not the language of the plates. Lucy Mack Smith, History, 1844–45, book 4, MS 1.

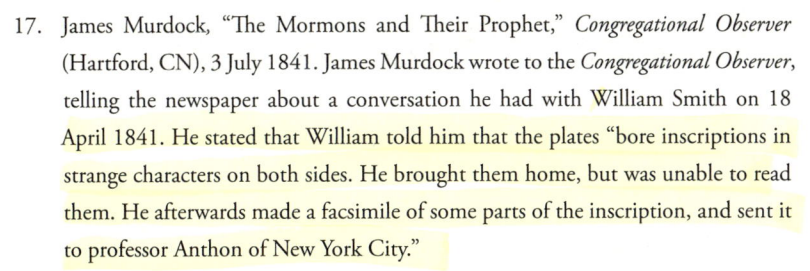

17. James Murdock, "The Mormons and Their Prophet," *Congregational Observer* (Hartford, CN), 3 July 1841. James Murdock wrote to the *Congregational Observer*, telling the newspaper about a conversation he had with William Smith on 18 April 1841. He stated that William told him that the plates "bore inscriptions in strange characters on both sides. He brought them home, but was unable to read them. He afterwards made a facsimile of some parts of the inscription, and sent it to professor Anthon of New York City."

18. See Don Cameron Allen, "The Predecessors of Champollion," *Proceedings of the American Philosophical Society* 104, no. 5: 527–47.

19. See Champollion, *Lettre à M. Dacier relative à l'alphabet des hiéroglyphes phonétiques*, 1822. See also Lesley and Roy Adkins, *The Keys of Egypt: The Obsession to Decipher Egyptian Hieroglyphs* (HarperCollins, 2000); and Daniel Meyerson, *The Linguist and the Emperor: Napoleon and Champollion's Quest to Decipher the Rosetta Stone* (Random House, 2005).

20. Fayette Lapham, "Interview with the Father of Joseph Smith, the Mormon Prophet, Forty Years Ago. His Account of the Finding of the Sacred Plates," *Historical Magazine*, May 1870, 305–9.

21. See Erin Jennings, "Charles Anthon," *JWHAJ* (Fall/Winter 2012): 177; Luther Bradish to Thomas Appleton, 1 July 1824.

22. Jennings, "Charles Anthon."

23. Knight Sr., History, 3. Though he may have initially stopped in New York City to speak with scholars, there are no records of his stay or his interactions there at that time. If he spent any time there it is possible that someone in New York City prompted him to carry on to Philadelphia. James Gordon Bennett suggests that Harris met with Charles Anthon first and then left to visit others, like Samuel Mitchill, before he returned to meet with Anthon again. If Anthon is correct, Bennett is in error because Anthon claimed that Mitchill sent Harris to meet with him, James Gordon Bennett, "Mormonites," *Morning Courier and Enquirer* (New York), September 1, 1831. It is difficult to know who Bennett received his information from, because members of the Church of Christ had moved from New York, where he apparently gathered his information, by the spring of 1831. Bennett was likely told the story secondhand from someone who was not involved.

24. American Philosophical Society, *Transactions*, 4, 1799.

25. Atwater authored *Descriptions of the Antiquities Discovered in the State of Ohio and other Western States* in 1820, and Rafinesque wrote *Ancient History, or, Annals of Kentucky: with a Survey of the Ancient Monuments of North America* in 1824.

26. See Charles Boewe, "C. S. Rafinesque and Ohio Valley Archaeology," *Ancient America* Monograph Series (Barnardsville, NC: Center for Ancient American Studies), 6.
27. See Caleb Atwater, *Remarks Made on a Tour to Prairie de Chien,* 1831, 75–97.
28. See Lee Eldridge Huddleston, *Origins of the American Indians: European Concepts, 1492–1729* (Austin: University of Texas Press, 1967); and Robert Wauchope, *Lost Tribes and Sunken Continents: Myth and Method in the Study of American Indians* (Chicago: University of Chicago Press, 1962). For works cited by these authors, see the following for examples of late-nineteenth-century authors that include histories of the origin theories: John T. Short, *The North Americans of Antiquity: Their Origin, Migration, and Type of Civilization Considered* (1879) (see especially 131–55); and Samuel G. Drake, *The Aboriginal Races of North America* (1860).
29. For a few examples, see Richard Hakluyt, *The Principal Navigations, Voyages, Traffiques and Discoveries of the English Nation* (London, 1589); Isaac de la Peyrere, *A Theological System upon the Presupposition That Men Were before Adam* (London, 1655); Ira Hill, *Antiquities of America Explained* (1831); and George Jones, *The History of Ancient America, Anterior to the Time of Columbus* (1843).
30. See William Penn, *A Letter from William Penn, Proprietary and Governour of Pennsylvania in America, to the Committee of the Free Society of Traders* (1683).
31. See James Adair, *History of the American Indians* (1775); and Charles Hudson, "James Adair as Anthropologist," *Ethnohistory* 24, no. 4 (1977): 311–28.
32. See Ethan Smith, *View of the Hebrews; or, The Tribes of Israel in America* (1825).
33. See Michael A. Wadyko, "Alexander Von Humboldt and Nineteenth-Century Ideas on the Origin of American Indians" (PhD diss., West Virginia University, 2000).
34. Oliver Cowder to W. W. Phelps, "Letter VII," *Messenger and Advocate*, July 1835, 1:155–59.
35. Leaving after the Lord confounded the language of the people in Babel, a group travelled in unique dish-shaped barges to the Americas. See Ether 6:7–12.
36. Toward the end of the reign of Zedekiah, the last king of Judah, the Book of Mormon explains that his only surviving son, Mulek, took "as many as would hearken unto the voice of Lord" and sailed to America (Omni 1:15–16). The Book of Mormon explained that Mulek's escape from the Babylonian conquest of Jerusalem forced a group of Jews from the homeland to the Americas, including Zedekiah's royal bloodline. Helaman 6:10 reads, "Now the land south was called Lehi, and the land north was called Mulek, which was after the son of Zedekiah; for the Lord did bring Mulek into the land north, and Lehi into the land south."

37. See Alma 10:3, which states, "And Aminadi was a descendent of Nephi, who was the son of Lehi, who came out of the land of Jerusalem, who was a descendant of Manasseh, who was the son of Joseph who was sold into Egypt by the hands of his brethren."
38. See Mitchill to Samuel Burnside, *Archaeologia Americana*, 1:314–15. The earliest records, found in 1829 New York newspaper accounts, verify that Mitchill was not only the person Harris was sent to, but that he was the central figure in the story. Jonathan Hadley, who was the first printer to publish anything about Harris's visit, explained that "among the number [of scholars] was Professor Mitchell of New York," as if Mitchill were the most notable figure he visited. Just weeks later, the *Rochester Advertiser and Telegraph* on 31 August 1829 reproduced Hadley's article, claiming that Harris took the characters to see if someone could "English them" and placed Mitchill at the center of the story. By 5 September 1829, the *Rochester Gem* reported that "Harris states that he went in search of someone to interpret the hieroglyphics, but found no one was intended to perform that all-important task but Smith himself."
39. Much of Mitchill's work focused upon the area around New York State, in which he argued that the region was much older than Europe. In 1818, Mitchill wrote *Observations on the Geology of North America*, which was published alongside the work of the renowned French naturalist and comparative anatomist Georges Cuvier. See Georges Cuvier, *Essay on the Theory of the Earth*, 1818.
40. Samuel L. Mitchill, "No. III: The Original Inhabitants of America Consisted of the Same Races with the Malays of Australia, and the Tartars of the North," *Archaeologia Americana*, 1.
41. Bennett, "Mormonites."
42. See David Cowen, *Medical Education: The Queen's-Rutgers Experience, 1792–1830* (New Brunswick, NJ: Rutgers University, 1966).
43. See Robert Hall, *A Scientist in the Early Republic: Samuel Latham Mitchill* (Columbia, 1934); and Samuel Latham Mitchill, "Specimen of the Poetry and Singing of the Osages," *Archaeologia Americana*, 1:315–17. In 1858, J. W. Francis reflected back upon Mitchill's work and commented that he translated many ancient glyphs. J. W. Francis, *Old New York* (1858), 90. Even Mitchill's doctoral dissertation included over 150 translations that he had done between 1804 and 1818, though these are limited to the few that he included to make his point in the dissertation.
44. See *Detroit Gazette*, 7 March 1823, 2; *Nile's Weekly Register*, 3 May 1823, 130.

❖ FROM DARKNESS UNTO LIGHT

45. *Detroit Gazette*, 7 March 1823, 2.
46. *Detroit Gazette*, 16 May 1823, 2.
47. *Detroit Gazette*, 16 May 1823, 2.
48. Bennett, "Mormonites."
49. In 1841, Anthon clarified that it was "Dr. Samuel L. Mitchell" who had sent Harris to him, in a letter to Thomas Winthrop Coit, on 3 April 1841. *Church Record*, 17 April 1841, 231–32. Charles Anthon, who Harris visited next, wrote on 17 February 1834 to E. D. Howe: "Some years ago, a plain, and apparently simple hearted farmer, called upon me with a note from Dr. Mitchell of our city, now deceased, requesting me to decipher, if possible, a paper, which the farmer would hand me, and which Dr. M. confessed he had been unable to understand." E. D. Howe, *Mormonism Unvailed*, 270.
50. E. D. Howe, *Mormonism Unvailed*, 270.
51. Henry Drisler, "Commemorative Discourse" (New York: 1868), 12–15.
52. Washington Irving, "Philip of Pakanoket: An Indian Memoir," in *The Sketch-Book of Geoffrey Crayon, Gent.* (1819–20). See Edmund Henry Barker, Thetford England to Charles Anthon, New York City, 9 July 1827, Edmund Henry Barker, Letters, 1827–31, Rare Book and Manuscript Library, Columbia University Library, New York.
53. Edmund Henry Barker, Thetford England to Charles Anthon, New York City, 9 July 1827, Edmund Henry Barker, Letters, 1827–1831, Rare Book and Manuscript Library, Columbia University Library, New York.
54. Edmund Henry Barker, Thetford England to Charles Anthon, New York City, 29 September 1827, Edmund Henry Barker, Letters, 1827–31, Rare Book and Manuscript Library, Columbia University Library, New York.
55. Edmund Henry Barker, Thetford England to Charles Anthon, New York City, 11 December 1827, Edmund Henry Barker, Letters, 1827–31, Rare Book and Manuscript Library, Columbia University Library, New York.
56. If Mitchell sent Harris to Anthon, he did not likely recognize Native American characters, especially those found in Humboldt's book, which he was certainly familiar with.
57. See Jennings, "Charles Anthon."
58. Joseph Smith, History, vol. A-1, 9.
59. "Golden Bible," *Palmyra Freeman*, 11 August 1829; *Rochester Advertiser and Telegraph*, 31 August 1829.
60. 2 Nephi 27:15, 17–18.

61. Joseph Smith, History, ca. summer 1832, 5.
62. Joseph Smith, History, vol. A-1, 9.
63. See forthcoming article presented at the 2013 BYU Church History Symposium by Michael MacKay titled "Git Them Translated." The article will be published in the symposium's compiled and edited volume.

*The spectacles and plates. Watercolor by Anthony Sweat.*

# 4

# Learning to Translate

Though LDS history traditionally assumes that Joseph Smith knew exactly how to translate once he received the gold plates and the Nephite interpreters in September 1827, there was a steep learning curve until he began translating "by the gift and power of God" in the winter of 1828.[1] In 1956, when speaking of this learning period, Joseph Fielding Smith declared that "nothing was done towards translating the record that year [1827]." He explained that Joseph Smith "was busy studying the characters and making himself familiar with them." He insinuated that Joseph Smith had to become familiar with "the use of the Urim and Thummim" before using them to translate. Joseph "had a great deal more to do than merely to sit down and with the use of the instrument prepared for that purpose to translate the characters on the plates."[2]

Though Joseph's initial instincts were to find a translator to decipher the characters on the plates, the need for God's hand in the translation became readily apparent upon the return of Martin Harris from New York City. If Harris's original intention was to find a scholar who could help Joseph translate the ancient writings on the gold plates, he returned to Harmony in failure. The scholars he had consulted had either been unable

## FROM DARKNESS UNTO LIGHT

to provide any information on the cryptic characters or had been unwilling to entertain the notion that they were prophetic writings delivered by an angel. Nonetheless, Joseph had drawn the characters off the plates and sent for their translation.

In hindsight, Harris's failure was a step forward in their progress toward translating the plates. In Joseph's earliest account of Martin Harris's disappointing return from New York City, Joseph remembered that Harris told him that the scholars could not translate the characters. Once Joseph understood that scholars could not translate the characters, he realized that with the aid of the Nephite interpreters, he would translate the plates.[3] Though this conveniently fits the narrative of the Isaian prophecy and the fact that Joseph may have supposed he would eventually use the Nephite interpreters to translate the plates, Joseph wrote that he knew upon Harris's return that "the Lord had prepared spectacles for [him] to read the Book." Shortly thereafter he began to use those spectacles and "commenced translating the characters and thus the Prophecy of Isaiah was fulfilled."[4] So what were the Nephite interpreters, and why did Joseph take months to learn how to use them?

## The Spectacles

The spectacles (or interpreters, as the Book of Mormon calls them) that Joseph retrieved along with the gold plates and the breastplate were not like ordinary nineteenth-century eyeglasses. The frame was not meant to sit on a person's nose or wrap around their ears; in fact, the seer stones in place of the lenses did not even improve one's vision in the way glasses were intended. Though they were often called spectacles, they were apparently "about one and half inches longer than those used at the present day, the [lenses] not of glass, but of diamonds."[5] Lucy Smith and others called the stones in the spectacles "diamonds" to emphasize that they were more than just rocks—they were *seer stones*.[6] To express the value of the stones and to set them apart from others, Orson Pratt called them crystals, and they were often described as transparent or clear, but possibly in the same way that an unpolished diamond or crystal was translucent.[7] The cloudy crystalline stones were later described by Martin Harris and David Whitmer, both of whom saw the spectacles and the plates in June 1829.

62

LEARNING TO TRANSLATE ❖

*Replica of the spectacles. Photo by Gerrit J. Dirkmaat.*

Martin Harris recounted that they looked "like polished marble, with a few gray streaks," and David Whitmer said they were "whitish stones."[8] Whitmer also explained they were "shaped like a pair of ordinary spectacles, though much larger, and at least half an inch in thickness."[9] Harris observed that "the two stones set in a bow of silver were about two inches in diameter, perfectly round, and about five-eigths of an inch thi[c]k in the center." He also stated that they were convex on both sides, forming magnifying glass–like lenses and appearing to be much more like stones wrapped in a frame than actual glasses. The crystalline lenses were much thicker than ordinary lenses and shaped in a way that might magnify if they were transparent.[10] Additionally, instead of wrapping around the ears, the frame for the spectacles was connected to the breastplate with a single metal rod. Joseph Smith's history stated that "these stones fastened to the breast plate,"[11] a plate that was intended to be strapped to Joseph's chest.[12] The spectacles were held conveniently in front of the face of the individual wearing the breastplate, and the person could freely use his or her hands to do other things while looking into the spectacles.

Joseph Smith would later learn while translating the Book of Mormon that devices like the spectacles had been used by ancient seers and that the instrument he had retrieved had been "kept and preserved by the hand of the Lord" for his use.[13] By at least 1833, Joseph Smith and members of the Church began using the biblical term "Urim and

63

> *The spectacles were not originally called a "Urim & Thummin"*

❖ FROM DARKNESS UNTO LIGHT

Thummim" to refer to any seer stone, including seer stones Joseph found before 1827.[14] The name was apparently adopted to reflect the Old Testament's use of the Urim and Thummim that the high priest of Israel used for revelatory guidance.[15] However, the Book of Mormon explains that the spectacles were handed down to Joseph Smith from ancient American prophets, and though the term was used in the early 1830s, they were not originally called the Urim and Thummim.[16]

The spectacles had an ancient American past, dating back much further than when the ancient prophet Moroni prepared the stone box that stored the plates, the breastplate, and the spectacles. Moroni did not make the spectacles; they had been passed down by a long series of ancient seers before Moroni buried them in the Hill Cumorah. The Book of Mormon states that "the spectacles were prepared from the beginning, and were handed down from generation to generation, for the purpose of interpreting languages."[17] They were not even originally created on the American continent, nor were they created by any man. They were first given to an early prophet in the Book of Mormon known only as "the brother of Jared" before his voyage to the Americas. The Book of Mormon explains that Jared and his people fled from their homeland.[18] Jared's brother built eight barges to carry them to a promised land in the Americas, and in the process he asked the Lord to touch sixteen stones, which would then glow—providing light within the barges (two in each barge). The brother of Jared also left the Lord's presence with more than he had asked for: the Lord gave him two additional stones. The Lord explained, *(Ether 3:23-24)* "These two stones will I give unto thee, and ye shall seal them up also with the things which ye shall write. For behold, the language which ye shall write I have confounded; wherefore I will cause in my own due time that these stones shall magnify to the eyes of men these things which ye shall write."[19] The brother of Jared took the two stones with him in the barges and carried them to America. After his people arrived in the Americas, the Lord commanded him "that he should seal up the two stones which he had received, and show them not, until the Lord should show them unto the children of men." *(Ether 3:28)* [20]

Hundreds of years later, around 120 BC, some of the seafaring Israelites in America found the record of the Jaredites. The record, which consisted of twenty-four gold plates, was taken to Mosiah, the king of the

64

## LEARNING TO TRANSLATE

*[handwritten note: Joseph Smith did not understand at first that the spectacles were provided to help translate the Gold Plates]*

Nephites, who "translated them by the means of those two stones which were fastened into the two rims of a bow ... for the purpose of interpreting languages." The Book of Mormon explains that the stones had been "kept and preserved by the hand of the Lord, that he should discover to every creature who should possess the land the iniquities and abominations of his people; and whosoever has these things is called seer, after the manner of old times."[21]

Though the Book of Mormon does not articulate a history of all of the prophets who possessed the spectacles, they were presumably passed down from one prophet to the next along with the records of God's people in America. Sometime before AD 385, the prophet Mormon had been entrusted with the Nephite records and abridged them as the gold plates, which Joseph Smith would retrieve in 1827. After Mormon's death, his son Moroni finished the record and buried it along with the spectacles for Joseph Smith to retrieve. In some of Mormon's final words written on the plates, he admitted that no one knew the language which he had written on them. However, as he explained, "the Lord knoweth the thing which we have written, and also that none other people knoweth our language; and because that none other people knoweth our language, therefore he hath prepared means for the interpretation thereof."[22] *[handwritten: Mormon 9:34]*

## Learning to Use the Spectacles

When Joseph took the plates and the spectacles from their stone box in 1827, he focused most of his interest and attention upon the spectacles. Four years earlier, Moroni explained to Joseph that the spectacles were "what constituted seers in ancient or former times and that God had prepared them for the purpose of translating the book."[23] However, Joseph did not begin translating the plates immediately, and he did not seem to understand Moroni's statement that the spectacles were included with the plates to enable him to translate them. He originally only used the spectacles to help protect the plates.

Though Joseph's visits with Moroni detailed many of the challenges that he would face in the coming years, Moroni may not have told Joseph how to use the spectacles. He had explained that Joseph was supposed to translate the plates, but Joseph remembered that it was not until around February

1828 that he fully realized how the spectacles were supposed to be used.²⁴ Before then Joseph used the spectacles to keep the plates safe and identify people who were going to help him translate them.²⁵ Joseph's efforts to translate the plates were primarily focused upon studying the characters without the spectacles. Lucy Smith recalled that during the period before February 1828, "Joseph was very solicitous about the work but as yet no means had come into his hands of accomplishing it."²⁶

Joseph's actions during this period demonstrate that he was trying to find someone else who could translate the plates, as mentioned previously. He actively worked at transcribing the characters from the plates and sent Harris to obtain a secular translation. If Joseph Smith was intending to translate the plates with the spectacles anyway, there would have been little reason for him to send Harris to several scholars in hopes that one of them could translate the characters. Joseph apparently believed for a time that someone else, someone more learned, would take the leading role in the translation of the plates. Because of the ill intentions of people like Willard Chase in Palmyra, Joseph kept his cards close to his chest during the autumn of 1827 to protect the plates.²⁷ However, those who were part of his inner circle, like Lucy Smith and Joseph Knight Sr., remembered clearly that Joseph's earliest intentions were to have the plates translated and at the very least have the language identified.²⁸ Knight, for example, recalled that soon after receiving the plates from the angel Moroni, Joseph expressed his desire to have the plates translated. Soon after Joseph brought the gold plates home, he described the plates to Knight and told him that "they are written in Caracters and *I want them translated*." Interestingly, Joseph also told Knight about the spectacles and related to him that he could see anything in them, yet he still emphasized his need to find someone else to translate the plates. In the process of finding someone who could translate the plates, Joseph copied "of[f] the Caricters exactley like the ancient and sent Martin Harris to *see if he Could git them Translated*."²⁹ Lucy Smith similarly asserted that as Joseph took "some measures to accomplish the translation . . . he was instructed to take off a facsimile of the . . . characters" and by sending it to "learned men," he could acquire a "translation of the same."³⁰

Even when Martin Harris was upon his deathbed, some of his final words declared that Joseph sent him to New York City to get the characters translated. Martin avowed that he "went by the request of the Prophet

Joseph Smith to the city of New York, and presented a transcript of the records of the Book of Mormon to Professor Anthon and Dr. Mitchell and ask[ed] them to translate it."[31]

## The Book of Mormon Seer Stone

Joseph seemed to be initially unaware that he had within his possession a device that could enable him to translate the characters himself. In the fall and winter of 1827, Joseph used the spectacles in ways that seemed natural to him and were based upon his past experiences since 1822, when he was initially introduced to the duties of a seer. Joseph had also retrieved at least one seer stone of his own that he used to find lost items and buried treasure before 1827. That said, Joseph's use of seer stones before 1827 helps us understand why he only used the Nephite interpreters to protect the plates. He used the spectacles like a seer stone, to identify or find lost items, unlike his later use of them as instruments to translate ancient characters.

Joseph's possession of additional seer stones is generally not included in traditional LDS history, which focuses upon the use of the "Urim and Thummim." Some LDS histories and art typically depict Joseph with the spectacles as if they were the only device Joseph Smith used in the translation. Yet Church leaders and Church-sponsored histories have identified the fact that Joseph did not use just the spectacles.[32] Recently, historians of the Joseph Smith Papers Project carefully analyzed all of the known accounts about the translation to document the use of the seer stone.[33] It turns out that Joseph's seer stone was prepared by God, according to the Book of Mormon, and like the Nephite interpreters, was buried in the earth where Joseph would eventually find it. Brigham Young remembered Joseph telling him that the stone was found "fifteen feet underground."[34]

The Book of Mormon describes more devices than just the spectacles. It identifies the compass-like Liahona,[35] which was a ball of "fine brass." Not only did this ball operate like a compass, but at various times words appeared on it, providing revelatory instruction to the seer that looked upon it. The Book of Mormon also mentioned another translating device possessed by King Mosiah. The book explained that with this device Mosiah could "translate the records; for he has wherewith that he can look, and translate all records that are of ancient date; and it is a gift

67

❖ FROM DARKNESS UNTO LIGHT

from God. And the things are called interpreters, and no man can look in them except he be commanded, lest he should look for that he ought not and he should perish. And whosoever is commanded to look in them, the same is called seer."[36] But, more particularly, the Book of Mormon mentioned a single seer stone referred to as "Gazelem." When the aging prophet Alma entrusted the records of the Nephites and the spectacles to his son Helaman, he also quoted a prophecy: "The Lord said: I will prepare unto my servant Gazelem, a stone, which shall shine forth in darkness unto light."[37] This stone, like the spectacles, was intended to help bring forth the translation of ancient records, but it was different from the spectacles—it was a single seer stone.

In fact, that seer stone was prepared for Joseph Smith and was apparently delivered to him in 1822, five years before he was given the spectacles. After having seen and held the stone, Wilford Woodruff stated that it was "the seer stone known as 'Gazelem', which was shown by the Lord to the Prophet Joseph to be some thirty feet under ground, and which he obtained by digging under the pretense of excavating for a well."[38] Woodruff valued the stone deeply, recording in his journal on 18 May 1888, when the Manti Utah Temple was dedicated, that he "consecrated upon the Altar the seers Stone that Joseph Smith found by Revelation some 30 feet under the Earth."[39]

Remarkably, the name Gazelem may have even referred to Joseph himself rather than the stone. According to William W. Phelps, who was Joseph Smith's close associate, Joseph's original name in the premortal realm was Gazelem, a name he was given before his birth. In a eulogy for Joseph, Phelps declared, "Joseph Smith, who was Gazelam in the spirit world, was, and is, and will be in the progress of Eternity:—The Prince of Light."[40] Joseph had also received a revelation in April 1843 that connected this other name with the seer stone. Speaking of the kingdoms of postmortal glory, the revelation stated, "A white stone is given to each of those who come into the celestial kingdom, whereon is a new name written, which no man knoweth save he that receiveth it. The new name is the key word."[41] Hence the name Gazelem could have applied to either the servant or his stone, or both.[42] Therefore, the prophecy in the Book of Mormon could be read to mean: "The Lord said: I will prepare unto my servant [Joseph Smith], a stone, which shall shine forth in darkness unto light."

Only two years after Joseph Smith saw God the Father and Jesus Christ in a grove near his home, he had been inspired to find this specially prepared seer stone.[43] But Joseph never used this seer stone in a way that would have helped him understand how to translate the plates with the spectacles. Instead, he used it to see visions of people, places, and lost items. He had not ever used this early seer stone to translate languages or ancient text.[44] Thus, despite his prior experience with a seer stone, he was left with very little practical understanding of how he could use the seer stones in the spectacles to translate the gold plates.[45]

## Using the Spectacles

After years of using his seer stone to see items and places in vision, when Joseph received the spectacles in 1827 he naturally used them to protect the plates by keeping track of their location. Lucy recalled that Joseph could see where the plates were located at any time by looking into the spectacles. Worried about how he would store the plates, just before he left to take possession of the plates Joseph asked Lucy Smith if she had a box to put them in. When Joseph hid them in a log, he brought the spectacles home and told his mother, "Do not be uneasy mother, all is right see here, I have got a key." He showed her the spectacles wrapped in a thin handkerchief and comforted her through his ability to track the location of the plates with the spectacles. Lucy uniquely called the spectacles a "key"—possibly referring to the spectacles as a replacement for the unavailable lock box.[46]

Lucy Smith wrote that "Joseph kept the urim and thumim constantly about his person as he could by this means ascertain at any moment if the plates were in danger." In one instance, mentioned earlier, Joseph also saw Emma in the spectacles. When he was in Macedon, soon after Moroni gave him the plates,[47] Joseph "looked into them before Emma got there [and] perceived her coming and came up out of the well and met her."[48]

However, Joseph apparently learned to see translated text in the spectacles. He apparently noticed this ability before Martin Harris left on his journey and began translating the plates in February 1828, but he did not know what to make of the text that appeared in the stones.[49] After making copies of the characters on the plates, it appears that Joseph also began looking in the spectacles for the translation of some of these

❖ FROM DARKNESS UNTO LIGHT

copied characters. But he did not begin translating the text of the Book of Mormon generally until Harris left for New York City (though he may have been curious to know whether what he saw in the spectacles was in fact the translation of the gold plates).

Along with Joseph's 1832 history, the Book of Mormon manuscript, produced in 1829, explained that the translation would not begin until after Harris returned from New York City. Speaking prophetically about the episode with Charles Anthon, it states, "*Then* shall the Lord God say unto him: The learned shall not read them, for they have rejected them, and I am able to do mine own work; wherefore thou shalt *read the words* which I shall give unto thee."[50] Though this prophecy predicted what would take place in 1828, it implies that Smith would not translate until *after* the "learned" had tried to translate the characters. In 1839, however, Joseph remembered copying both untranslated characters and translated characters onto paper for Harris—all *before* Harris left for New York City.[51] Joseph had not officially begun translating the plates, but he remembered that it was not until after Harris returned that he began translating the plates in earnest. Assuming that what he saw in the spectacles was the translation of the gold plates, he apparently sent Harris with a sample of what appeared in the seer stones, hoping that the scholars would verify the translation. The printer of the *Palmyra Freeman* published in 1829 said that Joseph told him that Harris "took some of the *characters interpreted by Smith*, and went in search of some one, besides the interpreter, who was learned enough to English them; but all to whom he applied happened not to be possessed of sufficient knowledge to give satisfaction! Harris returned, and set Smith to work at interpreting the [gold plates]."[52]

Harris told Joseph Smith that "Professor Anthon stated that the translation was correct, more so than any he had before seen translated from the Egyptian." Harris also told Joseph that Anthon had given him a certificate, verifying "that the translation of [the characters] as had been translated [by Joseph] was ... correct."[53] Nevertheless, Joseph's initial response once Harris returned and told him that he should translate the characters was skepticism. He stated, "I ... cannot for I am not learned." Despite this, Joseph's confidence in what he saw in the spectacles grew, and he recalled that "the Lord had prepared spectacles for [him] to read the Book." Following his acceptance of his role in this divine work, he then "commenced translating the characters and thus the Prophecy of Isaiah was fulfilled."[54]

The months between September 1827 and early 1828, when Joseph copied characters from the plates and had scholars examine them, served as a time of preparation for Joseph Smith to learn to translate the plates. In a similar situation, more than a year later, the Lord told Oliver Cowdery in a revelation that he had been given the gift to translate ancient records just like Joseph Smith.[55] Like Joseph in 1827 after being told that he would translate the gold plates, Cowdery discovered that it was not as simple as having possession of the record and a device for translating.[56] He was given a revelation after failing to translate, which told him that he was wrong to believe that the Lord "would give it unto you, when you took no thought save it was to ask me." Cowdery was also told that he had to "study it out in [his] mind" before he could translate.[57] After months of preparation and study in 1827, Joseph apparently fulfilled that requirement and learned to translate.

Joseph declared throughout the remainder of his life that he translated by the power of God. Beginning in the preface of the Book of Mormon, he wrote, "I would inform you that I translated, by the gift and power of God." That statement was distributed with the first five thousand copies of the Book of Mormon, and Joseph reiterated it in 1842 when he declared, "With the records was found a curious instrument which the ancients called Urim and Thummim, which consisted of two transparent stones set in the rim of a bow fastened to a breastplate. Through the medium of the Urim and Thummim I translated the record by the gift and power of God."[58] As the Book of Mormon prophesied, the word of God "shall shine forth in darkness unto light."[59] With the "gift and power of God" Joseph read the translated words that appeared on the seer stones and his scribes recorded them as the text of the Book of Mormon, a concept that will be further elaborated upon in following chapters.

## Notes

1. Title page to the Book of Mormon.
2. Joseph Fielding Smith, *Doctrines of Salvation* (Salt Lake City: Bookcraft, 1956), 3:215–16.

❖  FROM DARKNESS UNTO LIGHT

3. Isaiah 29:11. Joseph framed the story in his 1832 history as the fulfillment of a prophecy made in the Book of Isaiah, which states, "the words of a book that is sealed, which men deliver to one that is learned, saying, Read this, I pray thee: and he saith, I cannot, for it is sealed."
4. Joseph Smith, History, 1832, 6.
5. Fayette Lapham, "II.—The Mormons," *Historical Magazine*, May 1870, 307. Lapham was around in 1828 and claimed that he got his information from Joseph Smith Sr. He apparently lived in Perrington, New York, but conducted some of his business in Palmyra.
6. See Mark Ashurst-McGee, "Pathway to Prophethood: Joseph Smith Jr. as Rodsman, Village Seer, and Judeo-Christian Prophet" (master's thesis, Utah State University, 2000), 306n496. See also A. W. Benton, "Mormonites," *Evangelical Magazine and Gospel Advocate*, 9 April 1831, 120.
7. In 1840 Orson Pratt explained that they "consisted of two transparent stones, clear as crystal" in the most popular Mormon pamphlet in the late 1830s. Before printing the pamphlet in Edinburgh, Scotland, he likely met with Joseph Smith in New York. Orson Pratt, *Interesting Account of Several Remarkable Visions*, 1840, 8–9; see also *Journal of Discourses*, 19:214.
8. Tiffany, "Mormonism," August 1859, 165–66. Harris was also quoted by Edward Stevenson to have said they were "two clear stones." *Deseret Evening News*, 13 December 1881, 4. Orsamus Turner, who lived in Palmyra before Joseph Smith retrieved the gold plates, stated that the stones were opaque to all who looked into them except for Joseph. Orsamus Turner, *History of the Pioneer Settlement*, 215. William Smith apparently also claimed that he "put the Urim and Thummim before his eyes, but could see nothing, as he did not have the gift of a Seer." J. W. Peterson, "The Urim and Thummim," *Rod of Iron*, February 1924, 7. On other occasions David Whitmer was recorded as saying that they were transparent and opaque. See "Mormon Relics," *Inter Ocean*, 17 October 1886, 17; and Zenas H. Gurley interview, 14 January 1885, Richmond, MO, Church History Library. For a survey of the various descriptions of the spectacles, see Ashurst-McGee, "Pathway to Prophethood," 309–19.
9. "The Golden Tables," *Chicago Times*, 7 August 1875, 1.
10. Tiffany, "Mormonism," August 1859, 165–66.
11. Joseph Smith, History, 1838–1856, 5.
12. Lucy Mack Smith explained that the breastplate had four straps "for the purpose of fastening it to the breast." Lucy Mack Smith, *Biographical Sketches* (Liverpool: S. W. Richards, 1853), 107.

13. Mosiah 28:14–15.
14. See "The Book of Mormon," *The Evening and the Morning Star*, January 1833, 2.
15. See, for example, Exodus 28:30; Leviticus 8:8; and Numbers 27:21. Cornelis van Dam, *The Urim and Thummim: A Means of Revelation in Ancient Israel* (Winona Lake, IN: Eisenbrauns, 1997).
16. Joseph Smith, History, 1832, 6.
17. Mosiah 28:14.
18. See Genesis 11:1–9.
19. Ether 3:23–24.
20. Ether 3:28.
21. Mosiah 28:13–16.
22. Mormon 9:34.
23. Joseph Smith, History, vol. A-1, 5. See also Mosiah 8:13–17 and Ether 4:5.
24. Joseph Smith, History, ca. Summer 1832, 6; Joseph Smith, History, vol. A-1, 9.
25. David Sloan argues that he needed to study it out in his mind (D&C 8) before the Lord revealed the translation to him. David Sloan wrote: "Although the 1839 history clearly records that Joseph Smith translated a number of characters off the plates before the Harris-Anthon encounter, Nephi's prophetic account and a number of historical accounts indicate that Joseph Smith was initially unable to translate the Book of Mormon and sought the assistance of learned men to help with the translation. Evidence also exists that Joseph referred to experimental and preliminary attempts as translating, regardless of the outcome. For this reason, Joseph could consistently refer to translated characters even at a time when he had been completely unsuccessful in his efforts. This is exactly the process of human effort and study that one would expect from reading Doctrine and Covenants 9." David E. Sloan, "The Anthon Transcripts and the Translation of the Book of Mormon: Studying It Out in the Mind of Joseph Smith," *Journal of Book of Mormon Studies* 5, no. 2 (1996): 57–81. In 1956, Joseph Fielding Smith declared that "nothing was done towards translating the record that year [1827]." See also Joseph Fielding Smith, *Doctrines of Salvation* (Salt Lake City: Bookcraft, 1956), 3:215–16.
26. Lucy Mack Smith, History, 1845, book 6, [5–7].
27. Lucy Mack Smith recounted that her son had explained, "the angel of the Lord says that we must be careful not to proclaim these things or to mention them abroad, for we do not any of us know the weakness of the world, which is so sinful, and that when we get the plates they will want to kill us for the sake of the gold,

if they know we have them." Lucy Mack Smith, History, 1845, [53–60]. Outside of the Smith family, only Josiah Stowell and Joseph Knight Sr. were at the Smiths' Manchester house when he retrieved the plates.

28. A few of Emma's relatives remembered that even before then, Joseph did not plan on translating the plates. Isaac Hale seemed to believe that Joseph told him that a "young child" would translate the plates, after which one of Isaac Hale's wife's relatives went further by stating that only Emma's unborn child could open the plates without dying. Sophia Lewis, who was a resident of Harmony until 1843, stated that "she heard Smith say 'the Book of Plates could not be opened under penalty of death by any other person but his first-born, which was to be a male.'" She says she "was present at the birth of this child, and that it was still-born and very much deformed." Isaac Hale explained, "I inquired of Joseph Smith Jr., who was to be the first who would be allowed to see the Book of Plates? He said it was a young child. After this I became dissatisfied, and informed him that if there was any thing in my house of that description, which I could not be allowed to see, he must take it away; if he did not, I was determined to see it. After that, the plates were said to be hid in the woods." Joshua McKune, whose father owned property adjoining Joseph Smith's property in Harmony, stated, "Joseph Smith, Jr. told him that (Smith's) first-born child was to translate the characters, and hieroglyphics, upon the plates into our language at the age of three years: but this child was not permitted to live to verify the prediction." "Mormonism," *Susquehanna Register*, 1 May 1834, 1. Local Manchester resident and fellow treasure hunter Willard Chase recounted that Martin Harris had said that Emma "June following would be delivered of a male child that would be able when two years old to translate the Gold Bible. Then, said he, you will see Joseph Smith, Jr. walking through the streets of Palmyra, with a Gold Bible under his arm, and having a gold breastplate on, and a gold sword by his side." E. D. Howe, *Mormonism Unvailed*, 248.

29. Knight Sr., History, 3; emphasis added. Other accounts also suggest that Joseph created the documents to verify them as ancient characters and to identify the language. See "Additional Testimony of Martin Harris (One of the Three Witnesses) to the Coming Forth of the Book of Mormon," *Millennial Star*, 20 August 1859, 21:545–46; "Incidents in the Life of Martin Harris," *Deseret Evening News*, 13 December 1881, 4; "Martin Harris's Testimony," *Millennial Star*, 4 December 1893, 55:793–94; "The Three Witnesses to the Book of Mormon," *Millennial Star*, 5 July 1886, 48:421; and Stevenson, *Reminiscences of Joseph, the Prophet, and the Coming Forth of the Book of Mormon*, 30–33. In his 1834 letter to E. D. Howe,

Charles Anthon explained that Harris asked him to "decypher, if possible, a paper." According to Anthon, Joseph Smith had asked Harris to pay for the publication of the Book of Mormon, a decision that Harris was reticent to make until he could be assured that the plates were ancient and the characters were genuine. Charles Anthon to E. D. Howe, 17 February 1834, in Howe, *Mormonism Unvailed*, 270–72. John A. Clark related that Harris stated that he "started off with some of the manuscripts that Smith furnished him on a journey to New York and Washington to consult some learned men to ascertain the nature of the language in which this record was engraven." "Gleanings by the Way," *Episcopal Recorder*, 5 September 1840, 94. Anthon wrote that he was asked to "examine, and give [his] opinion upon, a certain paper, marked with various characters." Charles Anthon to Thomas Winthrop Coit, 3 April 1841, in Clark, *Gleanings by the Way*, 233–38.

30. Lucy Mack Smith, History, 1844–1845, book 6, [3].
31. "Martin Harris, Jr., Reports Death and Testimony of His Father," *Adventure* 1, no. 4.
32. For the talks of two Apostles who address this issue, see Neal A. Maxwell, "'Apply the Atoning Blood of Christ,'" *Ensign*, January 1997, 38–39; and Russell M. Nelson, "A Treasured Testament," *Ensign*, July 1993, 62–63. Historian Richard Lloyd Anderson also addressed the issue in a Church-sponsored publication, "'By the Gift and Power of God,'" *Ensign*, September 1977, 77–85.
33. Volume 1 Introduction, in *JSP*, D1: xxix–xxxii.
34. Kenney, *Wilford Woodruff's Journal*, 5:382–83.
35. Alma 37:38–41. Lehi found the Liahona at his tent: "it was of fine brass. And within the ball were two spindles; and the one pointed the way whither we should go into the wilderness. . . . We did follow the directions of the ball." Additionally, Lehi was told by the Lord, "Look upon the ball, and behold the things which are written." 1 Nephi 16:10, 16, 26.
36. Mosiah 8:9–13.
37. Alma 37:23. In this enigmatic passage, it is unclear whether Gazelem was the name of the servant or the stone prepared for the servant.
38. George A. Smith Papers, box 174, folder 26, Manuscripts Division, Marriott Library, University of Utah.
39. Kenney, *Wilford Woodruff's Journal*, 2:144; 8:500.
40. W. W. Phelps, "The Funeral Sermon," MS, 13 June 1866, Church History Library. Phelps reconstructed his funeral sermon in 1855.
41. D&C 130:11.
42. See Ashurst-McGee, "Pathway to Prophethood," 274–80.

43. See Steven C. Harper, *Joseph Smith's First Vision: A Guide to the Historical Accounts* (Salt Lake City: Deseret Book, 2012).
44. Joseph told Joseph Knight Sr. that he could see anything with the spectacles, but Joseph had yet to use the spectacles to translate. Joseph had apparently seen places and people in vision through his seer stone, such as when he first used another seer's stone to locate his own seer stone. When he looked into the stone, "He was greatly surprised to see but one thing, which was a small stone, a great way off. It soon became luminous, and dazzled his eyes, and after a short time it became as instense as the mid-day sun. he said that the stone was under the roots of a tree or shrub as large as his arm, situated about a mile up a small stream that puts in on the South side of Lake Erie, not far from the New York and Pennsylvania line." William D. Purple, "Joseph Smith, the Originator of Mormonism: Historical Reminiscences of the Town of Afton," *Chenango Union*, 2 May 1877, 3. This source should be used cautiously because it is such a late reminiscence, but it does correlate with other descriptions of how Smith used his seer stones. See John Phillip Walker, ed., *Dale Morgan on Early Mormonism*, 329–31, for a discussion of the validity of Purple's memory. Harris also reported that during one of his first encounters with Joseph Smith, before the fall of 1827, Joseph pulled the seer stone from his pocket and found a toothpick Harris had recently dropped and could not find. Tiffany, "Mormonism," August 1859, 164. Even though Harris and Joseph Smith Sr. had gotten down on their hands and knees in search of the toothpick, they could not find it until Joseph looked into his stone, and without looking up he found the toothpick. Describing a similarly visionary experience, Josiah Stowell apparently testified in Joseph Smith's defense in 1826, in the court of Justice Neely, that he had witnessed Smith peering into his seer stone. Stowel explained that Smith "looked through [a seer] stone and described Josiah Stowel's house and out houses, while at Palmyra" miles away and before he had ever seen or visited Stowel's residence. *People of State of New York v. Joseph Smith*, 20 March 1826, Bainbridge, NY, in "A Document Discovered," *Utah Christian Advocate* (Salt Lake City), January 1886, 1. Lorenzo Saunders explained that "Jo. Could see in his peep stone what there was in that cave" and that "young Joe could . . . see a man sitting in a gold char. Old Joe said he was king i.e. the man in the chair; a king of one of the . . . tribes who was shut in there in the time of one their big battles." Lorenzo Saunder, interview with E. L. Kelley, 12 November 1884, Kelley Papers, CCLA.

45. Bushman, *Joseph Smith and the Beginnings of Mormonism*, 79; Bushman, *Joseph Smith: Rough Stone Rolling*, 57; Ronald W. Walker, "Joseph Smith: The Palmyra Seer," *BYU Studies* 24, no. 4 (Fall 1984): 461–72; and Wesley P. Walters, "Joseph Smith's Bainbridge, N.Y. Court Trials," *Westminster Theological Journal* 36, no. 2 (1974): 141–42; compare Gordon Madsen, "Joseph Smith's 1826 Trial"; H. Michael Marquardt and Wesley P. Walters, *Inventing Mormonism*, 67–77, 222–30; and Dan Vogel, ed., *Early Mormon Documents*, 4:239–66; Joseph reportedly stated in court that "he had a certain stone, which he had occasionally looked at to determine where hidden treasures" were located. He also stated that he "frequently ascertained in that way where lost property was . . . that he has occasionally been in the habit of looking through this stone to find lost property for three years." "A Document Discovered," *Utah Christian Advocate*, January 1886. See also Charles Marshall, "The Original Prophet. By a Visitor to Salt Lake City," *Fraser's Magazine*, February 1873, 225–35; *Eclectic Magazine*, New York, 17 April 1873, 479–88; Daniel S. Tuttle, "Mormons," *A Religious Encyclopaedia*, ed. Philip Schaff (1883), 2:1576; The Council of the First Presidency and the Quorum of the Twelve Apostles, "Council," 30 September 1855; and minutes taken by Thomas Bullock, MS, General Church Minutes Collection, Church History Library.
46. Lucy Mack Smith, History, 1845, book 6, [1].
47. Lucy Mack Smith, History, 1845, book 5, [10].
48. Lucy Mack Smith, History, 1845, book 5, paper fragment inserted after [10]. This is also similar to Josiah Stowell's experience when he saw Joseph peer into the stone to view an image of his house and out buildings. Samuel Lawrence went to the "hill Cumorah" with Joseph Smith and saw in his seer stone a vision of the spectacles in the hillside. Smith also apparently saw Martin Harris in his seer stone to alert him to the fact that Harris was supposed to help him bring forth the Book of Mormon. See Tiffany, "Mormonism," August 1859, 166.
49. Though Joseph was not known to have used his seer stones to translate anything before he retrieved the spectacles, he may have seen something like an American Indian pictograph. In Joseph's 1826 trial, Josiah Stowell was reported to have said that Joseph had once "told about a painted tree, with a man's head painted upon it, by means of said stone." "A Document Discovered," *Utah Christian Advocate*, January 1886. A questionable source, from William Hine of Colesville, claims that Joseph "saw writing cut on the rocks in an unknown language telling where [Captain] Kidd buried it, and he translated it through his peep-stone." This

❖ FROM DARKNESS UNTO LIGHT

statement was given by Hine to Arthur B. Deming in 1885, nearly fifty years after the fact. Dan Vogel explained, "Hine's statement should be approached with caution since it makes claims contrary to established chronology and history." Vogel, *Early Mormon Documents*, 4:181.
50. 2 Nephi 27:20.
51. Joseph Smith, History, vol. A-1, 9. The history Joseph initiated in 1838 stated, "I commenced copying the characters off the plates. I copied a considerable number of them, and by means of the Urim and Thummim I translated some of them."
52. "Golden Bible," *Palmyra Freeman*, 11 August 1829.
53. Joseph Smith, History, vol. A-1, 9.
54. Joseph Smith, History, 1832, 6.
55. Revelation, April 1829–A [D&C 6], in *JSP*, D1:35–37.
56. Revelation, April 1829–D [D&C 9], in *JSP*, D1:49–50.
57. *JSP*, D1:34–48. See Revelation, April 1829–A [D&C 6]; Revelation, April 1829–B [D&C 8]; Revelation, April 1829–D [D&C 9]; and Account of John, April 1829–C [D&C 7].
58. See *Times and Seasons*, 1 March 1842, 708.
59. Alma 37:23.

# 5

# Translation and the Lost Book of Lehi

Learning and accepting his own ability to translate the plates through the seer stones was only the first obstacle Joseph Smith faced as he began to translate the Book of Mormon. Most people still did not believe in his claims, which appeared to some to be both fanciful and fantastical. Even those who had shown an early interest in the gold plates and in their potential translation eventually became staunch opponents, hindering rather than helping the work, regardless of the fact that Joseph and others continued to offer a glimpse of the plates by showing copies of the characters.

The characters Joseph copied onto paper did not remain private, especially after Martin Harris asked scholars in New York to examine them. Even after Joseph's death in 1844, a Church newspaper created unique metal type of the characters to print copies of them more broadly as a memorial of Joseph. They represented his work with the plates during his life and his prophetic calling. The story of Joseph's copies of the characters is a simple narrative about a few slips of paper, but it also highlights his early efforts to translate the plates and the power the gold plates had in the lives of believers, even if they only saw small samples of the characters.[1]

❖ FROM DARKNESS UNTO LIGHT

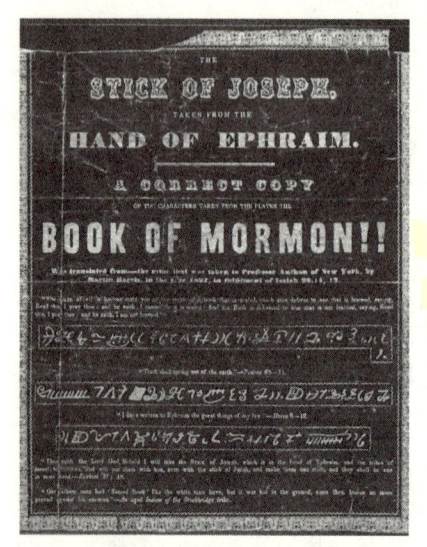

Stick of Joseph, Taken from the Hand of Ephraim, *broadside (New York: The Prophet, 1844), Church History Library.*

The sense of the validity of the characters was not universal, however. Sometime in early 1828, Martin Harris took copies of the characters to an Episcopal preacher in Palmyra named John Clark. According to Clark, Harris "had occasionally attended divine service in our church. . . . If I mistake not, at one period [Harris was] a member of the Methodist Church, and subsequently had identified himself with the Universalists."[2] Harris's boldness, approaching Clark with stories of Joseph Smith and his visit from Moroni, caused the local pastor to view Harris as a fallen parishioner and to declare that Harris's "religious views . . . seemed to be floating upon the sea of uncertainty." To convince his former pastor that the plates existed, Harris declared to Clark that Joseph "had transcribed [characters] from one of the leaves of [the gold plates]" for all to see. Harris dramatically revealed his evidence, "carefully unfold[ing] a slip of paper, which contained three or four lines of characters."[3] Though the size of the paper and the number of characters that were included on each line are unknown, Clark's description offers a small witness of the characters, without positive effect.

Nonetheless, Martin Harris embraced the characters as evidence for the existence of the plates and showed them to numerous people, anticipating that they too would believe that Joseph Smith had the ancient records in his possession. He apparently showed some of the characters in early spring 1828 to his family, who were highly skeptical of Joseph Smith's claims. Lucy Harris was outwardly unimpressed. She conjured a plan to duplicate the characters in order to lessen their impact upon others as Martin showed them his copy of the characters. She convinced her daughter's suitor, Flanders Dyke, to sneak into Martin's house to find Harris's copy of the characters and duplicate them. In return, Lucy Harris

> *Lucy Harris secretely copied the characters her husband Martin Harris had.*

## TRANSLATION AND THE LOST BOOK OF LEHI ❖

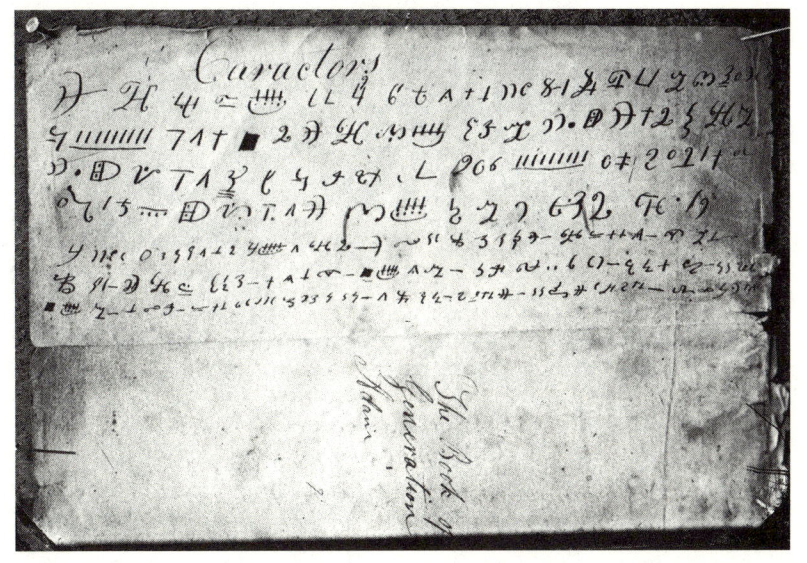

*Glass plate negative of the "Caractors" document by Jacob H. Hicks, 1886. Photo courtesy of Clay County Museum and Historical Society, Liberty, Missouri.*

agreed to allow Dyke to marry her daughter. Once Lucy Harris had her copy, she conveniently pulled it from her pocket each time her husband displayed his copy to others in order to prove that "Smith was not the only one that was in possession of this great curiosity." Lucy Smith remembered that Lucy Harris "had the same characters and they were quite as genuine as those displayed to them by Mr. H[arris]."[4] Lucy Harris's possession of the characters opened a new avenue for people to see them, expanding the number of potential viewers.

According to Lucy Mack Smith, few made as deep and lasting an impact as did the intractable Lucy Harris. Once Martin Harris returned from New York City in 1828, Lucy's attitude toward the plates and Joseph Smith himself became increasingly more acerbic. She actively tried to prevent Martin from maintaining his relationship with Joseph Smith and participating, financially or otherwise, in the translation of the plates. Her husband's abrupt departure for New York City apparently created further suspicion in Lucy's mind about the authenticity of the plates and her husband's involvement in the translation. She had asked Martin to let her travel with him to New York, but he had declined. Worse still, upon his return he began offering to help pay for the enormous costs associated with

81

❖ FROM DARKNESS UNTO LIGHT

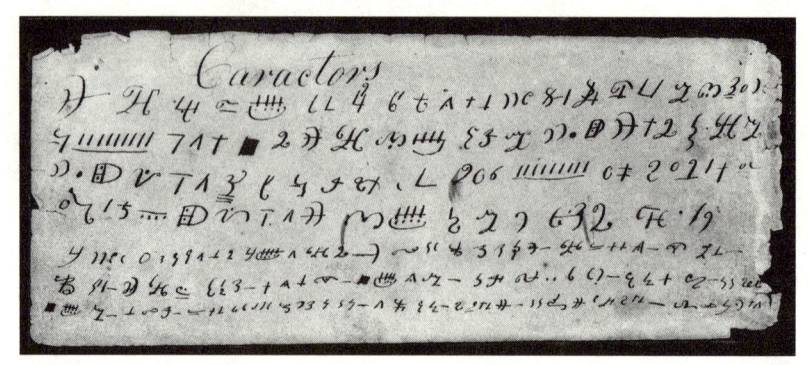

*"Caractors" document. Photo courtesy of Community of Christ's Library-Archive, Independence, Missouri.*

translating and publishing the book—all this after an expensive trip to New York. Even though she and her daughter had held the plates in the box, she eventually doubted that her experience offered her any evidence that the plates actually existed. She demanded to see them before she supported her husband's enthusiasm and financial commitment to the endeavor. Lucy was so angry with Martin by the time he returned from New York that she refused to sleep in the same room with him and repeatedly insisted that when he returned to Harmony that she would accompany him, in order to convince Joseph Smith to let her see the plates.[5]

Martin reluctantly acquiesced, and Lucy Harris made the weeklong trip to Harmony alongside her husband. When they arrived in Harmony, Lucy immediately confronted Joseph, even more aggressively than she had in October 1827, demanding that he show her proof that the plates existed.[6] But Joseph, citing the commandment he had received, still refused to show her the plates. Wary of her intentions, Joseph took a moment while Lucy was distracted to remove the trunk and the plates from the house and bury them in the woods on the northern side of his property. This move proved fortuitous. The next morning Lucy reportedly began "ransacking every nook & corner of the house chest cupboard trunk &c." To her dismay, she found nothing. Teetering back and forth between her doubts about whether the plates existed and her experience holding the plates in the box in October 1827, she persisted in her search for them throughout the house. The next day, she searched the surrounding property and "hunted the ground over," looking for the spot where Joseph had buried the plates—examining the

*Lucy Harris and the large black snake*

ground for holes and recently moved dirt. From early in the morning until late in the afternoon, she continued her search before she returned to the house to find warmth. When she finally returned, she seemed perplexed by an experience she claimed to have had while scouring the grounds.[7]

As she desperately looked for the plates and walked through the woods, she was apparently startled by a "tremendous great black snake" that "stuck up its head" in front of her, just before she had turned around to return to the house. In a very threatening manner, the snake "commenced hissing at me," Lucy Harris exclaimed to Emma once she was back at the house. Distraught and disappointed that she could not find the plates, she left the house to stay at a nearby inn. She apparently told her hostess the story of the black snake, explaining that she had found the spot where Joseph had buried the plates and just before she began scraping away the recently disturbed snow, leaves, and earth, "she encountered a horrible black snake which frightened her so [b]adly that she ran to the house as fast as possible."[8]

As Lucy Harris repeated her story in Harmony of the hissing snake, the tale came to resemble other folk stories in which a mythical treasure guardian prevented discoverers from obtaining the buried riches. Rather than using her failed attempts to find the plates to deny any divine involvement with Smith at all, she instead used her encounter with the snake to reinforce the idea of supernatural powers aiding Joseph Smith, just dark and foreboding ones. She began a public campaign to discredit him in the surrounding community, according to Lucy Mack Smith. For the next two weeks before she returned to Palmyra, she reportedly did "all that her ingenuity could contrive to injure Joseph in the estimation of his neighbors."[9] The discovery of the snake, however, was hardly something only explainable by the lore of dark magic surrounding buried treasure. In her frantic search in the woods, Lucy likely stumbled onto the nest of the indigenous black rat snake of Pennsylvania, which reaches lengths of seven to eight feet in length. She likely disturbed the reptile from its late hibernation period, where it had been coiled sleeping underground. Such snakes usually hibernated in a small cave or holes, under decayed trees, and other naturally concealed places where she would have been likely looking for the buried plates.

Lucy's experience in Harmony did not end with her completely denying that Joseph possessed the plates; she seemed to believe that they

❖ FROM DARKNESS UNTO LIGHT

existed. She accepted the fact that they were real by frantically searching for them and assigning a supernatural evil to the protection of their hiding place.[10] Interestingly, Lucy Mack Smith remembered the story secondhand and recorded it in her history.

Lucy Harris may have been one of the earliest antagonists to associate Joseph's experience with local treasure guardian lore in order to defame him and rouse public opinion against him. She continued telling her same vitriolic tale once she returned to Manchester and Palmyra.[11] Whether others took her claims seriously or not, others soon described Joseph's interaction with the angel Moroni in the terms of a treasure guardian. By 1830, the editor of the *Reflector* also identified Moroni as a treasure guardian. The newspaper reported that "It is well known that Jo Smith never pretended to have any communion with angels, until a long period after the pretended finding of his book, and that the juggling of himself or father, went no further than the pretended faculty of seeing wonders in a 'peep stone,' and the occasional interview with the spirit, supposed to have the custody of hidden treasure."[12] Reporting Joseph's experience far earlier and utterly contradicting the *Reflector* and Lucy Harris, Jonathan Hadley of the *Palmyra Freeman* wrote in August 1829, "a person by the name of *Joseph Smith*, of Manchester, Ontario County, reported that he had been visited in a dream by the spirit of the Almighty."[13]

Martin Harris returned to Manchester not long after his wife left. He promised Joseph that he would return to help him translate the gold plates and "write for a season," regardless of his wife's insistence that he abandon his interest in the plates. Making the weeklong wagon ride, again Harris traveled to Harmony to help Joseph translate the plates from mid-April until mid-June 1828. Martin's choice to return to Harmony created an indelible wedge between himself and Lucy. While Martin was in Harmony acting as Joseph's scribe, Lucy Harris had a legal document drawn up that guaranteed her the rights of one-third of Harris's property in Palmyra, New York.[14] By giving Lucy Harris the equivalent of her dowry rights, Martin attempted to calm her fears about losing all of their property if Martin invested his time and money into the translation and publication of the Book of Mormon.[15] Nevertheless, at that point, he had only donated $50 and his own time into the translation and coming forth of the Book of Mormon.[16]

## Translating with Emma

Once the translation began, Emma Smith and her brother Reuben Hale were the first of a series of scribes that recorded Joseph's dictation as he miraculously read the words from the ancient text as it appeared on the spectacles. Joseph's indigent circumstances forced him to rely on close family members rather than a paid professional to help him record the translation on paper. Joseph Knight Sr. remembered, "Now when he Began to translate he was poor and was put to it for provisions and had not one to write for him But his wife and his wifes Brother would sometimes write a little for him through the winter."[17] Very little is known about Reuben Hale and his participation in the translation, but Emma soon became Joseph's first primary scribe.

Emma's experience as Joseph's scribe formed a cherished memory that she reflected back upon throughout her life, especially in the decades after Joseph died. In one instance, she stated, "When my husband was translating the Book of Mormon, I wrote a part of it, as he dictated each sentence, word for word."[18] In an interview with Joseph's son Joseph Smith III, Emma remembered, "I frequently wrote day after day, often sitting at the table close by him." She explained that Joseph used the spectacles to translate, but not by looking through them at the plates, but instead by placing them in a large-brimmed hat with which he could block out the light. As Joseph excluded the light and looked onto the seer stones in the hat, he dictated the words he saw "hour after hour with nothing between us."[19] Emma explained that he was not looking anywhere but at the stones in the hat; he was not looking at the plates and "had neither manuscript nor book to read from." When asked directly if Joseph could have been, as detractors later claimed, reading from a hidden manuscript or book, she replied emphatically, "If he had had anything of the kind he could not have concealed it from me."[20]

Latter-day Saint art in the past has depicted the translation by excluding the spectacles or by showing Joseph looking through them at the plates. Yet none of Joseph's scribes left any accounts that fit those descriptions. In fact, only one early account includes the concept of looking *through* the spectacles, an interpretation given by Truman Coe, a pastor of the Old South Church in Kirtland, Ohio, and an antagonist of the Church.[21] Bothered by members of the Church in Kirtland, he wrote to a newspaper editor

❖ FROM DARKNESS UNTO LIGHT

in 1836 warning the public about a "sect of Religious Fanatics, who are collected in this town." His warning, written to demonstrate his incredulity, revealed how he believed Joseph translated the Book of Mormon. He wrote, "The manner of translation was as wonderful as the discovery [of the plates]. By putting his finger on one of the characters and imploring divine aid, then looking through the Urim and Thummim, he would see the import written in plain English."[22] The word "spectacles" or "interpreters" likely

Emma Smith. *Painting by Lee Greene Richards.* © Intellectual Reserve, Inc. All rights reserved.

## TRANSLATION AND THE LOST BOOK OF LEHI

> *Handwritten annotations at top:* Joseph Smith never read from the plates as he dictated their contents to his scribe. So what was the purpose of having the plates if he didn't read from them ??

led many to believe they were like eyeglasses, but it is clear that Joseph usually held the spectacles in the bottom of a hat, with no possibility of looking through them.

Furthermore, the plates were the object of inspiration, not the object of analysis and careful secular translation. Joseph did not place his finger on the plates to translate, as Coe bemoaned. According to Emma, the plates "often lay on the table without any attempt at concealment" other than a small linen tablecloth that Emma had provided to keep them covered from the glance of the naked eye. Joseph apparently never removed the thin covering to examine the leaves as he translated or to inspect the characters to see if they matched those that appeared on the spectacles, but Emma "once felt of the plates, as they thus lay on the table, tracing their outline and shape" with her finger. She felt them through the linen, explaining, "They seemed to be pliable like thick paper, and would rustle with a metallic sound when the edges were moved by the thumb, as one does sometimes thumb the edges of a book." When her son Joseph III asked if she ever pulled the cover off the plates, Emma replied, "I did not attempt to handle the plates, other than I have told you, nor uncover them to look at them." However, she "moved them from place to place on the table, as it was necessary in doing my work." Her belief in the plates was not the result of a heavenly vision, nor was it simply blind faith in the words of her husband. She had physically handled the plates. They were as real as the table they lay upon; they were actual plates, with separate leaves that could be tangibly separated from each other. In her mind, she had little need to see what was under the linen. She told her son, "I was satisfied that it was the work of God, and therefore did not feel it to be necessary" to remove the cloth.

So, what was the purpose of having the plates if Joseph left them covered during the translation? Though Emma explained that Joseph did not use the plates, as a traditional translator would have, they were still deeply important to the translation. They represented where the words originated—demonstrating their historicity, and forming a sense of reality about the individuals described in the Book of Mormon. The plates were in essence the body for the spiritual words that fell from Joseph Smith's lips as he translated. They created confidence in the minds of Joseph and his family and friends. They offered believers something physical and tangible to understand how and where the text of the Book of Mormon originated.

❖ FROM DARKNESS UNTO LIGHT

They were also invaluable for demonstrating that Joseph Smith was a chosen seer. The relationship between the plates, Joseph, and God was indelible for communicating the nature and purpose of the Book of Mormon. Without the plates, the translation was empty, and without Joseph's gift, it was not from God.

Emma explained that it would have been impossible for Joseph to dictate the translation without the power of God and the use of the spectacles, especially since he was not looking at the plates.[23] Emma argued that Joseph "could neither write nor dictate a coherent and well-worded letter; let alone [dictate] a book like the Book of Mormon," and yet Joseph dictated passages for hours and days at a time. Emma went on to explain, "Though I was an active participant in the scenes that transpired, and was present during the translation of the plates, and had cognizance of things as they transpired, it is marvelous to me, 'a marvel and a wonder,' as much so as to anyone else." Fascinated by Joseph's gift, she declared, "as [Joseph] dictated each sentence, word for word," she recalled, "proper names he could not pronounce, or long words, he spelled them out, and while I was writing them, If any mistake in spelling, he would stop me and correct my spelling, although it was impossible for him to see me writing them down at the time."[24]

Emma apparently never saw Joseph using the spectacles and the breastplate together; in fact, she never even mentioned that she saw Joseph wearing the breastplate. Martin Harris and Oliver Cowdery, who were both scribes and witnesses of the translation process, left no accounts about the use of the breastplate during the translation either. Yet, it seems that once the Nephite interpreters and Joseph's seer stone were called the Urim and Thummim, they also took on qualities of the Old Testament device,[25] such as the Urim and Thummim's relationship with the priestly breastplate, which the Book of Mormon never describes, but Joseph eventually describes the Nephite interpreters as part of the breastplate. The most notable account that draws direct comparisons with the Urim and Thummim and the Nephite interpreters comes from an interview of William Smith in 1891. J. W. Peterson published the interview years later in 1924, but there is no way of knowing if it was an accurate reproduction of what William remembered in his eightieth year of life. It is also difficult to know what William knew firsthand and what he had heard or extrapolated from others. William explained that, like the priestly Old Testament breastplate, "A pocket was prepared in the breastplate on the left side, immediately over the heart. When not in use the [interpreters were] placed in this pocket, the rod being of just the right length to allow it to be so deposited."[26] The breastplate was ostensibly intended to be fastened to the chest and the spectacles were then supposed to be fastened to the breastplate.[27] Though this was possible, since Joseph's history stated that he was given a breastplate with the Nephite interpreters, early accounts only describe Joseph setting the breastplate aside.[28]

Outside of pulling the straps tighter, the breastplate was neither adjustable nor easy to work with, and the Book of Mormon explained that it was "large."[29] Frustrated, Joseph apparently stopped using it even before Emma ever started writing for him. By having the spectacles connected to the breastplate, there was no way of adjusting them back and forth to achieve the optimum viewing distance. As an alternative to the breastplate, he placed the spectacles into the bottom of a hat, allowing him to better control the distance from his eyes to the surface of the stones. The hat allowed Joseph to move the spectacles up and down as needed so he could focus on the translation; it also darkened the area around the seer stones to allow them, as the Book of Mormon explains, to "shine forth in darkness unto light."[30]

## Translating with Martin Harris

Like Emma's experience acting as Joseph's scribe, Martin Harris also witnessed the process. From mid-April to mid-June 1828, Martin Harris stayed at Joseph's house in Harmony, recording for him as he dictated the words that appeared on the spectacles. After observing the miraculous translation in Harmony, Martin Harris marveled at the fact that "Joseph knew not the contents of the Book of Mormon until it was translated."[31] The process fascinated him and he was convinced that Joseph's dictation was only possible through the power of God.

Once Martin arrived in Harmony in April, he picked up where Emma had left off in her scribal work. He and Joseph completed a large manuscript called "the Book of Lehi" that Joseph and Emma had been working on for quite some time. Upon reflection, Harris expressed that "he was favored to write direct from the mouth of the Prophet Joseph Smith." He

❖    FROM DARKNESS UNTO LIGHT

*Replica of the breastplate. Photo by Gerrit J. Dirkmaat.*

further described that by the "aid of the seer stone, sentences would appear and were read by the Prophet and written by [Martin], and when finished he would say, 'Written,' and if correctly written, that sentence would disappear and another appear in its place, but if not written correctly it remained until corrected." Though Harris was never able to look into the spectacles like Joseph, this process forced Joseph to explain to Martin what was happening, as he required him to change what he had written because it was incorrect or the text in the spectacles would not change.[32]

While it is unknown how long Emma had spent recording Joseph's translation before Martin arrived, Martin stayed in Harmony to write for Joseph for around two full months before he returned to his home in Palmyra. Emma had likely already written the majority of the "book of Lehi" before Harris ever arrived. Martin remembered, "There were not many pages translated while he [Martin] wrote; after which Oliver

90

Cowdery and others did the writing." Martin stated that he wrote "about one third of the first part of the translation of the plates as [Joseph] interpreted them by the Urim and Thummim."[33]

While Latter-day Saints commonly teach that Joseph Smith used a sheet to veil the plates while he translated with Martin Harris, it seems to be something that occurred before the translation began. The idea appears to have come from the confused statements of those who heard Harris describe how Joseph copied the characters from the plates. But because Harris had already hefted the plates and their box, and because they were often left lying on the table with nothing but a linen cloth over them, it is hard to believe that Smith hung a sheet up between them during their translation in the summer of 1828. Though Joseph Smith may have used a sheet at one point to hide the plates from others who were in the room, it was evidently before Harris began writing for Smith in April 1828.[34]

Some of the confusion surrounding reports of a sheet being involved in the translation process stems from Charles Anthon's 1833 derogatory letter, in which he claimed that Martin had explained the translation process to him in February 1828 and had included the story of a sheet separating the two men.[35] Yet, despite Anthon's version of events, Harris had not, by February 1828, participated in any *translation* of the Book of Mormon with Joseph. It would have been impossible for him to give an eyewitness account about how Joseph translated until several months after his trip to the East. Much more likely, Anthon was confusing Harris's description of how Smith copied the characters with later reports of the actual translation process. At that early stage, Smith may have divided the room with a sheet to keep the plates hidden from Martin Harris, Reuben Hale, and Emma Smith, who were all apparently involved in creating or receiving copies of the characters. While it later became a popular way to describe Joseph's translation, it seems that Joseph only used the sheet when he had the plates exposed in front of him while he transcribed the characters from the plates in the winter of 1827. John Clark, who saw copies of the characters before Harris helped Joseph with the translation, was the only other person to describe a sheet being used to separate Joseph and his scribe.[36]

In any case, Harris was one of the few people who served as a scribe during the early translation of the gold plates, and he provided numerous testimonies of both the process and the plates. Long before he claimed to have a visionary experience in which an angel miraculously showed him the plates, Harris had other witnesses. Harris lifted the box of plates numerous times and was present for over two months as Joseph Smith dictated the translation of the ancient record. In one later interview, Harris reported, as did Emma Smith, that Joseph simply had the plates "on a table in the room in which Smith was translating, covered over with a cloth."[37] Though the plates largely remained in the house, they were also hidden outside in the woods.[38] In addition to numerous physical witnesses of the gold plates, Harris also apparently saw the spectacles Smith had retrieved with the gold plates. He later explained the spectacles to one newspaperman: "The stones were white, like polished marble, with a few gray streaks. I never dared to look into them by placing them in the hat, because Moses said that 'no man could see God and live.'. . . And beside, we had a command to let no man look into them, except by the command of God. Lest [anyone] should 'look aught and perish.'"[39] Martin later explained to Edward Stevenson that as the seer stones rested in the bottom of a hat "the Prophet would read sentence by sentence as Martin wrote."[40]

Martin Harris further explained that at one point during the translation, in order to make the mechanics of translation easier, Joseph stopped using the spectacles. He had already stopped using the cumbersome breastplate, and the apparently large and unwieldy spectacles were also making the long hours of translating more difficult. One local Palmyra resident heard "that the glasses were as big as a breakfast plate."[41] Another claimed that Joseph described them as "having very large round glasses, larger than a silver dollar."[42] For his part, Martin Harris explained that the spectacles were around "eight inches" long.[43] Rather than continuing to work with the awkwardly large spectacles, according to Harris, Joseph began using a single seer stone instead of the spectacles. He stated that Joseph "possessed a seer stone, by which he was enabled to translate as well as from the Urim and Thummim [spectacles], and for convenience he then used the seer stone."[44] For Wilford Woodruff, this transition from the device containing two stones to a single one was seen as a fulfillment of the prophecy in the Book of Mormon that "Gazelem," *a* seer stone, would be used to bring forth the ancient records of the Nephites.[45]

*Mid Summer 1828*

TRANSLATION AND THE LOST BOOK OF LEHI ❖

## Losing the Book of Lehi

Regardless of the particular method of translation used, by mid-summer 1828 Joseph and Martin had finished a significant manuscript.[46] In an attempt to placate his wife, Lucy, however, Harris pressured Joseph Smith repeatedly for permission to take the manuscript home to "read to his friends that peradventure he might convince them of the truth."[47] Joseph explained that he "inquired of the Lord and the Lord said unto [him] that [Harris] must not take" the manuscript home to New York.[48] Not deterred by this initial rebuff, over the next two months, Harris inquired two more times. Joseph Smith later explained that "after much solicitation" he "enquired of the Lord, and permission was granted [for Harris] to have the writings on certain conditions," which included showing them to only a specified number of people in Palmyra.[49]

Harris, ecstatic to have finally received permission to show the manuscript to his wife and others, hurriedly left for his home in Palmyra, New York, in mid-June. Just a day after Harris's departure with the pages, Emma Smith gave birth to a stillborn son in an exceptionally difficult and painful delivery that nearly took her life. For nearly three weeks, Joseph cared for his bedridden wife, who appeared at times to be near death. As Emma finally began to recover in early July, she became concerned over the duration of Harris's extended absence with the manuscript that she had worked so hard to transcribe. She encouraged Joseph to "repair to Palmyra, for the purpose of learning the cause of Mr. Harris's absence as well as silence."[50] Joseph responded immediately to her concern and, despite the expense, took the first stagecoach north to Palmyra while Emma's mother helped care for her in his absence.[51]

The first available stagecoach, however, did not take him directly to his parents' house. Instead, its route apparently only got as close as Geneva, twenty miles southeast of Palmyra. From there Joseph began a long walk at around ten o'clock at night. The walk was all the more difficult because of his distraught condition. He was visibly upset from the recent loss of his first child and still worried about his ailing spouse as he staggered through the dark on the dusty road to Palmyra. Although the walk was difficult, Joseph was not alone; Lucy Smith reported that a Good Samaritan on the stagecoach had recognized Joseph's distress. Joseph had apparently

93

❖ FROM DARKNESS UNTO LIGHT

*[handwritten: Martin Harris loses the manuscript — "The Book of Lehi"]*

not eaten and had slept very little during the long ride from Harmony, which alarmed the passenger enough that he felt pity for Joseph and kindly accompanied him on his walk until dawn when they reached Joseph Smith Sr.'s house. During their walk Joseph told the man "he had left his wife in so low a state of health that he had reason to fear that he would not find her alive when he returned[. And] he had buried his first and only child but a few days previous to leaving home."⁵² Lucy Smith also recalled that "there was heavy trouble laying at his heart that he did not dare to mention," thinking of the translated manuscript that Martin Harris had for some reason not already returned. When Joseph arrived at his parents' home, someone was sent to bring Martin Harris to breakfast so they could discuss the manuscript.

However, although Joseph had exerted himself throughout the night, taking no rest in order to learn the fate of the pages, Martin did not come immediately when he was called. Instead, the Smiths sat anxiously waiting for hours, wondering why Harris had not yet arrived. Finally, without his usual horse or buggy, Martin was seen slowly walking down the small dirt road leading to the Smiths' house. Lucy explained that Harris's eyes were "fixed thoughtfully upon the ground" as he made his way to the gate in front of their house. There, "he stopped, instead of passing through, and got upon the fence, and sat there some time with his hat drawn over his eyes." At this point expecting the worst, the Smiths welcomed him in the house and sat him at the table for his long-delayed breakfast. Before he could eat, Martin finally cried out, "Oh, I have lost my soul! I have lost my soul!" Having feared something had befallen the sacred manuscript all throughout the night and into the morning, Joseph's anger and frustration over his own recent difficulties were manifest. He sprang from his chair and interrogated Martin: "Have you broken your oath, and brought down condemnation upon my head, as well as your own?" With deep anguish and regret, Harris timidly replied, "Yes, it is gone." Lucy Smith wrote that "sobs and groans . . . filled the house," with Joseph "weeping and grieving like a tender infant." The next morning Joseph set out for Pennsylvania to return to his ailing wife and relate to her the catastrophic news. As he left, he and his family "parted with heavy hearts."⁵³

Exactly what happened to the lost manuscript pages, which Joseph referred to as "the Book of Lehi," remains a mystery. Lucy Smith explained that Harris began displaying the manuscript as soon as he brought it home in June, but initially only to those whom the Lord had specified. His wife "seemed highly pleased with what she heard and entered into the spirit of it so much that she gave her husband the privilege of locking it up in a set of drawers which she had never before permitted him to look into." It seems, however, that Lucy Harris was more interested in locking the manuscript up to control it herself rather than to keep it safe from others. Not many days later, a "very particular friend made [Martin] a visit," at which time Harris told him the story of the gold plates and his experience translating with Joseph Smith. Without contemplating the consequences of betraying his promise to show the manuscript to only those the Lord identified or considering the reaction of his wife, Martin broke the lock to Lucy's cabinet and pulled the manuscript out to show his friend. After showing the manuscript once, it became easier for him to continue showing it to others, all in violation of the previous oath he had made. Once Lucy Harris found out that Martin had broken the lock, she was enraged, and "her irracible temper knew no bounds and an intolerable storm ensued throughout the house which descended with greatest force upon the head of the devoted husband." Lucy Smith believed, citing Lucy Harris's anger at Martin and her continued opposition to the work, that once Lucy Harris found the lock was broken she surreptitiously took the manuscript and hid it where Martin could not find it.[54]

If she did steal the manuscript, what she did with pages after taking them is not known. Years later, several rumors circulated among former New York residents about what Lucy did with the pages. One local resident said that he heard Lucy Harris "say she burned the papers. She was pretty high on combativeness." He went on to explain, "She says she burned them up. And there was no mistake, but she did. They never was found; never came to light."[55] Another former New Yorker contrarily claimed that she stole the manuscript and passed it off to "a certain Dr. Seymour." In any case, if Lucy took the pages of the book of Lehi she likely did so to stop her husband from investing his time and money into the translation and publication of the Book of Mormon.[56]

For his part, Joseph Smith believed that the manuscript had been stolen by "evil and designing persons." A revelation declared to him in the voice of the Lord that "wicked men have taken them from you." By the time he penned the preface to the Book of Mormon a year later, he wrote of the lost manuscript that "some person or persons [had] stolen and kept [it] from [him], notwithstanding [his] utmost exertions to recover it again." The purpose for their treachery had been to "destroy [him], and also the work." Joseph believed that someone planned at some future point to reveal the lost manuscript in order to discredit the Book of Mormon. He wrote that the Lord told him that he "should not translate the same over again, for Satan had put it into their hearts to tempt the Lord their God, by altering the words, that they did read contrary from that which I translated and caused to be written; and if I should bring forth the same words again, or, in other words, if I should translate the same over again, they would publish that which they had stolen, and Satan would stir up the [hearts] of this generation, that they might not receive this work."[57] Not only had Harris's failure to secure the manuscript prevented the world from reading the book of Lehi, but the loss of the manuscript could have potentially derailed the entire translation project.[58] Harris's failure also had the potential to sever the men's relationship entirely and thus endanger Joseph's chances to secure funding from Harris to publish the book.

Joseph Smith recalled that "Immediately after my return home [to Harmony] I was walking out a little distance, when Behold the former heavenly messenger appeared and handed to me the Urim and Thummin again (for it had been taken from me in consequence of my having wearied the Lord in asking for the privilege of letting Martin Harris take the writings which he lost by transgression) and I enquired of the Lord through them and obtained the folowing revelation."[59] Apparently some distance from his house and likely without paper, ink, or a quill, it is unlikely that he recorded the revelation immediately. Once Smith returned to his house, Emma or his brother-in-law Reuben Hale, who had served as his scribes even before Harris began writing for him, may have recorded the revelation.[60]

The revelation rebuked Joseph Smith for his misdeed in asking repeatedly to allow Harris to take the manuscript and commanded him to repent before he could resume the translation of the gold plates. The angel announced that because Smith "had sinned in delivering the manuscript into the hands of a wicked man, . . . [he] would of necessity have to suffer the consequences of his indiscretion."[61] As an initial consequence, Smith

> *The Angel Moroni takes away the plates and spectacles, then later returns them to Joseph Smith.*

reported that the plates and spectacles were taken from him twice—once prior to the revelation after asking a third time to let Harris take the manuscript and once afterwards: "After I had obtained [this] revelation, both the plates, and the [spectacles] were taken from me again, but in a few days they were returned to me."[62]

After Joseph returned to Harmony, his family in Palmyra was unaware of what was transpiring in Harmony, but they knew Joseph had left them very distraught from the loss of the manuscript and fearful of Emma's health. Wondering what had happened to Joseph since he left their Manchester home in July 1828, Lucy and Joseph Smith Sr. traveled to Pennsylvania in September to see Joseph and Emma. Just before they arrived on this unplanned visit, Joseph prophetically told Emma that his parents were approaching their property. Trusting this impression, and without yet seeing them in the distance, he walked nearly a mile to meet his parents on the road. Lucy explained: "He met us with a countenance blazing with delight and it was very evident that his joy did not arise wholly from seeing us."[63]

That evening Joseph told Lucy the story of his repentance, stating, "God was pleased with my faithfulness and humility and loved me for my penitence and diligence in prayer." She was pleased to know that the plates were safely stored in Emma's bureau, in a Moroccan trunk that she first saw as she entered their house. Joseph and Emma had apparently pulled themselves from a dark hole of despair, and Joseph's prophetic revelation gave him direction, coupled with the return of the spectacles and the gold plates. Though Joseph and Emma would face a hard winter that year, they seemed rejuvenated that September as Lucy and Joseph Smith Sr. left to return to their home in Manchester.[64]

## Notes

1. MacKay, Dirkmaat, and Jensen, "The 'Caractors' Document," 131–52.
2. John A. Clark, *Gleanings by the Way* (Philadelphia: W. J. & J. K. Simon, 1842), 217. G. W. Stoddard, who was a farmer in Wayne County, New York, claimed Harris was a Universalist and a Methodist. See Howe, *Mormonism Unvailed*, 260–61.
3. John A. Clark, *Gleanings by the Way*, 217, 222–31.
4. Lucy Mack Smith, History, 1844–1845, book 6, [9].
5. Lucy Mack Smith, History, [74–75]; Joseph Smith, History, vol. A-1.

6. Lucy Harris apparently stated that she "had come to see the plates and would never leave until she attained her object." Lucy Mack Smith, History, 1844–1845, book 6, [11].
7. Lucy Mack Smith, History, 1844–1845, book 6, [13].
8. Lucy Mack Smith, History, 1845, book 6, [10–11]. Original spelling has been preserved throughout the chapter.
9. Lucy Mack Smith, History, 1845, book 6, [10–11].
10. It appears that Lucy Harris was the first of many who identified Joseph's recovering of gold plates after visits from an angel as money digging and interaction with a treasure guardian. Mark Ashurst-McGee analyzed this kind of literature after Lucy's claim and concluded that "a closer look at what the treasure-guardian sources actually say clearly demonstrates that their source is not Joseph Smith but rather run-of-the-mill treasure-lore superimposed upon his story." Ashurst-McGee, "Moroni," 44–47.
11. Abigail Harris, Lucy Harris's sister-in-law, explained that Martin was involved in the gold plates to make money, and she also couched the angelic experience in the language of treasure lore. Howe, *Mormonism Unvailed*, 253–54.
12. *Reflector* (Palmyra, NY), 28 February 1831, 1.
13. "Golden Bible," *Palmyra Freeman*, 11 August 1829.
14. In 1825 Martin Harris had apparently signed over one-third of his property to Lucy Harris. The deed, which guaranteed Lucy the equivalent of her dowry rights (one-third of her husband's property), was lost or more likely not formally recorded by the court in 1825. On 13 May 1828, a copy was created to assure Lucy Harris's claim to one-third of Martin Harris's property.
15. Harris and Martin, Indenture to Peter Harris, Wayne Co., NY, 29 November 1825, mortgage record, US and Canada Record Collection, Family History Library; Lucy Mack Smith, History, 1844–1845, book 6, [8–10]. In May 1828, she had her husband deed that portion of his property to Peter Harris, Lucy's brother, who immediately deeded the land to Lucy Harris to make it a legal transaction that allowed her to take possession of her dowry rights without a divorce from Martin.
16. Joseph Smith, History, vol. A-1, 9. See also Howe, *Mormonism Unvailed*, 254.
17. Knight Sr., History, 4.
18. Edmund C. Briggs, "A Visit to Nauvoo in 1856," *Journal of Mormon History*, October 1916, 454.
19. Joseph Smith III, "Last Testimony of Sister Emma," *Saints' Herald*, 1 October 1879, 289–90.
20. Joseph Smith III, "Last Testimony of Sister Emma," 289–90.

*The process of translation*

TRANSLATION AND THE LOST BOOK OF LEHI ❖

21. There are actually two, but the second is more complicated. An Ohio Shaker who had spoken with Oliver Cowdery wrote in his journal, "Two transparent stones in the form of spectacles thro which the translator looked on the engraving & afterwards put his face into a hat & the interpretation then flowed into his mind." See Christian Goodwillie, "Shaker Richard McNemar: The Earliest Book of Mormon Reviewer," *Journal of Mormon History* 37, no. 2 (Spring 2011): 143.

22. "To the Editor," *Ohio Observer*, 11 August 1836, 46.

23. The process of translation was, in itself, evidence to Emma that it was undeniably God's work. She witnessed the spectacles and saw her husband use them. Joseph Smith would later describe the spectacles in his history, explaining that the instrument consisted of "two stones," used by ancient seers, "in silver bows." A minister of the Reformed Church in Fayette, Diedrich Willers, recalled that "by the aid of certain mysterious seer stones," Joseph translated the plates. Diedrich Willers, "joseph Smith," n.d., manuscript, Diedrich Willers Papers, Seneca Falls Historical Society, Seneca Falls, New York, box 3, folder 2, item 10; as seen in Ashurst-McGee, "A Pathway to Prophethood: Joseph Smith Junior as Rodsman, Village Seer, and Judeo-Christian Prophet" (master's thesis, Utah State University, 2000), 302. The stones were apparently around one and one-half to two inches across and one-half inch thick. Martin Harris stated, "The two stones set in a bow of silver were about two inches in diameter, perfectly round, and about five-eighths of an inch thick at the centre; but not so thick at the edges where they came into the bow." Tiffany, "Mormonism," August 1859, 165–66; Fayette Lapham recalled a conversation with Joseph Smith Sr., who apparently told him that they were "a pair of Spectacles, about one and half inches longer than those used at the present day." Lapham, "II.—The Mormons," *Historical Magazine,* May 1870, 307. Joseph Knight, one of Joseph Smith's close friends that gave money and food to aid in the translation, later recalled, "Now the way he translated was he put the urim and thummim [the spectacles] into his hat and Darkned his Eyes then he would take a sentance and it would apper in Brite Roman Letters then he would tell the writer and he would write it then that would go away the next sentance would Come and so on But if it was not spelt rite it would not go away till it was rite so we see it was marvelous thus was the hol translated." Knight Sr., History, 4.

24. Edmund C. Briggs, "A Visit to Nauvoo in 1856," *Journal of History* 9 (October 1916): 454.

25. Cornelis Van Dam, *The Urim and Thummim*, 221–22, chapters 10 and 11. See Exodus 28:30 and Leviticus 7:8. Compare Mosiah 8:10; and Ether 3:27–28, 4:5.

99

26. J. W. Peterson and W. S. Pender, interview of William Smith, 1891, *The Rod of Iron* 1, no. 3 (February 1924): 7.

27. See Joseph Smith History, vol. A-1, 5; Howe, *Mormonism Unvailed*, 246–47, 253, 267.

28. In the Book of Mormon, the people of Limhi found the brother of Jared's gold plates and the spectacles. It also explains that they found multiple breastplates, seemingly associated with armor. One of these breastplates may have been the one Joseph retrieved in 1827, but it is unknown and the Book of Mormon does not account for a priestly breastplate associated with the spectacles. See Mosiah 8:8–11.

29. This is assuming that the breastplates described in Mosiah 8 included the breastplate given to Joseph along with the plates and the spectacles. See previous footnote.

30. See Alma 37:23.

31. Collier and Harwell, *Kirtland Council Minute Book*, 21.

32. *Deseret Evening News*, 13 December 1881.

33. *Saints' Herald*, 24 May 1884, 324. Possibly contradicting this point, Anthony Metcalf claimed that Harris told him that he "wrote a great deal of the Book of Mormon . . . as Joseph Smith translated or spelled the words out in English." Anthony Metcalf, *Ten Years before the Mast* (Malad City, ID: Research Publications, 1888), 70–71.

34. In a late interview with Frederick G. Mather, Sally McKune, who lived in Harmony next to the Smiths, stated, "The translating and writing were done in the little low chamber of Joe Smith's house. The Prophet and his precious trust were screened even from the sight of his clerks by blankets nailed to the walls. The nails remained for many years just as they were driven by the Prophet, and it was not until some repairing was done a short time ago that they were drawn out." "The Early Mormons. Joe Smith Operates at Susquehanna," *Binghamton Republican*, 29 July 1880.

35. Charles Anthon stated from his interaction with Harris in February 1828 that Joseph Smith "was placed behind a curtain, in the garret of a farm house, and, being thus concealed from view, put on the spectacles." Howe, *Mormonism Unvailed*, 270–72.

36. Even though John A. Clark, whom Harris had shown the characters, seemed to believe that Smith was translating behind the sheet and dictating the text to a scribe, he clarified that he only had knowledge of the earliest interaction with plates. He explained, "What other measures they afterwards took to transcribe or translate from these metallic plates, I cannot say, as I very soon after this removed to

another field of labour where I hear no more of the matter till I learned the BOOK OF MORMON was about being published." John A. Clark and Charles Anthon claimed that Joseph Smith would hang a large sheet from the ceiling to stop Harris from seeing what he was doing during the translation. Clark wrote that "although in the same room, a thick curtain or blanket was suspended between them, and Smith concealed behind the blanket, pretended to look through his spectacles, or transparent stones, and would then write down or repeat what he saw, which, when repeated aloud, was written down by Harris, who sat on the other side of the suspended blanket. Harris was told that it would arouse the most terrible divine displeasure, if he should attempt to draw near the sacred chest, or look at Smith while engaged in the work of deciphering the mysterious characters." Clark, *Gleanings by the Way*, 217, 222–31.

37. Metcalf, *Ten Years Before the Mast*, 70–71. Eber D. Howe wrote that Martin Harris explained that "he never saw the wonderful plates but once, although he and Smith were engaged for months in deciphering their contents." *Mormonism Unvailed*, 13.
38. See Knight Sr., History, 3–4; Lucy Mack Smith, History, 1844–45, book 6, MS 9.
39. Tiffany, "Mormonism," August 1859, 163–70.
40. Edward Stevenson, "The Three Witnesses to the Book of Mormon. No. II," *Millennial Star*, 21 June 1886, 366. Harris told William Pilkington that "Joseph dictated to [him] from the plates of Gold as the characters theron assumed through the Urim and Thummim the forms of Equivelent modern words which were familiar to the understanding of the Prophet and See." William Pilkington, "Martin Harris' Dying Testimony," affidavit, 3 April 1934, Church History Library; see also *Deseret News*, 5 May 1934.
41. Footnote in W. Wyl, *Joseph Smith the Prophet, His Family and His Friends* (Salt Lake City: Tribune Print and Publishing Co., 1886), 276.
42. Henry G. Tinsley, "Origin of Mormonism," *San Francisco Chronicle*, 14 May 1893, 12.
43. Tiffany, "Mormonism," August 1859, 165–66.
44. *Deseret Evening News*, 13 December 1881, 4.
45. See Alma 37:23; Kenney, *Wilford Woodruff's Journal*, 2:144, 8:500; George A. Smith Papers, box 174, folder 26, Manuscripts Division, Marriott Library, University of Utah.
46. Joseph Smith, History, vol. A-1, 9. They may have not actually had 116 pages; evidence suggests that this was the title given to this manuscript by Joseph Smith

in the preface of the Book of Mormon. See Preface to Book of Mormon, circa August 1829, in *JSP*, D1:92–94.

47. There are signs that Lucy and Martin Harris had a troubled marriage prior to Martin's involvement with Joseph Smith and the gold plates. In May 1828 the Harrises concluded a jointure agreement giving Lucy Harris her marital or dower interest, which was similar to a postnuptial settlement. Lucy's legal rights to her portion of the property were subsequently deeded to her by Martin by way of her brother Peter, a document which was backdated to 1825. Since Lucy Harris was opposed to Martin's involvement in the translation of the gold plates at the same time, she may have forced Martin to execute this legal agreement as a result of her fear that Martin would invest in the translation and printing of the Book of Mormon. Aside from the legal agreement, Lucy Harris had also recently traveled to Harmony to see the plates herself, but left in anger, having not been shown them by Joseph Smith. Metcalf, *New Approaches to the Book of Mormon*, 395n1; Royal Skousen, "Critical Methodology and the Text of the Book of Mormon," *FARMS Review of Books on the Book of Mormon* 6, no. 1 (1994): 137.
48. Joseph Smith, History, circa Summer 1832, in *JSP*, H1:15.
49. Joseph Smith, History, vol. A-1, 9. See also Revelation, March 1829 [D&C 5], in *JSP*, D1:13–19.
50. Lucy Mack Smith, *Biographical Sketches*, 118.
51. Lucy Mack Smith, History, 1844–1845, book 2, [7].
52. Lucy Mack Smith, History, 1844–1845, book 4, [7].
53. Lucy Mack Smith, History, 1844–1845, book 6–7.
54. Lucy Mack Smith, History, 1844–1845, book 7–9.
55. Lorenzo Saunders, interview by E. L. Kelley, 12 November 1884, E. L. Kelley Papers, "Misc," CCLA; William Pilkington to Vern C. Poulter, Letter, 28 February 1930, Church History Library.
56. Arthur Deming, *Naked Truths About Mormonism* (Oakland, CA: Deming & Co., 1888), 2.
57. See Revelation, Spring 1829 [D&C 10], in *JSP*, D1:37–44; see also Preface to Book of Mormon, circa August 1829, in *JSP*, D1:92–94.
58. How much of the manuscript Smith and Harris had finished by mid-June is not known with certainty. In the preface he wrote for the Book of Mormon, Joseph explained that he "translated, by the gift and power of God, and caused to be written, one hundred and sixteen pages, the which I took form the Book of Lehi." The manuscript was replaced with the translation of the plates of Nephi,

which just so happened to be 116 pages (and two lines) long in the printer's copy of the finished Book of Mormon manuscript. This is significant because the original manuscript of the Book of Mormon was approximately three pages shorter than the printer's manuscript at that point in the manuscript, and the 116 pages is unique to the printer's manuscript. On the other hand, John Gilbert stated that the printer's manuscript was copied and handed to him in twenty-four-page groups as they set the type and that the first group was given to him in late August 1829, after the preface was written. Nonetheless, it is likely that the 116 pages mentioned in the preface was the number of pages that replaced the book of Lehi, and the printer's manuscript may have had over 116 pages finished by the time Joseph Smith wrote the preface. Therefore, the size of "the Book of Lehi" was likely not 116 pages long; it may have been more, and it may have been less.

59. Joseph Smith, History, vol. A-1, 10.
60. The earliest known copy was created in the spring of 1831, so it is possible that Smith dictated the revelation to either of them, or even to another scribe at a later time before 1831.
61. Lucy Mack Smith, *Biographical Sketches*, 125.
62. Joseph Smith, History, vol. A-1, 11. Lucy Mack Smith added a dimension to this account when she wrote that after losing the plates and Urim and Thummim a second time, Joseph "continued [his] supplications to God, without cessation, and . . . had the joy and satisfaction of again receiving the Urim and Thummim." Lucy also explained that Joseph had told her that the angel "seemed pleased with me when he gave me back the Urim and Thummim, and he told me that the Lord loved me, for my faithfulness and humility." Lucy Mack Smith, *Biographical Sketches*, 126. The reminiscent accounts of Joseph and Lucy Mack Smith differed slightly on the details of the events. Joseph, for example, said the Urim and Thummim was returned, along with the plates, "a few days" after he received the July 1828 revelation. See Joseph Smith, History, vol. A-1, 11. Lucy, however, quoted Joseph as saying the Urim and Thummim was returned "on the twenty-second of September [1828]." Lucy Mack Smith, *Biographical Sketches*, 126. Conversely, Lucy Mack Smith remembered visiting Joseph and Emma in September 1828, at which time Joseph was given the spectacles again by an angel. Whether they were returned in July or October, Emma apparently translated a little more before Joseph went to work on his small farm. Knight Sr., History, 4–5.

❖ FROM DARKNESS UNTO LIGHT

63. Lucy Mack Smith, History, book 7–8.
64. Lucy Mack Smith, History, book 7–9.

# 6

## Returning to the Translation

It is unknown to what extent Martin Harris maintained his zeal to publish the Book of Mormon in the months that followed the loss of the book of Lehi. Once Joseph made his 150-mile trip back to Harmony that summer, a temporary rift formed between Joseph and Martin. The distance between them, coupled with the painful loss of the manuscript, severed any personal contact between them for nearly eight months. After placing so much trust in Martin to protect the manuscript, Joseph's disappointment in its loss likely discouraged him from writing letters to him or from updating him about his own attempts to begin translating again. Nevertheless, Martin maintained his interest in the translation of the gold plates and likely maintained contact with the Smiths in Palmyra.[1] After spending the fall of 1828 working on his farm, Joseph Smith once again made new, determined efforts to translate the plates in 1829, but by that point, he turned to others to help him with the translation.[2]

In early 1829, Joseph dictated a revelation that made a very distinct prophetic call to all who would listen, declaring that the Lord needed all those who were willing to help bring forth his work. Joseph Smith Sr. may have shown Martin Harris this revelation and informed him of Joseph's immediate

❖ FROM DARKNESS UNTO LIGHT

*The Martin Harris Farm. Martin mortgaged this farm to Egbert B. Grandin to ensure payment of the costs to publish 5,000 copies of the Book of Mormon. Photo by George Edward Anderson. Courtesy of Church History Library.*

Feb 1829

intentions to recommence the translation sometime in February 1829. Joseph Knight Sr., a family friend and early supporter from Colesville, New York, wrote that Joseph Sr. and Samuel Smith stopped at his home in Colesville on their way to Harmony. Knight wrote, "I told [Joseph Smith Sr.] they had traviled far enough, [and] I would go with my sley and take them Down [to Harmony] to morrow[.] I went Down and found them well and the[y] were glad to see us[.] we conversed about many things. in the morning I gave the old man a half a Dollar and Joseph a little money to Buoy [buy] paper to translate."[3] Knight's provision of paper provided Joseph Smith with essential materials needed to resume the translation. During their visit Joseph dictated a revelation for Joseph Smith Sr. that spoke of a "marvelous work," explaining through an apocalyptic metaphor that the "field is white already to harvest," fostering an urgency to bring forth the translation of the gold plates. Some of Joseph's other revelations perpetuated the same sense of urgency in the spring of 1829. They all developed imagery of an impending harvest, while demonstrating Joseph's prophetic voice and determination to translate the plates.[4]

In the months before March 1829, Emma and Samuel Smith helped Joseph with the translation of the plates by recording his words as he dictated the translation.[5] Joseph's history stated, "Now my wife had written some for me to translate and also my Brothr Samuel H Smith but we had become reduced in property and my wives father was about to turn me out

106

RETURNING TO THE TRANSLATION ❖

of dores."[6] Their immediate material needs prevented the translation from moving forward quickly; it was difficult for them to afford even the paper for recording Joseph's translation. It was not until February that Joseph Knight Sr. arrived and provided them money for paper and supplies.[7]

## Martin Harris

According to Isaac Hale, Harris returned to Harmony in March to receive a "greater witness" of the gold plates. This need for a great witness may have been the result of a lawsuit threatened by his wife.[8] Hearing from the Smiths and others in Palmyra that Joseph was once again translating the plates, Harris had "a great desire to go down to Penn[sylvania] to see how they were prospering for himself."[9] After the disastrous loss of the manuscript the previous summer, Harris was eager to speak with Joseph, but his wife Lucy resumed her opposition and tried to stop Harris from reengaging in the translation with Joseph. When Lucy Harris heard about Smith's intentions of beginning the translation again, she worked towards finding another "means of hindering [Martin Harris] perhaps entirely from accomplishing the work which he was about."[10]

Lucy Harris apparently tried to build opposition against Joseph Smith among local residents in Palmyra who knew about the gold plates and Joseph's plan to translate them. Lucy Smith recalled that Martin's wife "mounted her horse [and] flew through the neighborhood like a dark spirit from house to house making diligent enquiry at every house for miles where she had the least hope of gleaning anything that would subserve her purpose." She apparently searched for anyone who had information about the plates that would incriminate Joseph Smith. She believed that if she could find someone who could prove that the plates were fakes, she could demonstrate in a court of law that Joseph Smith was committing fraud by asking her husband to fund the publication of the Book of Mormon. She hoped to prove that Joseph had counterfeited the plates "for the express purpose of obtaining money from those who might be so credulous as to believe him." According to Lucy Smith's history, Lucy Harris may have begun threatening a lawsuit against Joseph as early as March, but did not enter a formal complaint before a magistrate until early August in Lyons, New York.[11]

Lucy Harris's threats of a lawsuit concerned her husband and others very deeply. Referencing Lucy's threat, Martin Harris remembered that his consternation about the potential lawsuit prompted him to travel to Harmony in March to see Joseph Smith. Harris recalled that "In March [1829] the People Rose up & united against the Work gathering testimoney against the Plates & Said they had testimony Enough & if I did not Put Joseph in Jail <& his father> for Deseption they Would me."[12] In essence, they were telling Martin that if the plates were fakes, he too was guilty of fraudulently misleading the public into buying copies of the translation. Lucy Harris and others had apparently gathered witnesses who would testify in court that Joseph Smith was fraudulently perpetuating the existence of the gold plates simply to make money from the publication of the pretended text. Lucy Harris was well aware of the fact that her husband had never actually seen the plates with his own eyes, and she had already discounted her own experiences of lifting and hearing the plates in the box. She knew that no one had seen the plates with their own eyes. Using this knowledge to her advantage, she gathered at least three witnesses that would testify that they knew what was inside of the cryptic box. Since no one had seen the plates, it was one person's word against another's. One witness claimed that it was only sand in the box, failing with such a claim to explain the metallic sound the plates made when they shifted and the clear sense that there was a large, solid object in the box.[13] A second witness claimed that Joseph confided in him that he filled the box with a large bar of lead. However, this claim too contradicts the experiences of friends and family who heard and felt the plates as individual metal sheets. Furthermore, as Martin Harris later retorted, the Smiths did not have the money to pay for fifty to sixty pounds of lead, let alone the financial wherewithal to turn such lead into individual metal sheets to form the "plates." The final witness's claim was perhaps the most absurd. He claimed that Joseph told him that there was nothing in the box. However, even several of Joseph Smith's detractors, including Lucy Harris and Isaac Hale, had felt the weight of plates in the box.[14]

These witnesses claimed to have spoken with Joseph Smith personally about the plates. Each of them claimed that Joseph had admitted to them that the plates did not actually exist and that he was claiming their existence with the aim of making money. Their claims presented a possible threat to Joseph Smith because he could not quiet their charges by simply showing them the plates, making it their word against his. For his part, even though Harris had experienced a heavenly vision proclaiming to him

> Mr. Rogers & Lucy Harris' plan to expose the plates as a fraud.

RETURNING TO THE TRANSLATION ❖

the truthfulness of the work, he had never seen the plates himself without a cover. Though he believed that they were real after witnessing the translation and lifting the box they were stored in, the threat of the lawsuit motivated him to ask Joseph to show him the gold plates.

To prove that Joseph fabricated the plates, Lucy Harris devised a plan to replace the speculation of guessing what was in the box with actual evidence. When Martin left for Harmony, she persuaded a "Mr. Rogers" to travel with her husband with the purpose of finding a way to expose the plates once they arrived. Having heard the stories of Joseph leaving the plates unprotected on the table with only a cloth to cover them, Rogers hoped to catch Joseph in a vulnerable moment when he could quickly cut the cloth from the plates to see them with his own eyes.[15] By doing so, Rogers hoped to prove that the gold plates were not under the covering and that they were fakes created to rob Harris and others of their money. While Rogers made the journey to Harmony, there is no evidence that he either attempted to or succeeded in cutting the cloth off the plates and exposing them. In any case, he apparently failed to undermine Harris's belief in the plates.

Regardless of the fact that neither Mr. Rogers nor Martin Harris saw the plates during that March visit, it appears that Joseph Smith wanted to show the plates to others. Joseph understandably wanted someone else to shoulder the burden of affirming that the plates were real. Harris later explained, "Joseph wished me to see them." He told Harris, "I am afraid you will not believe unless you see them."[16] Before asking the Lord if Harris could see the plates, perhaps remembering the disastrous result of the early inquiry to allow Harris to show the book of Lehi to others, Joseph apparently constructed a plan for Harris to see them if it was the will of the Lord. According to Isaac Hale, Harris arranged with Joseph to follow his footprints in the snow to the place where he hid the plates, so that Harris could see the plates without Joseph showing them to him.[17] If Joseph wanted to show Harris the plates he could have easily uncovered them and handed them to him, but instead he buried them in the woods for Harris to find them—if it was the will of the Lord.

Still, according to Isaac Hale, Harris was not successful in his quest to see the plates on that occasion either. Instead, Joseph Smith dictated a revelation for him that addressed his concerns by stating that the revelation was to be seen as "a witness that my Servant Joseph hath got the things

> The proof of the Book of Mormon lies not in the plates but in the contents of the book itself.

## FROM DARKNESS UNTO LIGHT

which he hath testified," but it reiterated the fact that Joseph Smith could not show the plates to anyone. Nevertheless, the revelation did promise Harris that "if he will go out & bow down before me & humble himself in mighty prayer & faith in the sincerity of his heart" he would eventually see the plates and become a witness of them.

While Harris was in Harmony, he may have informed Smith of the mounting opposition in Palmyra and the potential lawsuit. The revelation Joseph had recently received stated, "There are many that lie in wait to destroy thee," perhaps an allusion to those preparing the lawsuit against him. The revelation declared that "the Swoard of Justice" hung above the people of that generation, and if they would "persist in the hardness of their hearts the time cometh that it must fall upon them." The book's authenticity, the revelation asserted, was evidenced not primarily by the plates but by the message found within the pages of the translation. It explained that an examination of the plates would not satisfy those who did not believe, but that the only real proof of the plates was the text of the Book of Mormon itself. These skeptics believed both the plates and the translation process to be fraudulent, positing that the Book of Mormon's text was not provided to Joseph by revelation but by Joseph Smith Sr., his father. Martin Harris reported that those preparing a lawsuit in opposition to the Book of Mormon wanted to "Put Joseph in Jail <& his father> for Deseption."[18] On Harris's trip back to Palmyra he shared a stagecoach ride with William S. Sayre, who recalled that one of the other passengers "did not believe that Jos[eph] was capable of composing anything, but that Jo's father was a man of some education & cunning & shr[ewd] . . . & was duping others through Joe, & that there [they] were cheating" Harris out of his money.[19] The incredulity with which some viewed Joseph Smith's claim to write the Book of Mormon, given his lack of education, persisted well into the summer. The editor of the *Palmyra Freeman*, Jonathan Hadley, exclaimed, "Now it appears not a little strange that there should have been deposited in this western world, and in the secluded town of Manchester, too, a record of this description; and still more so, that a person like this Smith (very illiterate) should have been gifted by inspiration to find and interpret it."[20]

> many did not believe that J.S. was capable of writing a book

Even though Harris never saw the plates during his visit to Harmony, Smith translated more of them while he was there, and Harris acted as his scribe for a short period. Isaac Hale explained that Smith and Harris "were engaged in their translation of the Book,"[21] and Smith's revelation to Martin

110

*Martin Harris switches out the seer-stone*

RETURNING TO THE TRANSLATION ❖

Harris occurred in that context and directed Harris to translate "a few more pages." While they were working on it, Harris apparently devised his own test he could use to prove to others that Joseph Smith indeed did have the ability to translate through the seer stones. On one occasion as the men took a break from their translation efforts, Harris replaced Joseph's seer stone in the hat with a similar rock he picked up by the Susquehanna River. When Smith returned to continue translating, Joseph peered into the hat as he usually did, but the stone did not shine with the writing. He exclaimed to Harris that it was as "black as Egypt" in the hat, probably recognizing very quickly what Harris had done. When questioned, Harris explained to Smith that he had done it "to stop the mouths of fools, who had told him that the prophet had learned those sentences and was merely repeating them."[22] Joseph's further response is unknown, but Harris believed he could use the event to prove to others that Smith was actually reading words as they appeared miraculously on the stone rather than reciting from previously prepared manuscript, as so many detractors had claimed.

Though he had not seen the plates as he had hoped, Harris returned to Palmyra with renewed enthusiasm for the project. William S. Sayre wrote that in April 1829 he was traveling in a stagecoach between Bainbridge and Geneva, New York, when a man boarded the stage and began telling the other passengers about Joseph Smith. Harris, who was presumably that passenger, explained that Joseph Smith "had found a gold bible & stone in which he looked & was thereby enabled to translate the very ancient [chara[c]ters]." Further, "Smith [had] read to him a good deal of the bible & [Harris] repeated to those in the Stage verse after verse of what Smith had read to him."[23] While he had not seen the plates, he had heard the voice of the Lord promise him in one of Joseph's revelations that he would.

## Joseph's Prophetic Voice

Like Harris's revelation, Joseph's early revelatory words generally lay carefully scribbled on a small scrap of paper, but shone forth like a beacon of light from the pockets of the early believers where they were stored, inspiring them to give up their lives to bring forth the Book of Mormon and build God's church. Joseph often received his revelations in response to questions that arose among believers. Those addressed by the revelations believed that the Lord was speaking to them personally through Joseph Smith. Other revelations addressed the entire body of believers. Like Harris, those who accepted Joseph Smith's teachings regarded the revelatory communications as divine commandments from God and followed them with deep devotion. Some members of the Church copied Joseph's revelations into their notebooks and journals. The Church would eventually edit and publish most of these early revelations as a book of scripture, which encouraged later readers to view the revelations as a collection rather than as individual documents, but Joseph did not seem to realize that he would begin collating the revelations into one volume until the summer of 1830.

Joseph never recorded some of his earliest revelations, such as the revelations that he received through spectacles telling Harris that he could take the book of Lehi home in June 1828. This was partly due to Joseph's lack of consistent scribal assistance. Quite literally, any of the communications that Joseph received after his First Vision of Deity and as early 1822, when he received his first seer stone, could be seen as a revelation. For example, when Joseph saw a vision of Martin Harris in the spectacles, soon after he retrieved them from the stone box on Cumorah, this was a type of unwritten revelation. Shortly after the founding of the Church of Christ in 1830, Joseph Smith apparently stopped using the seer stones as a means of regular revelation. Instead, he dictated them directly to a scribe as they flowed into his own mind. His revelations also included visits from angels and visions of eternity. Eventually, other texts produced by Joseph Smith would also be canonized by the Church as revelations of Joseph Smith, such as the minutes of the meeting in which the high council was established, the text of the Kirtland Temple dedicatory prayer, letters he wrote to buoy up the Church membership, and even portions of his history. Some of the revelations may have been initially intended to be documents that would later be updated as needed. However, regardless of the initial intent, Joseph felt free to alter and update them as he felt so inspired. He made revisions himself and instructed others to make revisions also throughout his life.[24]

## Oliver Cowdery

Even before Joseph Smith began translating the plates again, the man who would serve as his most prolific scribe became deeply interested in the gold plates. Originally born in Wells, Vermont, Oliver Cowdery and his brothers had moved to western New York. In 1828, Oliver's brother Lyman was hired as a teacher in the Palmyra area. To Oliver's benefit, Lyman did not accept the offer, and the local school committee, which included Hyrum Smith, took Oliver as a replacement. Possibly because of Hyrum's connection with the committee, Cowdery rented a room from Joseph Sr. and Lucy Smith in their frame home in Manchester, New York.[25] By the fall of 1828, Cowdery had heard from Palmyra area residents about the gold plates and Joseph Smith. In particular, a resident from Fayette, New York, named David Whitmer piqued Cowdery's curiosity about the strange rumors emanating from the town. The excitement about the gold plates continued in Palmyra and Manchester long after Joseph Smith moved to Harmony in the winter of 1827, and rumors eventually reached both Cowdery and Whitmer. According to Whitmer's memory, Cowdery was originally more interested and was the first to be convinced that the plates existed. Contrarily, Whitmer was initially more skeptical, wondering if the plates were simply a rumor. Cowdery apparently exclaimed that "there must be some truth in the story of the plates, and that he intended to investigate the matter."[26] Whitmer too investigated the claims further by discussing the matter with others that had worked with Joseph Smith as they dug for buried ore. Those associates of Smith convinced Whitmer that the plates were real by describing to him their experience discovering the hole in the earth from which Joseph retrieved the plates.[27]

Lucy Smith recalled that Cowdery was so obsessed with the plates that he could not speak of anything else. Before ever meeting Joseph Smith, Oliver Cowdery reportedly had a divine manifestation that encouraged him

*Daguerreotype thought to be Oliver Cowdery. Photo by Patrick A. Bishop. © BYU Studies.*

❖ FROM DARKNESS UNTO LIGHT

to inquire of Joseph Smith Sr. about the gold plates. Joseph explained that the "Lord appeared unto a young man by the name of Oliver Cowdery and shewed unto him the plates in a vision and also the truth of the work and that the Lord was about to do through me his unworthy Servant."[28] Lucy Smith recalled that "one night after he [Cowdery] had retired to bed, he called upon the Lord to know if these things were so," and "the Lord . . . manifested to him that they were true."[29] Cowdery further explained to Joseph Smith Sr. that he "had been in a deep study all day and it had been put into his heart that he would have the privilege of writing for Joseph."[30] Accordingly, Cowdery left Palmyra for Harmony near the end of March to work with Joseph Jr. on the translation as his vision had commanded.[31] Cowdery arrived on 5 April 1829 and began taking dictation for Smith's translation of the plates on 7 April.[32] On his way there, he had stopped in Fayette, New York, to meet with his friend David Whitmer. In the ensuing months, he would write several letters to Whitmer that reported on the progress of the translation of the gold plates.[33] That progress, now that Joseph had an educated and reliable scribe, continued much more swiftly than the previous months of translation. In fact, Oliver Cowdery recorded nearly the entire Book of Mormon within the next three months as Joseph dictated it to him.

David Whitmer. *Portrait by Lewis A. Ramsey.*

## Notes

1. Just a couple of months after Joseph left Palmyra, distraught about the loss of the book of Lehi, Lucy and Joseph Smith Sr. traveled to Harmony in the fall of 1828 to check on Joseph and to discover what happened once he returned after losing the manuscript. Lucy wrote that an angel told Joseph, "If you are

sufficiently humble and penitent that you will receive them [the plates] again on the 22 of September." Upon their return, they likely informed Harris of Joseph Smith's plans to continue the translation and that the Lord had given Joseph the plates back. Lucy Mack Smith, History, 1845, book 7, MS 9.

2. Lucy Mack Smith, History, 1845, MS 90.
3. Knight Sr., History, 5. Original spelling has been preserved throughout the chapter.
4. See, for example, Revelation, April 1829–A [D&C 6:1, 3]; Revelation, May 1829–A [D&C 11:3]; Revelation, May 1829–B [D&C 12:1, 3]; and Revelation, June 1829–A [D&C 14:1, 3] in *JSP*, D1.
5. Lucy Mack Smith, History, book 7, [9]. Lucy Smith explained that Joseph began translating again in the fall of 1828 with Emma Smith as his scribe.
6. History, circa Summer 1832, in *JSP*, H1:16. See also "Last Testimony of Sister Emma," *Saints' Herald*, 1 October 1879, 289–90.
7. Even though Martin Harris visited in March 1829 and recorded a small portion of the translation, it was not until April that Joseph began translating the gold plates every day. There are no samples of Emma's, Samuel's, or Martin's handwriting. There are several theories about what portions of the manuscript they translated during this period, but one can only speculate about how much and what they recorded.
8. See Howe, *Mormonism Unvailed*, 264.
9. Lucy Mack Smith, History, 1844–1845, book 8, [5]. Lucy recounted that Samuel Smith visited Martin Harris after his return from Harmony that sparked Harris's interest in the translation again. Lucy Mack Smith, History, 1844–1845, book 8, [4]. This may be incorrect, because David Hale's ledger book places Samuel in Harmony in March. "David Hales Book," 20 March 1829, [19], digital copy, Harold B. Lee Library. This suggests that Joseph Smith Sr. returned home without Samuel and that Joseph Sr. likely brought the information that "roused" Harris's interest in the plates.
10. Lucy Mack Smith, History, 1844–1845, book 8, [5].
11. When Harris filed his complaint with the magistrate cannot be known because there is no extant legal record of it. Lucy Mack Smith, History, 1844–1845, book 8, [5].
12. "Testimony of Martin Harris," 4 September 1870, Edward Stevenson Collection, Church History Library.
13. Compare Peter Ingersoll statement in Howe, *Mormonism Unvailed*, 236.
14. Lucy Mack Smith, History, 1845, book 8, [7–8].
15. Rogers cannot be positively identified, although there was a "Joseph Rogers" who lived near Manchester in Phelpstown and later gave a negative account about the Smiths and claimed to have affidavits demonstrating that the Smiths were thieves.

115

See "Joseph Rogers' Statement," in *Startling Revelations! Naked Truths about Mormonism*, ed. Arthur B. Deming (Oakland, CA: n.p., 1888), 1. Edward Stevenson records the only brief account we have of him from Martin Harris. After hearing of the threat of a lawsuit, Harris stated, "So I went from Waterloo 25 mls South East of Palmyra to Rogerses in Suscotua [?] Co N.Y. & to harmony Pensylvania 125 & found Joseph. Rogers unknown to me had agreed to give my wife 100 Dollars if it was not A Deseption & had Whet his Nife to cut the covering of the Plates as the Lord had forbid Joseph exhibiting them openly." "Testimony of Martin Harris."

16. Tiffany, "Mormonism," August 1859, 166.
17. Howe, *Mormonism Unvailed*, 264.
18. "Testimony of Martin Harris."
19. William S. Sayre, Bainbridge, NY, to James T. Cobb, 31 August 1878, Theodore A. Schroeder Papers, Wisconsin State Historical Society.
20. "Golden Bible," *Palmyra Freeman*, 11 August 1829.
21. Howe, *Mormonism Unvailed*, 265.
22. Edward Stevenson, "One of the Three Witnesses," *Deseret Evening News*, 13 December 1881, 4. The use of a seer stone for translation in this account suggests that the incident occurred during Harris's 1829 visit to Harmony rather than during his 1828 scribal work on the lost book of Lehi. According to Emma Smith, Joseph Smith stopped using the "spectacles" after July 1828. Emma Smith, Nauvoo, IL, to Emma Pilgrim, 27 March 1870, in John T. Clark, "Translation of Nephite Records," *Return* (Davis City, IA), 15 July 1895, 2. "Now the first that my <husband> translated, was translated by the use of the Urim, and Thummim, and that was the part that Martin Harris lost, after that he used a small stone, not exactly, black, but was rather a dark color." David Whitmer stated explicitly that "Martin wrote some" as Joseph Smith dictated from the seer stone after the loss of the book of Lehi and that it was at this time that Martin Harris attempted to trick Joseph Smith by switching the stone. See Edward Stevenson, Sandusky, OH, to Franklin D. Richards, 10 January 1887, in Stevenson, Journal, 28:106–13, Church History Library; and Edward Stevenson, "A Visit to David Whitmer," *Juvenile Instructor*, 15 February 1887, 55. The quote above also indicates that some people who Harris knew had been informed about how the translation took place, yet before Harris arrived in 1828 to scribe for Joseph, only Emma and Reuben Hale had seen the translation. It is unlikely that someone would have replied to Martin with the above quote in 1828. By March 1829, Harris had likely told

others about the translation and they retorted that Joseph had prepared what he was going to say before he dictated the words of the translation. Nonetheless, this experience may have occurred in the second half of Harris's work with Joseph Smith in the summer of 1828, but it is less likely.

23. William S. Sayre, Bainbridge, NY, to James T. Cobb, 31 August 1878, Theodore A. Schroeder Papers, Wisconsin State Historical Society. Although Sayre called the man "Richards," he admitted that he was not certain of the name. The details of Sayre's account leave little doubt that the man was Harris. For example, he dates the incident to April 1829, and Harris was known to be in the area in March. The description of the man as a Palmyra resident accurately describes Harris, and his identification as the financier of the Book of Mormon's publication is unique to Harris also.

24. See *JSP*, D1: xxvii–xxviii; Minute Book 2, 8 November 1831, Church History Library.

25. The exact timing and sequence of events related to Oliver Cowdery's relationship with the Smith family are not clear. According to David Whitmer, Cowdery said that "he was acquainted with the Smith family" when Whitmer and Cowdery first met, but Whitmer offered no dates (other than the year 1828) and said nothing about Cowdery's staying with the Smiths. "Mormonism," *Kansas City Daily Journal*, 1 June 1881. Lucy Mack Smith, on the other hand, indicated that Cowdery began boarding with the Smith family right after he accepted the teaching position, but she said nothing about Cowdery's meeting Whitmer and, like Whitmer, gave no specific dates. Lucy Mack Smith, History, 1844–1845, book 7, [12].

26. "Mormonism," *Kansas City Daily Journal*, 1 June 1881. Whitmer had conversations with "several young men" who claimed that they knew Joseph Smith had the plates and that they had seen "the place in the hill that he took them out of." For the correction from "plates" to "place" in the last passage, see *Kansas City Daily Journal*, 13 June 1881.

27. "Mormonism," *Kansas City Daily Journal*, 1 June 1881.

28. History, circa Summer 1832, in *JSP*, H1:16.

29. Joseph Smith History, vol. A-1, 13.

30. Lucy Mack Smith, History, draft, book 8, [1].

31. Lucy Mack Smith, History, 1845, [93].

32. Joseph Smith History, vol. A-1, 13; Oliver Cowdery to W. W. Phelps, 7 September 1834, 14.

33. David Whitmer interview, *Kansas City Daily Journal*, 1 June 1881.

*Joseph translating with Oliver Cowdery as his scribe. Watercolor by Anthony Sweat.*

# 7

# Oliver Cowdery and the Translation of the Book of Mormon

Oliver Cowdery arrived providentially at Joseph Smith's doorstep in Harmony, Pennsylvania, on 5 April 1829. He came after the Lord appeared to him and showed him the gold plates in a vision, commanding him to go to Harmony to record the translation as Joseph Smith dictated the text.[1] His response to that manifestation marked the beginning of a series of men who would serve as recorders, scribes, and historians writing down the words and prophecies given by Joseph Smith until his death in 1844. Like Emma Smith and Martin Harris before him, Oliver recorded Joseph's translation of the plates, but he also ushered in an era in which the number of documents created by Joseph increased dramatically.[2] By the end of June, not even three months later, Cowdery had recorded the entire Book of Mormon on a series of hundreds of sheets of paper as well as a dozen of Joseph's revelations.[3] In addition, Cowdery would copy nearly the entire Book of Mormon manuscript later that fall and spring as they prepared it for publication.

Almost as soon as Oliver arrived in Harmony on the 5th, he and Joseph began recording the Book of Mormon. Cowdery wrote, "On Monday the 6th, I assisted him in arranging some business of a temporal nature, and on Tuesday the 7th, commenced to write the book of Mormon."[4] Joseph

❖ FROM DARKNESS UNTO LIGHT

remembered that "two days after the arrival of Mr. Cowdery (being the seventh of April) I commenced to translate the book of Mormon and he commenced to write for me."[5] Oliver was a far more capable scribe than Martin or Emma, and the pace of the translation was faster than it had ever been before. Yet, even though they translated nearly all of the Book of Mormon in less than ninety days, they accomplished far more than just the translation during that period.

Seated at a small table in Joseph's framed house, the topic of translation apparently filled their conversations in between the long hours of dictation and writing. Joseph Smith explained that "having continued [the translation] for some time I enquired of the Lord through the Urim and Thummin and obtained" a revelation for Oliver that explained to him that there were additional "records which contain much of my gospel, which have been kept back because of the wickedness of the people." With quill and ink in hand, Oliver went on to record the revelation, which promised him, "if you have good desires, a desire to lay up treasures for yourself in heaven, then shall you assist in bringing to light, with your gift, those parts of my scriptures which have been hidden because of iniquity." To his amazement, the revelation told Cowdery that he possessed the "gift" to translate, like Joseph. It stated, "I give unto you, and also unto my servant Joseph, the keys of this gift, which shall bring to light this ministry." After Cowdery had observed Joseph's gift to translate—which he could only comprehend as the "power of God"—he likely saw the comparison between him and Joseph as incredible, if not untenable.

Additional revelations provided Oliver Cowdery with directions for learning how to translate, apparently through a similar process to what Joseph Smith himself went through in the winter of 1827 when he learned to translate.[7] The Lord authoritatively declared to Oliver in one revelation, "Behold I am Jesus Christ, the Son of God" and affirmed that the words Joseph dictated from the seer stone were actually Christ's words. The revelatory words that fell from Joseph's lips read as if the words shining forth on the seer stone represented the Lord. They beckoned Cowdery to translate in the same manner as Joseph Smith. The Lord told Oliver, "I am the light which shineth in the darkness, and the darkness comprehendeth it not." The Lord had also prophesied centuries earlier to the Book of Mormon prophet Alma that the light shining forth in darkness would unveil the

OLIVER COWDERY AND THE TRANSLATION

Lord's words. Alma explained to his son Helaman that "the Lord said: I will prepare unto my servant Gazelem, a stone, which shall shine forth in darkness unto light."[8] These parallels between the way in which Joseph dictated revelations from words appearing on the seer stone and the similar way he translated the pages of the Book of Mormon may have taught Cowdery that the power of the Lord was the driving force behind Joseph's gift. These revelations should have inspired him to recognize his own gift to translate.

Further piquing Oliver's interest, the text of the Book of Mormon, which Joseph was dictating to Oliver, described the gift of translation and even mentioned lost manuscripts and records. Within the first portion of their translation work, Cowdery recorded the story of King Limhi, who possessed an ancient set of twenty-four gold plates that were "filled with engravings" that neither he nor his people could read. Searching for someone that could translate those plates, he was fortuitously visited by a missionary named Ammon, who knew of a man (King Mosiah) who had the gift to translate and a device that enabled him to do so. The words Cowdery recorded stated that "For he hath wherewith that he can *look*, and translate all records that are of ancient date; and it is a gift from God. And the things are called interpreters . . . And whosoever is commanded to look in them, the same is called seer . . . revelator, and a prophet."[9]

Cowdery's desire to translate, therefore, increased as he recorded Joseph's dictation of the Book of Mormon throughout April. Furthermore, Joseph received another revelation that again encouraged Oliver to translate.[10] Reflecting back upon that moment, Joseph Smith wrote that Cowdery "became exceedingly anxious to have the power to translate bestowed upon him."[11] The previous revelation had motivated Cowdery by declaring that he would "know mysteries which are great and marvelous."[12] Edging him forward, the revelation told Cowdery about the particulars of how to translate.[13] It commanded him to ask with "an honest heart" and faith in Christ to receive the power to translate. Explaining that the translation was not just enveloped within the stone, but that the Lord would "tell [him] in [his] mind & in [his] heart by the Holy Ghost," the revelation enlightened Cowdery to gifts that he already possessed that were relative to his attempts to translate. He apparently already possessed the "spirit of Revelation," which was the same spirit "by which Moses brought the children of Israel through the red Sea on dry ground." Encouraging him to

121

❖ FROM DARKNESS UNTO LIGHT

translate, the revelation also explained that Cowdery's "gift of working with the sprout," or his ability to use a divining rod to find underground pockets of water and buried ore, was a blessing from God.

The Lord compared Oliver's newly bestowed gift to translate to his previous skill at using a divining rod in order to equate translation with something he already understood. In fact, the Book of Mormon translation would soon teach Cowdery this concept prophetically, declaring, "The Lord God giveth light unto the understanding; for he speaketh unto men according to their language, unto their understanding."[14] The concept of working with a sprout, or newly torn Y-shaped branch of a young tree, represented the common belief that the unseen water under the ground would attract the water inside the branch. The diviner holding the sprout could reportedly feel the slight pull of the branch toward the water, located underground. Once the diviner found the location of the underground water, farmers and others could dig with more confidence for wells, knowing that there was water beneath them.[15] By using a combination of advice that would bring Cowdery closer to the Holy Ghost and connecting his previous experience using a divining rod, the revelation attempted to teach Cowdery to translate.

One of Joseph's April revelations even provided Cowdery with an increased understanding of how Joseph translated an ancient document. This revelation came as Joseph and Oliver used the seer stone to settle a "difference of opinion" that arose between them about whether John the Apostle "died, or whether he continued" on earth awaiting the Second Coming of Christ.[16] This question likely arose as a direct result of their translation work. The transcribed Book of Mormon text described the experience of the prophet Alma, who seemingly disappeared but actually was "taken up by the Spirit, or buried by the hand of the Lord." The passage went on to make a biblical comparison with Moses: "But behold, the scriptures saith the Lord took Moses unto himself; and we suppose that he has also received Alma in the spirit, unto himself; therefore, for this cause we know nothing concerning his death and burial."[17] The men likely wondered if John's fate was also similar to Alma's fate. In the final chapter of the Gospel of John, Peter asked Christ what would happen to his fellow Apostle John, to which Christ responded, "If I will that he should tarry till I come, what is that to thee?"[18] Whatever the impetus of the disagreement,

Joseph remembered that he and Oliver "mutually agreed to settle it by the Urim and Thummin."

What Joseph saw as he looked into the stone demonstrated to Cowdery, just as the text of the Book of Mormon had, that there were still ancient documents lost to the world that would come forth by the power of God.[19] As Joseph looked into the stone he saw a long-lost document that John had written centuries earlier, "translated from parchment, written and hid up" by John himself.[20] There are no accounts that suggest that Joseph ever possessed or held this parchment; in fact, he explained that he had obtained the translation of the parchment solely through "the Urim and Thummim."[21] The text of the revelation is in first-person voice of John the Apostle, who related Christ's statement on the fate of John, stating that he "shalt tarry until I come in my glory."[22] This experience clearly demonstrated to Oliver Joseph's ability as a seer and that the translation occurred only through the power of God by way of the seer stone.

Unfortunately for Cowdery, when he finally attempted to translate he was unsuccessful. Joseph received an additional revelation, which explained to him: "You have supposed that I would give it unto you, when you took no thought, save it was to ask me." It further explained, "The work which you are called to do, is to write for my servant Joseph."[23] However, the revelation also comforted Cowdery over his failure to translate and promised him that he would be able to translate at another future time.

## The Translation of the Gold Plates

Like the revelation Joseph had received about the lost parchment of John, in which the parchment was never laid in front of them, the gold plates were apparently never consulted during their translation either. Instead, Joseph always had them apparently covered with a cloth or concealed within a box. He did not check back and forth between the plates and the seer stone to assure he was translating the plates correctly. In fact, he likely never correlated any given character on the gold plates with the translated text that appeared on the seer stone. Even if he had checked back and forth, he would not have known what the characters meant without the seer stones. The only way that Joseph knew what portion of the plates he was translating was by reading the transcribed text of the Book of Mormon, which described the organization of the gold plates in several places.

*[Handwritten: The order of how the book in the Book of Mormon were translated]*

❖ FROM DARKNESS UNTO LIGHT

*The plates covered with a cloth during translation. Watercolor by Anthony Sweat.*

The translation apparently did not proceed chronologically from the first book in the Book of Mormon to the last, as they stand in the Book of Mormon today. The Book of Mormon explains that the prophet Mormon and his son Moroni compiled the plates. The prophet Mormon apparently began his creation of the gold plates by abridging "The Book of Lehi," which covered the period from around 580 BC to 120 BC, into the beginning of the large plates. Martin Harris lost that portion of the translation of the large plates, and then in April 1829, Joseph Smith and Oliver Cowdery began translating the rest of the large plates, which began with the remaining chapters of the book of Mosiah. By the end of May 1829, Joseph and Oliver had finished the last three-fourths of the Book of Mormon, which included all of the large plates (other than the lost book of Lehi), the writings of Mormon, the book of Ether, and the writings of the prophet Moroni.[24] Before the end of May, however, Joseph received a revelation that commanded him not to retranslate the book of Lehi that had been lost. The revelation declared that wicked men had changed the lost manuscript to discredit Joseph Smith, and that there was another set of plates that had been prepared centuries earlier to substitute for the book of Lehi. The gold plates apparently included the small plates of Nephi, and Mormon said that he "put them with the remainder of [his] record" just before the beginning of the large plates.[25]

The translation process in the spring of 1829 was slightly different than it was in the summer of 1828 when Joseph worked with Emma Smith and Martin Harris. Though many accounts describing the instrument that Joseph Smith translated with simply call it the "Urim and Thummim," Joseph Smith and his scribes described two separate instruments and

*Handwritten annotation at top:*
Instruments used by Joseph Smith:
1) spectacles
2) Seer-stone #1 (brown-shaped like a baby shoe) Gazelem
3) Seer-stone #2 (white-shaped like an egg)

## OLIVER COWDERY AND THE TRANSLATION

*Joseph translating with Martin Harris as his scribe. Watercolor by Anthony Sweat.*

possibly even three. Outside of the spectacles given to him by the angel with the plates, Smith had at least two other individual seer stones in his possession. After the summer of 1828, the spectacles were taken from Joseph Smith for a short time as a result of the circumstances surrounding the lost manuscript of Lehi. Around that time, he apparently stopped using the spectacles as a regular means of translation and instead used individual seer stones, as described in an earlier chapter.

Apart from the spectacles, Joseph appears to have possessed two other seer stones—one that was dark brown and shaped like a baby's shoe and one that was white and shaped like a large chicken egg. The first was reportedly discovered a few years after his First Vision, buried under a tree. The second stone was apparently found twenty-five feet below the ground in the process of digging a well. However, it is difficult to know which story applied to which seer stone.[26] Given Emma Smith's explanation of the translation process, it is likely that the brown stone was the one referred to as Gazelem, which the Book of Mormon prophesied had been prepared to help translate ancient Nephite records like the Book of Mormon.[27]

In any case, Oliver Cowdery viewed the translation as a miraculous process.[28] He explained in 1834, "Day after day I continued, uninterrupted,

125

to write from his [Joseph's] mouth, as he translated, with the Urim and Thummim, or, as the Nephites would have said, 'Interpreters.'" Whether he was using the spectacles or an individual stone, Joseph apparently used either instrument by placing it in the bottom of a hat in order to block out the ambient light so he could read the words that appeared on the stone. Joseph Knight Sr. explained that the hat "Darkned his Eyes," in order to see the sentences "apper in Brite Roman Letters then he would tell the writer and he would write it then that would go away the next sentance would Come and so on But if it was not spelt rite it would not go away till it was rite so we see it was marvelous."[29] Just as it is difficult at present to see a film being projected in a brightly lit space, it was apparently similarly difficult to view the writing on the stones without darkening the area.

Still, it is difficult to determine exactly which instrument Joseph was using to translate at any given time while translating with Oliver Cowdery. While Emma and Joseph Knight Sr. later described Joseph using a single stone for the majority of the process, Joseph apparently told Jonathan Hadley in 1829 that the translation was accomplished by using the spectacles buried in the bottom of a hat.[30] Regardless, Emma explained that her husband would read the words off the stone and that the scribe would record the words Joseph dictated. She further explained that during that process Joseph would pause and spell out unfamiliar words and "proper names he could not pronounce."[31] David Whitmer, who was at his father's house when Joseph and Oliver were translating there, described the process by calling the words appearing on the stone the "spiritual light." He gave a detailed account of the entire translation process: "A piece of something resembling parchment would appear, and on that appeared the writing. One character at a time would appear, and under it was the interpretation in English. Brother Joseph would read off the English to Oliver Cowdery, who was his principal scribe, and when it was written down and repeated to Brother Joseph to see if it was correct, then it would disappear, and another character with the interpretation would appear. Thus the Book of Mormon was translated by the gift and power of God, and not by any power of man." Though it is not known if Whitmer ever saw the words appearing on the stone himself, he was present at his father's house, where he witnessed the translation for days at a time.

Oliver Cowdery used his experience as a scribe during the translation of the gold plates as a missionary tool, often referencing the translation to convince others of the truthfulness of Joseph Smith's claims. For instance, Cowdery declared that he "wrote with my own pen the intire book of mormon (Save a few pages) as it fell from the Lips of the prophet." Cowdery further explained, "As he translated it by the gift and power of god, By means of the urum and thummim, or as it is called by that book holy Interperters. I beheld with my eyes. And handled with my hands the gold plates from which it was translated. I also beheld the Interperters." Focusing upon his experiences while they translated, he emphatically stated, "That book [The Book of Mormon] is true."[32]

When Cowdery told others how Joseph translated the plates, he apparently primarily referred to the spectacles, rather than an individual seer stone. An early convert, Josiah Jones, explained that Cowdery "affirmed while [Joseph] looked through the stone spectacles another sat by and wrote what he told them."[33] Jones's account is important because it does not confuse the seer stone and the Nephite interpreters by calling them the Urim and Thummim. Instead, he clearly eliminates the seer stone by

*Replicas of the gold plates and spectacles. Photo by Gerrit J. Dirkmaat.*

calling the device "the stone spectacles." Similarly, on his first missionary journey after the Church was established in 1830, Cowdery apparently explained the translation process in an attempt to convince Shakers of Joseph Smith's prophetic calling. He told a Shaker in Union Village, Ohio, that "The engraving being unintelligible to learned & unlearned. there is said to have been in the box with the plates two transparent stones in the form of spectacles thro which the translator looked on the engraving & afterwards put his face into a hat & the interpretation then flowed into his mind. which he uttered to the amanuensis who wrote it down."[34] Though both of these accounts describe the function of the interpreters differently than direct accounts of the witnesses, they are both secondhand accounts derived from Cowdery that claim Joseph translated with the spectacles.

It is unknown whether Cowdery saw Joseph using both the spectacles and the individual seer stones, as Emma did. Josiah Jones, for example, an early parishioner of Sidney Rigdon, was baptized by Cowdery and his missionary companions when they passed through Kirtland, Ohio, on their way to proselytize Native Americans west of Missouri. He wrote that "In the last part of October, 1830, four men appeared here . . . with a book, which they said contained what was engraven on gold plates found . . . about three years ago by a man named Joseph Smith Jr. who had translated it by looking into a *stone or two stones*, when put into a dark place, which stones he said were found in the box with the plates."[35] Charles Anthon was apparently told by Martin Harris that Joseph stopped using the spectacles because they were too big, arguing that they "were so large, that if a person attempted to look through them, his two eyes would have to be turned towards one of the glasses merely, the spectacles in question being altogether too large for the breadth of the human face."[36] Anthon's account may also explain why Cowdery generally described the translation process as involving the "interpreters" or spectacles, while others stated that the latter part of the translation was done with only a single seer stone. In fact, it is possible that Joseph may have even removed one of the lenses from the spectacles in order to more easily use it. He also may have simply focused upon *one* of the two lenses while the spectacles lay in the bottom of the hat.[37] The earliest account, apparently informed by Joseph Smith, was printed in the *Palmyra Freeman* in August 1829 by Jonathan Hadley. It simply declared that Joseph placed the spectacles in the hat in order to translate, but this article does not eliminate the possibility that only one part of the spectacles was placed in the hat.[38] Jones seemed to think that Joseph used one or two seer stones that were all provided to Joseph with the plates. If he is being clear, he is suggesting that sometimes Joseph used just one of the two seer stones that constituted the Nephite interpreters.

In any case, some of those who were present during the later period of translation when Oliver Cowdery was acting as a scribe, like David Whitmer, wrote that they believed that Joseph was using a single brown seer stone when he translated. Whitmer explained that "Joseph Smith would put the seer stone into a hat, and put his face in the hat, drawing it closely around his face."[39] To make things more complicated, Joseph Smith and members of the Church generally stopped differentiating between the seer stones and the spectacles by simply calling all of them the Urim and Thummim. By 1833, for example, W. W. Phelps published an article in the Church newspaper in Missouri, *The Evening and the Morning Star*, that declared that Joseph translated the plates "by the gift and power of God . . . through the aid of a pair of Interpreters, or spectacles—(known, perhaps, in ancient days as Teraphim, or Urim and Thummim)."[40] By the time Joseph Smith's later history was written in 1839, Joseph was using the term Urim and Thummim to reference *any* seer stone. Thus it is impossible to tell from his own later accounts precisely which device he was using to translate the Book of Mormon or to receive revelations.

While all of the accounts of the translation of the Book of Mormon highlight the essential role of the seer stones in the production of the translated text, there was another aspect to the translation that was apparently just as important in order for the miraculous work to proceed. David Whitmer explained that Joseph Smith had to be personally right with God as well in order to have the powers of a seer. He explained that Joseph "could not translate unless he was humble and possessed the right feelings towards everyone." He had learned this powerful truth about the seer's ability to translate firsthand. Apparently one morning Joseph had gotten upset when "something went wrong about the house . . . that Emma, his wife, had done." When he came upstairs to resume the translation shortly thereafter, "he could not translate a single syllable." Recognizing the problem, Joseph went "out into the orchard and made supplication to Lord [and] was gone about an hour." When Joseph came back in from praying he went to his wife and asked her forgiveness for his previous actions. Obtaining it from her, he humbly made his way back up the stairs and resumed the translation, which now proceeded and "went on all right." From this experience, Whitmer concluded that although Joseph was the seer chosen by God to read the words on the stone, he "could do nothing save he was humble and faithful."[41]

## Immediate Effects of the Book of Mormon Manuscript

As they translated, Joseph and Oliver paid careful attention to the text that was miraculously written upon the seer stones that Cowdery recorded in the burgeoning Book of Mormon manuscript. The text itself led to questions about when and how to form Christ's church and specifically how to obtain God's authority to baptize and perform other sacred ordinances. Joseph and Oliver believed that the words Cowdery was recording were guiding them to ask God for his blessing to baptize in his name.

Joseph had wondered about authority and baptism for years. During his First Vision, Joseph had asked which church he should join and was told that he should join none of them. Jesus Christ told him that "the world lieth in sin and at this time and none doeth good no not one they have turned asside from the gospel and keep not <my> commandments they draw near to me with their lips while their hearts are far from me and mine anger is kindling against the inhabitants of the earth."[42] After that initial explanation, Joseph received further instruction on 22 September 1823 when the angel Moroni told him that some would eventually receive the holy priesthood and begin to baptize. Moroni told Joseph that "when they [the gold plates] are interpreted the Lord will give the holy priesthood to some, and they shall begin to proclaim this gospel and baptize by water, and after that they shall have power to give the Holy Ghost by the laying of their hands."[43] Though this declaration did not explain when Smith would receive the authority to baptize, it gave a timeline for when others could be baptized and obtain the priesthood connected to progress made translating the gold plates. Despite these early communications about authority, there are no existing records that suggest the topic of baptism was discussed by the followers of Joseph Smith before 1829. However, just days after he began dictating the Book of Mormon to Oliver Cowdery, the newly revealed text prompted major discussions about baptism.[44] As Joseph translated the story of Alma, one of the ancient prophets, the men learned that to obtain the kingdom of God, baptism was essential. One passage that the men could have readily related to was the story of Alma and Helam. In this account from the translated text, Alma led a group of believers away from a wicked civilization presided over by a wicked king and his false priests. Wanting to make themselves right before God, the believers wondered what they should do. They were told that if they were "desirous to come into the fold of God, and to be called his people, and are willing to bear one another's burdens, that they may be light; Yea, and are willing to mourn with those that mourn; yea, and comfort those that stand in need of comfort, and to stand as witnesses of God at all times and in all things, and in all places that ye may be in, even until death" they should then be "baptized in the name of the Lord, as a witness before him that ye have entered into a covenant with him."[45]

Only a few pages later, the importance of baptism was again reiterated by the text. Another prophet exhorted the people to "come and go forth, and show unto your God that ye are willing to repent of your sins and enter in to a covenant with him to keep his commandments, and witness it unto him this day by going into the waters of baptism." Not only did these passages reinforce the importance of baptism for believers, they also spoke about the establishment of God's church that believers united themselves to through their baptisms. One passage stated, "And they began to establish the church more fully; yea, and they were baptized in the waters of Sidon and were joined to the church of God; yea, they were baptized by the hand of Alma, who had been consecrated the high priest over the people of the church, by the hand of his father Alma."[46] Clearly identifying the need to baptize, another passage dictated by Joseph declared "that whosoever did not belong to the church who repented of their sins were baptized unto repentance, and were received into the church."[47]

In an almost cadence-like repetition, Smith dictated additional accounts of baptism week after week as part of the translation of the gold plates. The necessity of baptism was repeated, as Cowdery recalled, "day after day [as] I continued, uninterrupted, to write from his mouth, as <Joseph Smith> translated."[48] In fact, the revealed text of the book proclaimed the necessity of baptism nearly every day as Joseph dictated the translation.[49]

131

After all of the numerous references to baptism, the translated text then presented the commandment to be baptized from a source even more authoritative than any prophet. Before the middle of May 1829, Joseph dictated the account of Jesus Christ's American ministry, in which Christ bestowed power upon his leaders to baptize believers. In these passages, Christ spoke to his prophet Nephi: "I give unto you power that ye shall baptize this people when I am again ascended into heaven. And again the Lord called others, and said unto them likewise; and he gave unto them power to baptize. And he said unto them: on this wise shall ye baptize."[50] In fact, the manuscript described Christ addressing the importance of baptism almost immediately after his arrival, the first teaching of his ministry. Nephi and others were then given "power" to baptize and were told by Christ that only those who had this power could perform baptisms. The power that Christ gave to his disciples was not explained in detail in the translation. It seemed to be synonymous with authority, a divine permission given only to selected individuals who were empowered to perform ordinances that would be recognized by God as binding.

As a result of these powerful passages, both Smith and Cowdery recognized the necessity of baptism for salvation and the need for divine authorization and power to perform those baptisms. Cowdery later explained that "After writing the account given of the Saviour's ministry . . . it was easily to be seen . . . none had authority from God to administer the ordinances of the gospel." As the translation fell from Joseph's lips and was captured by Cowdery on paper, it served not only as sacred scripture and revelation, but as an effectual guide for the pair in April 1829. Christ explained to the believers in America about his calling of twelve disciples with power to baptize, saying, "I have chosen from among you to minister unto and to be your servants." Even though this referenced the twelve disciples specifically, it apparently prompted them to follow this same model for obtaining authority and power to baptize themselves. Joseph Smith's history stated, "We still continued the <work of> translation, when in the ensuing month (May, Eighteen hundred and twenty nine) we on a certain day went into the woods to pray and inquire of the Lord respecting baptism for the remission of sins as we found mentioned in the translation of the plates."[51] Joseph explained that in answer to their prayer on 15 May 1829 they were visited by a heavenly messenger that declared his name to be John the Baptist. He laid hands upon the men and said, "Upon you my fellow servants in the name of Messiah I confer the priesthood of Aaron, which holds the keys of the ministering of angels and of the gospel of repentance, and of baptism by immersion for the remission of sins."[52] Joseph later described the power given him by John the Baptist as the Aaronic priesthood.

Immediately following this experience in May 1829, Smith and Cowdery baptized Samuel Smith in Harmony, Pennsylvania, and others shortly thereafter in Fayette, New York. In fact, in June 1829, just weeks after their angelic visit, Cowdery penned, "The Articles of the Church of Christ," which explained that he had been given the authority to baptize and outlined the offices and duties of various positions in Christ's church as well as the prayers associated with the sacrament of the Lord's Supper and baptism.

This belief that they had received divine authority from God to perform proper baptisms became a point upon which others criticized and attacked Smith and his followers. When Cowdery and his missionary companions arrived in Ohio in the fall of 1830 to spread the gospel message, one local newspaper scoffed at the reports that Cowdery had "seen and conversed with Angels" and that the Mormons claimed to have God-given authority to baptize:

> Those who are the friends and advocates of this wonderful book, state that Mr. Oliver Cowdry has his commission directly from the God of Heaven, and that he has credentials, written and signed by the hand of Jesus Christ, with whom he has personally conversed, and as such, said Cowdry claims that he and his associates are the only persons on earth who are qualified to administer in his name. By this authority, they proclaim to the world, that all who do not believe their testimony, and be baptized by them for the remission of sins, and come under the imposition of *their* hands for the gift of the Holy Ghost, and stand in readiness to go to some unknown region, where God will provide a place of refuge for his people, called the "New Jerusalem," must be forever miserable, let their life have been what it may. If these things are true, God has certainly changed his order of commission.[53]

Another editor of an Ohio newspaper challenged the Mormons' authority to baptize only days after Joseph Smith and others had arrived in Kirtland to establish the Church there in February 1831. Incredulously, he asked about Mormon baptism, "When did Smith—and from whom did he receive the

Ordinance?" Ostensibly informed, he wrote, "The ordinance originated with these men, and the authority found vested in them to the exclusion of all others."[54] Yet the Mormon belief that proper authority was essential to the ordinance of baptism had originated with the very text Joseph had translated from the Book of Mormon in April 1829. This belief was codified when Joseph Smith and Oliver Cowdery were given the authority to baptize each other and then other believers, just as the Book of Mormon text described.

The experience they had on 15 May 1829 convinced them that only they had the authority to baptize believers in the name of Christ. Soon after the Church was organized on 6 April 1830, even those who wanted to unite themselves with the newly founded Church had to be rebaptized regardless of by whom or into what sect they had been baptized previously. Joseph Smith dictated a revelation on 16 April 1830 (D&C 22) that was often included as a part of the Articles and Covenants of the Church, the founding document later known as D&C 20. That 16 April revelation (D&C 22) was seen as part of the founding document that explained that the ordinance of baptism was only recognized by God when it was done by those in authority in his church. It read: "I say unto you that all old covenants have I caused to be done away in this thing; and this is a new and an everlasting covenant, even that which was from the beginning . . . because of your dead works that I have caused this last covenant and this church to be built up unto me, even as in days of old."[55] Years later Orson Pratt explained, "This is the reason why the Lord commanded this people—the Latter-day Saints—to rebaptize all persons who come to them professing to have been baptized before. In the early days of this Church there were certain persons, belonging to the Baptist denomination, very moral and no doubt as good people as you could find anywhere, who came, saying they believed in the Book of Mormon, and that they had been baptized into the Baptist Church, and they wished to come into our Church."[56] Such strong statements refuted all other claims to religious authority.

## Notes

1. History, circa Summer 1832, in *JSP*, H1:16; Joseph Smith, History, vol. A-1, 13.
2. Revelation, circa 8 March 1831–B [D&C 47], in *JSP*, D1:284. The experience he had in Palmyra before he traveled to Harmony in April, when the Lord appeared

to him, may have been his official calling as a recorder. Though he was not called the historian or recorder, John Whitmer was called to that position in March 1831, and the revelation that called him also stated that he replaced Oliver Cowdery.

3. See Royal Skousen, *Analysis of Textual Variants of the Book of Mormon*, vol. 4 of the Critical Text of the Book of Mormon series (Provo, UT: FARMS, 2004–9).

4. Oliver Cowdery to William W. Phelps, 7 September 1834, *Messenger and Advocate*, October 1834, 1:1.

5. Joseph Smith, History, vol. A-1, 13; Agreement with Isaac Hale, 6 April 1828, in *JSP*, D1:28.

6. Revelation, April 1829–A [D&C 6], in *JSP*, D1:34.

7. See Revelation, April 1829–A [D&C 6], in *JSP*, D1:34–37; Revelation, April 1829–B [D&C 8], in *JSP*, D1:44–47; Account of John, April 1829–C [D&C 7], in *JSP*, D1:47–48; and Revelation, April 1829–D [D&C 9], in *JSP*, D1:48–50.

8. Alma 37:23.

9. Mosiah 8:9, 13, 16.

10. Revelation, April 1829–B [D&C 8], in *JSP*, D1:44.

11. Joseph Smith, History, vol. A-1, 16.

12. Revelation, April 1829–A [D&C 6], in *JSP*, D1:25.

13. Revelation, April 1829–B [D&C 8], in *JSP*, D1:44.

14. 2 Nephi 31:3.

15. Ashurst-McGee, "Pathway to Prophethood," 126–48. See, for example, "The Divining-Rod," *Milwaukie Sentinel*, 7 September 1842, 1.

16. Joseph Smith, History, vol. A-1, 15.

17. Alma 45:19.

18. John 21:18–23. The meaning of this ambiguous passage was debated in the Bible commentaries of Joseph Smith's time. See Adam Clarke, *New Testament of Our Lord and Savior Jesus Christ, the Text Carefully Printed from the Most Correct Copies of the Present Authorised Version, Including the Marginal Readings and Parallel Texts, with a Commentary and Critical Notes . . . Vol. I.* (New York: B. Waugh and T. Mason, for the Methodist Episcopal Church, 1833), 631; Matthew Henry, *Exposition of the Old and New Testament . . . with Practical Remarks and Observations*, vol. 5, ed. George Burder and Joseph Hughes (Philadelphia: E. Barrington and Geo. D. Haswell, 1828), 957–59; and Thomas Scott, ed., *Holy Bible Containing the Old and New Testaments, according to the Authorized Version: with Explanatory Notes and Practical Observations*, vol. 5, 9th American Edition (Boston: Samuel T. Armstrong, 1823), 599.

❖ FROM DARKNESS UNTO LIGHT

19. Account of John, April 1829–C [D&C 7], in *JSP*, D1:47.
20. See Book of Commandments, 6; Joseph Smith, History, vol. A-1, 15.
21. Joseph Smith, History, vol. A-1, 15.
22. Compare to 3 Nephi 28:1–2, 6.
23. Account of John, April 1829–C [D&C 7], in *JSP*, D1:49.
24. This covers pages 153–588 of the 1830 edition of the Book of Mormon.
25. Revelation, Spring 1829 [D&C 10], in *JSP*, D1:37.
26. Brigham Young explained that Smith's first seer stone was found fifteen feet underground and that "He saw it while looking in another seers stone which a person had. He went right to the spot & dug & found it." Kenney, *Wilford Woodruff's Journal*, 5:382–83. It is unclear who this other seer was, but Joseph Smith Sr. apparently said the other seer used "a dark stone." Fayette Lapham, "The Mormons Part II," *Historical Magazine*, May 1870, 306. Ashurst-Mcgee suggests that Luman Walters (*Reflector*, 12 June 1830, 37), William Stafford (Howe, *Mormonism Unvailed*, 238), and Samuel Lawrence (*Naked Truths About Mormonism*, 2) may have been the seer Smith Sr. was referencing. William D. Purple, however, left the most detailed account that derived from an 1826 trial against Joseph Smith. Historian D. Michael Quinn concluded that Purple's account indicates that it was Sally Chase's stone that he looked into to find his own stone: "He said when he was a lad, he heard of a neighboring girl some three miles from him, who could look into a glass and see anything however hidden from others, that he was seized with a strong desire to see her and her glass. . . . he did so, and was permitted to look in the glass, which was placed in a hat to exclude the light. He was greatly surprised to see but one thing, which was a small stone, a great way off. It soon became luminous, and dazzeled his eyes, and after a short time it became as intense as the mid-day sun. He said that the roots of a tree or shrub as large as his arm, situated about a mile up a small stream that puts in the South side of Lake Eire, not far from the New York and Pennsylvania line." William D. Purple, "Joseph Smith the Originator of Mormonism," *Chenango Union*, 2 May 1877, 3. In an affidavit accusing Joseph Smith of theft, Willard Chase testified that he had hired Alvin and Hyrum Smith to dig a well for him and that Chase found the brown stone at that time, but Hyrum took and kept it without his permission. Howe, *Mormonism Unvailed*, 240. Chase's story is corroborated in part at least by another Palmyra resident, Lorenzo Saunders, who stated that Smith "dug one out of well on Chases Farm in the Shape of Baby's foot." Interview by Edmund Kelley, Reading, Michigan,

136

12 November 1884, in "Misc." E. L. Kelley Papers, CCLA. David Whitmer explained that the brown stone was given to Oliver Cowdery after the translation was finished and just before the Book of Mormon was published. After Cowdery's death, his widow gave Phineas Young, his brother-in-law, the brown stone. Phineas then gifted the stone to Brigham Young, his brother, and it has remained in the possession of The Church of Jesus Christ of Latter-day Saints since Brigham's death. See D. Michael Quinn, *Early Mormonism and the Magic World View* (Salt Lake City: Signature Books, 1987), 242. After Phineas Young gave the stone to Brigham Young, Brigham stated that "Oliver sent me Joseph's first Seer stone, Oliver always kept it until he sent it to me." Ashurst-Mcgee, "Pathway to Prophethood," 230n255.

27. She stated, "Now the first that my husband translated, was translated by the use of the Urim, and Thummim [i.e., the spectacles or interpreters], and that was the part that Martin Harris lost, after that he used a small stone, not exactly, black, but was rather a dark color." See also Alma 37:24.

28. When Cowdery arrived and began translating with Joseph after only knowing him for two days, he must have been mesmerized by Joseph's gift and the fact that he was receiving the translation, sentence by sentence, off of a seer stone buried in a hat. Cowdery recalled that "These were days never to be forgotten—to sit under the sound of a voice dictated by the inspiration of heaven, awakened the utmost gratitude of this bosom!" *Messenger and Advocate*, October 1834, 14.

29. Knight Sr., History. Original spelling has been preserved throughout the chapter.

30. "Gold Bible," *Palmyra Freeman*, 11 August 1829.

31. Describing the miraculous nature of the process, Emma explained, "While I was writing them, if I made any mistake in spelling, he would stop me and correct my spelling, although it was impossible for him to see how I was writing them down at the time. . . . When he stopped for any purpose at any time he would, when he commenced again, begin where he left off without any hesitation."

32. Reuben Miller, Journal, 21 October 1848.

33. Josiah Jones, "History of the Mormonites," *The Evangelist*, 1 June 1841.

34. Christian Goodwillie, "Shaker Richard McNemar: The Earliest Book of Mormon Reviewer," *Journal of Mormon History* 37, no. 2 (Spring 2011): 143.

35. Jones, "History of the Mormonites," 1 June 1841.

36. Charles Anthon to E. D. Howe, 17 February 1834, in Howe, *Mormonism Unvailed*, 270–71. Lyman Stowell, a local resident and county historian, remembered that he "found the prophet in the wood house searching earnestly, Smith explaining

❖ FROM DARKNESS UNTO LIGHT

that he had lost one of the magic glasses." *The Biographical Record of Henry County, Illinois* (Chicago: S. J. Clarke Publishing Company, 1901), 714.

37. See Ashurst-McGee, "Pathway to Prophethood," 322. Ashurst-McGee wrote: "Removing the lenses from their frame and placing them in the bottom of the hat would have allowed Smith to use both eyes. It also would have allowed him to view both stones, but the optical physics of such a scenario would have made it impossible to see one image in both lenses as one does when wearing glasses immediately over the eyes. Because Joseph had always looked at a single stone in his hat, he probably removed one of the lenses from the hat. At this point, substituting one of his earlier seer stones for the lens became a minute step. By doing so, he could reassemble the spectacles, reattach them to the breastplate, reinsert them in their protective pouch, and hide them in a safe place."
38. "Golden Bible," *Palmyra Freeman*, 11 August 1829.
39. David Whitmer, *An Address to All Believers in Christ* (Richmond, MO: 1887), 36.
40. "The Book of Mormon," *The Evening and the Morning Star*, January 1833, 2.
41. David Whitmer, *Address to All Believers*, 30. See also William H. Kelly and G. A. Blakeslee, 15 September 1882, in B. H. Roberts, *Comprehensive History of the Church*, 1:130–31.
42. Joseph Smith, 1832 History. Letterbook 1, Church History Library.
43. Joseph Smith, History, vol. A-1, 15.
44. See Oliver Cowdery to William W. Phelps, letter 1, 7 September 1834. "Day after day I continued, uninterrupted, to write from his mouth, as he translated with the *Urim* and *Thummim*, or, as the Nephites would have said, 'interpreters,' the history or record called 'The Book of Mormon.'"
45. Mosiah 18:8–10.
46. Alma 4:4.
47. Alma 6:2.
48. Oliver Cowdery to William W. Phelps, 7 September 1834.
49. Alma 4:4, "many were baptized in the waters of Sidon and were joined to the church of God"; Alma 5:3, "he did baptize his brethren in the waters of Mormon"; Alma 5:62, "Come and be baptized unto repentance, that ye also may be partakers of the fruit of the tree of life"; Alma 6:2, "And it came to pass that whosoever did not belong to the church who repented of their sins were baptized unto repentance, and were received into the church"; Alma 7:14, "come and be baptized unto repentance, that ye may be washed from your sins"; Alma 8:5, "And they were baptized throughout all the land"; Alma 8:10, "that he might baptize them unto

repentance"; Alma 9:27, "he cometh to redeem those who will be baptized"; Alma 15:13, "And Alma established a church in the land of Sidom, and consecrated priests and teachers in the land, to baptize unto the Lord whosoever were desirous to be baptized"; Alma 19:35, "as many as did believe were baptized; and they became a righteous people, and they did establish a church among them"; Alma 32:16, "blessed is he that believeth in the word of God, and is baptized without stubbornness of heart"; Alma 48:19, "they did baptize unto repentance all men whosoever would hearken unto their words"; Alma 49:30, "all those who had been ordained by the holy order of God, being baptized unto repentance, and sent forth to preach among the people"; Alma 62:45, "did cause them to repent of their sins and to be baptized unto the Lord their God"; Helaman 3:24, "thousands who did join themselves unto the church and were baptized unto repentance"; Helaman 3:26, "the Lord did prosper unto the baptizing and uniting the church of God"; Helaman 5:17, 19, "baptized unto repentance, and were convinced of the wickedness of the traditions of their fathers"; Helaman 16:1, "they confessed unto him their sins and denied not, desiring that they might be baptized unto the Lord"; 3 Nephi 1:23, "Nephi went forth among the people, and also many others, baptizing unto repentance"; 3 Nephi 7:24–26, "there were none who were brought unto repentance who were not baptized with water."

50. 3 Nephi 11:21–22.
51. Joseph Smith, History, vol. A-1, 17.
52. Joseph Smith, History, vol. A-1, 17.
53. "The Golden Bible," *Painesville Telegraph*, 16 November 1830; "The Book of Mormon," *Painesville Telegraph*, 7 December 1830.
54. *Observer and Telegraph* (Hudson, OH), 24 February 1831.
55. Revelation, April 1830–A, and Revelation, April 1830–B [D&C 22:1–3], in *JSP*, D1:130–33. For an early version see Sidney Gilbert Notebook of Revelations, MS 4583, box 1, folder 1, Church History Library. See also "The Golden Bible," *Painesville Telegraph*, 16 November 1830, [3].
56. Orson Pratt, in *Journal of Discourses*, 16:293.

*The gold plates. Watercolor by Anthony Sweat.*

*Oliver Cowdery & Joseph Smith run out of paper & food and forced to interrupt the translation and seek financial assistance from Joseph Knight Sr.*

# 8

---

# WITNESSES OF THE GOLD PLATES

By May 1829, after weeks of translating day after day in Harmony, Joseph Smith and Oliver Cowdery were in need of more provisions. They had been left with no time to earn money to buy more paper on which to record the translation. They had previously been given paper by Joseph Knight Sr. in February, but that supply was now almost entirely exhausted. To make matters worse, they were dangerously short on food and lacked the resources to purchase any themselves. Though Cowdery had brought some money with him when he started to write for Joseph, he had likely used it to make Joseph's first payment on his new home.[1] As a result, the men were forced to pause their translation and journey over twenty miles to Colesville, New York, where Joseph Knight Sr. lived, hoping that he would again help them by perhaps giving them food and supplies. Joseph Smith had come to rely on Knight's charity. Even before their trip to Colesville, Knight had already given Joseph $50 to make the second payment on his newly purchased house. To do this, Knight had been willing to sell one of his own wagons.[2] But after Joseph and Oliver made the day-long journey through the Susquehanna River Valley to Colesville, they found that Knight had left on business for the day, and they were forced to return to Harmony unsuccessful.

❖ FROM DARKNESS UNTO LIGHT

After making the twenty-six-mile trip back to Harmony, Joseph and Oliver had no choice but to stop translating and start searching for work in the surrounding area. Unfortunately, despite their best efforts, no one would give them even a day's work, and they returned to Joseph's house empty-handed and hungry. However, when Joseph Knight Sr. learned that his young friends had come to see him in a destitute condition, he took matters into his own hands. Without hesitation, he loaded his wagon with nine or ten bushels of grain, five or six bushels of potatoes, a pound of tea, and a barrel of mackerel. More importantly for their work translating the gold plates, he also packed enough paper to finish the translation.[3] He then made his way to Harmony the next morning with the wagon filled to overflowing.

Anxious to know if the Lord wanted even more of him, Knight then asked Joseph Smith what his duty was. Joseph inquired and received a revelation for Knight that declared, in an apocalyptic tone referencing the impending Second Coming of Christ, that "the field is white already to harvest; therefore, whoso desireth to reap, let him thrust in his sickle with his might, and reap while the day lasts."[4] The revelation further assured Knight that the words Joseph revealed were in fact the words of Jesus Christ, stating, "Behold, I am the light and the life of the world, that speak these words." It told him to "give heed with your might, and then you are called."[5]

Around this time, though the translation was moving along swiftly, the brief respite from public animosity Joseph had enjoyed for over a year quickly began to disintegrate. By May, even Joseph's father-in-law had ceased his tepid support of the couple as long as Joseph maintained his story about the gold plates and the visitation of angels. Joseph remembered that they had even "been threatened with being mobbed from time to time." Those who opposed Joseph and the translation may have also been provoked by local religious leaders as Joseph explained that the work was also being threatened "by professors of religion." Even though Isaac Hale had initially resisted mobocratic advances against the couple, his patience had worn thin. Joseph and Emma decided that their only choice was to either stop the translation or move away to a place where they would not be bothered as they continued it.[6]

Fortunately, Oliver Cowdery had formed a relationship with David Whitmer and his family before he began writing for Joseph Smith. The

*[Handwritten margin notes: "David Whitmer comes with horse & wagons to move Joseph Smith's family to his father, Peter Whitmer's home" / "Three strangers show up to sow the crop for David Whitmer"]*

## WITNESSES OF THE GOLD PLATES ❖

Whitmers were a German family from Pennsylvania who had settled in Fayette, New York, between Lake Cayuga and Lake Seneca. Joseph likely also knew the Whitmers from their acquaintance with his parents, who apparently stopped at the Whitmers' house on their way to visit Joseph in September 1828. Soon afterward, on "a business trip to Palmyra," David Whitmer met Oliver Cowdery there, at which time both men learned about the gold plates and Joseph Smith's attempts to translate them. In April 1829, on his way to Harmony for the first time to begin writing for Joseph as he translated, Cowdery stopped at Peter Whitmer Sr.'s farm. During that visit Cowdery promised to send letters to David Whitmer. The men subsequently corresponded with each other while Cowdery was in Harmony in April and May.[7]

After opposition began to emerge in Harmony, Cowdery wrote to David Whitmer asking if it would be possible to finish the translation at his father's farm in Fayette. David later explained that Cowdery told him "to come down into Pennsylvania and bring him and Joseph to my father's house, giving as a reason therefore that they had received a commandment [revelation] from God to that effect."[8] According to Joseph Smith's history, David Whitmer then "came to the place where we were residing, and brought with him a two horse wagon, for the purpose of having us accompany him to his father's place and there remain until we should finish the work."[9]

The Whitmers were eager to help and happy to have Joseph finish the translation at their house, but they were also themselves struggling, overwhelmed by the amount of work they had to do on their farm. David Whitmer, in particular, had to give up the better part of a week to move Joseph and Oliver to Fayette in the midst of spring plowing. He later explained that he was able to get the work done in half the amount of time that it would have normally taken him. Lucy Mack Smith later elaborated on that singular event. She claimed that three men unknown to the family had come and sown the seed in the Whitmer's field without any explanation or invitation, asking no money in return. Thus David had been enabled to go to Harmony almost immediately. That experience was only the beginning of the fortuitous events Whitmer and others later saw as miracles surrounding his involvement in the translation of the gold plates. For instance, David Whitmer later explained that as he was coming to retrieve them in his wagon, Joseph had been able to see through the seer stone precisely where Whitmer was along the way. In fact, Joseph reportedly knew

*The old man walking to Cumorah*

❖ FROM DARKNESS UNTO LIGHT

*The Whitmer home in Fayette, New York. Photo by John Telford.*

"where [Whitmer] put up at night and even the name on the sign board of the hotel where [he] stayed each night." On the two-and-a-half-day journey to Harmony, David believed that he had been guided by revelation and that the trip was filled with signs of God's work.[10]

Reflecting back upon these events decades later, David Whitmer apparently marveled at the things that had taken place during the bumpy journey back to Fayette with Joseph and Oliver. In 1887, Salt Lake City's *Deseret News* reported that Whitmer told of a story of their June 1829 trip back to Fayette. It was written that David never saw Joseph and Oliver heft the plates into the double-horsed wagon when he arrived. Once they had travel a considerable distance, they reportedly saw an old man walking down the road who told them that he was traveling to Cumorah, where Joseph had retrieved the plates. They offered the man a ride and he took a seat in the wagon. Once the old man told them he was headed for Cumorah, Whitmer turned to look at Joseph, startled by the response. Once his eyes returned to where the old man had been standing, he had disappeared.[11] Lucy Smith later wrote that Joseph had been commanded to let the man carry the plates and that he would deliver them to Joseph once he arrived at the Whitmers'.[12]

144

*Handwritten margin notes:*
- *An old man shows Mary Whitmer the Gold plates*
- *Joseph Smith baptizes David & Peter Whitmer in Lake Seneca; Oliver Cowdery baptizes Hyrum Smith*

WITNESSES OF THE GOLD PLATES ❖

David was not the only Whitmer who made a concerted effort to help Joseph comfortably finish translating the plates. Though each of the family members, five older boys and two girls, adopted a deep interest in the plates, Mary Whitmer, David's mother, was apparently especially rewarded for her devotion to Joseph's cause. After preparing her home for Joseph, Oliver, and eventually Emma, she went outside one day to milk the cows where she met an old man, who stated, "You have been very faithful and diligent in your labors, but you are tired because the increase of your toil, it is proper therefore that you should receive a witness that your faith may be strengthened." The old man then reportedly showed Mary the gold plates. According to David's later account, this would have been the very first time that anyone had been allowed to physically see the plates besides Joseph Smith.[13] Nevertheless, her experience was the first among nearly a dozen others in which men were allowed to see, handle, and testify of the reality of the gold plates. By early July 1829, eleven men were on record asserting that the plates existed and that Joseph had them.

## Building a Church

Even before additional witnesses of the gold plates were garnered, believers were baptized, and the Book of Mormon manuscript became an important guide to help them develop and organize a church. Once Joseph and Oliver arrived at Peter Whitmer Sr.'s house, empowered with the authority given them by John the Baptist, they began baptizing individuals who accepted Joseph's claims. Joseph Smith recalled that "upon our arrival, we found Mr Whitmer's family very anxious concerning the work, and very friendly towards ourselves."[14] The residents around Fayette were also much more inquisitive about what Joseph was doing and much more willing to listen. Joseph explained that amid their success, they traveled to the shores of Lake Seneca, where he waded into the lake with David and Peter Whitmer Jr. and personally baptized both of them. Following their baptisms, Oliver Cowdery then baptized Joseph's brother Hyrum. This was not all. In fact, Joseph's later history explained that "from this time forth many became believers, and were baptized, whilst we continued to instruct and persuade as many as applied for information."[15]

## FROM DARKNESS UNTO LIGHT

The baptisms were not just an expression of personal conviction—they were also a part of a process Joseph Smith was undertaking to establish God's church. As Joseph began dictating revelations more regularly after March 1829 and especially after April when Oliver Cowdery arrived in Harmony, several of the revelations began telling Joseph that God would soon establish his church through Joseph Smith. As early as March 1829, a revelation to Martin Harris declared, "I will establish my Church yea even the church which was taught by my Desiples."[16] In fact, within the first few days after Joseph and Oliver met, one of Joseph's revelations commanded Oliver to "seek to bring forth and establish the cause of Zion."[17] Soon thereafter another of Joseph's revelations declared directly that "if this generation harden not their hearts, I will establish my church among them."[18] By May, after John the Baptist gave Joseph and Oliver the power to baptize, they began talking about how they could establish a church. The text produced by the translation during the same period also gave them a blueprint to copy the foundation of Christ's postresurrection church described in the Book of Mormon.

Once they moved to Fayette, Joseph's revelations continued to encourage them to take steps in the process of establishing a church. David Whitmer, who had quickly become an ardent believer, was introduced to Joseph's revelations as Joseph dictated the words of a revelation from his seer stone that commanded David to "seek to bring forth and establish [the Lord's] Zion."[19] Another revelation to David Whitmer and Oliver Cowdery further commanded them to find twelve disciples to preach the gospel.[20] To Cowdery, this was a familiar charge because he had recently recorded part of the Book of Mormon in which Jesus Christ had descended from heaven and ministered to a group in the Americas from which he chose twelve Nephites to lead the church that he had established.[21] The twelve disciples Cowdery and Whitmer were charged to call were to fill a similar role, according to the revelation, to those whom Jesus had called in the Book of Mormon.[22] The revelation further declared to Oliver and David that its purpose was "relative to building up the church of Christ." Though it appears that they did not call twelve disciples in 1829, the commandment was later fulfilled and the revelation demonstrates the steps Joseph was taking in the summer of 1829 toward the formal establishment of a new church, a process that was eventually completed on 6 April 1830.

## WITNESSES OF THE GOLD PLATES

In addition to the commandment to call disciples, the revelation commanded Cowdery to "rely upon the things which are written; for in them are all things written, concerning [the Lord's] church, [the Lord's] gospel, and [the Lord's] rock."[23] In response, Oliver sifted through the passages of the Book of Mormon that Joseph had recently translated and compiled a document that was apparently intended to govern the believers who had recently been baptized and those who soon would be. Cowdery called the document the *Articles of the Church of Christ*. The articles prescribed to the baptized believers the baptismal prayer and a prayer to bless the Lord's Supper and also outlined several priesthood offices such as priest and teacher. The articles quoted directly from the text of the manuscript the men had been translating that would soon become the Book of Mormon. It used the teachings and phrases from the Book of Mormon as nearly a verbatim guide to regulating the affairs of modern believers.

At the same time, Oliver Cowdery deliberately left out major topics found within the passages he copied from the Book of Mormon manuscript, particularly passages describing the gift of the Holy Ghost and the office of elder. Likely connected to what was excluded from the articles, Joseph and Oliver were told by the Lord, in the chamber of Peter Whitmer Sr. during the translation, that they should not ordain each other as elders of the Church or begin giving the gift of the Holy Ghost until a later time. In April 1830, when the Church was established, they were ordained elders, and they began giving baptized members of the Church the gift of the Holy Ghost. Therefore, *Articles of the Church of Christ* was likely used by baptized believers before The Church of Jesus Christ of Latter-day Saints was established on 6 April 1830, but it was no longer used after the Church was formed. Joseph presented a new creedal statement to the Church called the *Articles and Covenants of the Church of Christ*, which later became known as Doctrine and Covenants section 20. It included all of the prayers and offices found in the early articles, but it was much more expansive, providing greater detail and explanation than could be found in just the Book of Mormon passages. Most importantly, now that the power to give the gift of the Holy Ghost and the office of elder had been established, *Articles and Covenants* outlined the duties of elders and provided directions for confirming members.[24]

Joseph later explained that during their efforts to establish a church in the summer of 1829, the Lord revealed to him that the Church would not be

147

❖ FROM DARKNESS UNTO LIGHT

Three Witnesses of the Book of Mormon. *Engraving by H. B. Hall & Sons, 1883, Church History Museum.*

established until 6 April 1830. As they delayed establishing the Church until the following year, they focused on finishing the Book of Mormon. One of the most significant aspects of preparing the book for publication was the inspired selection of eleven individuals who were to be shown the gold plates.[25]

## The Three Witnesses

In June, near the end of the translation of the Book of Mormon, Joseph dictated a passage that prophesied that when the gold plates would be brought forth again in modern times, three people would see them. This encouraged Oliver Cowdery to ask Joseph to inquire through the seer stone whether he was one of those who would see the plates. Joseph Smith remembered that it was "not many days after the [revelation] was given" that David Whitmer, Oliver Cowdery, and Martin Harris "agreed to retire into the woods, and try to obtain by fervent and humble prayer, the fulfilment of the promises given in this revelation; that they should have a view of the plates."[26]

Though numerous individuals had hefted and seen the plates under a cloth or covering, Joseph had stayed true to his promise that he would not allow anyone to view the plates themselves.[27] He always covered the plates and most often kept them in a box, in a trunk, or even hidden in the woods, buried or otherwise concealed. Even his scribes had never viewed the plates, though they were apparently placed on the table between them at times with a cover over them. Smith openly tried to reveal the plates in other ways, such as through the translation process and, as the revelation to Martin Harris stated in March 1829,[28] through the text of the translation.[29] In particular, Joseph even sent the early manuscript with Harris to show his family. However, after the manuscript was lost, Joseph kept the newly translated manuscript closely safeguarded until it was printed.

The temptation of seeing the plates, however, was overwhelming, especially for Martin Harris, who had on multiple occasions promised to pay for the cost of printing the Book of Mormon.[30] Beginning in March 1829, Joseph Smith's revelations had commanded his associates to "assist to bring forth" the work with the promise that they would be rewarded for their assistance. Soon after Joseph started translating the plates with Oliver Cowdery in April, he had received a revelation that had explained "in the mouth of two or three witnesses shall every word be established" and that God's words

❖ FROM DARKNESS UNTO LIGHT

would "be established by the testimony which shall be given."³¹ Cowdery had been commanded by that revelation to "assist to bring forth my work." This revelatory injunction was similarly given to Joseph Smith's father in February 1829 and again in May 1829 to his brother Hyrum. Each had commanded the men in the voice of the Lord to "assist to bring forth my work."³² Only a few months after all of these revelations referencing those that would assist the work, Joseph Smith dictated a passage from the Book of Mormon translation that explained that he, the translator of the gold plates, would show the plates "unto those who shall assist to bring forth this work." This passage reiterated Joseph's earlier revelation to Martin Harris that stated three individuals would see the plates "by the power of God" and testify of them.³³ David Whitmer was also "called to assist" and a revelation to him in June 1829 stated that he would "stand as a witness."³⁴

Smith further translated another passage from the gold plates that foretold of the time when three witnesses would see the plates and testify "to the truth of the book."³⁵ By the end of June, Whitmer, Cowdery, and Harris, apparently believing that they were to become the three special witnesses of the plates, "became so very solicitouss, and teazed [Joseph] so much, that at length [he] complied," by inquiring "through the Urim and Thummim" whether they would see the plates.³⁶ Through the interpreters Joseph received a revelation that the three men would finally be allowed to see the plates, the breastplate, the sword of Laban, the interpreters, and the Liahona.³⁷

Cowdery and Whitmer had apparently prepared themselves for the experience as they approached the end of the translation,³⁸ but Joseph Smith had to confront Martin Harris to reiterate the commandment he was given in March demanding that he humble himself. Lucy Smith later explained that "Soon after this these four [Smith, Cowdery, Whitmer, and Harris] left and went into a grove a short distance from the house where they continued in earnest supplication to God until he permitted an angel from his presence to bear to them a message."³⁹ Joseph's history related that they "retire[d] into the woods," where they knelt down and prayed to God, asking him to show them the plates. Each of the men took turns praying aloud and then repeated the process again, each time with no effect. At that point, sensing that his own shortcomings were the cause of their failure to receive a divine answer, Martin Harris excused himself from the group.⁴⁰ After Harris left, the three remaining men again began to pray. Joseph's history explained

## WITNESSES OF THE GOLD PLATES ✦

the miraculous result: "We beheld a light above us in the air of exceeding brightness, and behold, an angel stood before us; in his hands he held the plates which we had been praying for these to have a view of: he turned over the leaves one by one, so that we could see them, and discern the engravings theron distinctly."[41] They also heard a voice that stated, "These plates have been revealed by the power of God, and they have been translated by the power of God; the translation of them which you have seen is correct, and I command you to bear record of what you now see and hear."[42] Decades later David Whitmer remembered they "not only saw the plates of the Book of Mormon but also the brass plates, the plates of the Book of Ether, the plates containing the records of the wickedness and secret combinations of the people of the world down to the time of their being engraved, and many other plates." He also said they saw a table on which was placed the sword of Laban, the Liahona, and the interpreters—these were all objects described in the Book of Mormon translation which the previous revelation had promised the witnesses that they would see along with the plates.[43]

Soon after this visionary experience ended, Joseph Smith went in search of Martin Harris, who had wandered off, desperately petitioning the Lord for forgiveness in hopes of also being permitted to see the plates. Smith found Harris "a Considerable distance" away on his knees praying. Relieved, Smith joined Harris and again asked the Lord to see the plates, and they "once more beheld, and [saw], and heard the same things." Harris apparently cried out, "Tis enough, tis enough; mine eyes have beheld, mine eyes have beheld."[44]

Even though Harris's experience seeing the gold plates and the angel was separate from Cowdery's and Whitmer's, Smith explained that the same things were shown in both instances. The earliest account of the angelic visitation is found in a signed statement by all three of the witnesses, in which they attest to the shared experience. Their written statement was included with the manuscript pages of the Book of Mormon and was eventually printed in the back of the published book in 1830.[45]

## The Eight Witnesses

Though the experience of the Three Witnesses was both physical and visionary because they were shown the plates by a heavenly being, there were others that had a strictly physical witness of the plates. Only days after this first divine manifestation, Joseph Smith showed the gold plates to eight

151

❖ FROM DARKNESS UNTO LIGHT

other men. Like the Three Witnesses, the text of Smith's translation also foreshadowed the experience that these eight witnesses would have. The Book of Mormon stated: "Ye may be privileged that ye may shew the plates unto those who shall assist to bring forth this work; and unto three shall they be shewn by the power of God."[46] Additionally, a later passage stated: "There is none other which shall view it, save it be a few according to the will of God."[47] These lines of the text did not specify that there would be eight others that would testify of the plates, but they did identify two separate groups of people that would be shown them by Joseph Smith—the three and "a few" more.

It is not known whether Joseph Smith intended to select exactly eight people to give a written testimony of the plates, or if the "few" he felt guided to show happened to be eight in number. It is similarly unknown precisely why Joseph chose those who he did to be part of that group. The Book of Mormon stated that the witnesses would be chosen "by the power of God,"[48] yet there is no known revelation calling these specific people to be the Eight Witnesses, as there had been for the three earlier witnesses. In any case, the Book of Mormon gave the criterion that the witnesses would "assist to bring forth this work."[49] Clearly some other method of selection was also employed, because not all who had been assisting Joseph to translate and print the Book of Mormon were chosen for this privilege, including Peter Whitmer Sr. and Joseph Knight Sr.[50]

Christian Whitmer,[51] Jacob Whitmer,[52] Peter Whitmer Jr.,[53] John Whitmer,[54] Hiram Page,[55] Joseph Smith Sr.,[56] Hyrum Smith,[57] and Samuel Smith[58] were all chosen to see and handle the gold plates. Though Joseph had developed relationships with many in Harmony, Colesville, Fayette, and Palmyra, the Eight Witnesses were essentially all members of the Smith or Whitmer families, even Hiram Page, who had married Catherine Whitmer in 1825. Outside of Joseph Smith Sr., who was fifty-eight years old, the Eight Witnesses were relatively young men ranging from twenty-one to thirty-one years of age, suggesting that the relative standing of each in the community was not a major factor in the selection. Still, outside of Peter Whitmer Jr. and Samuel Smith, they were all older than Joseph Smith.

The Eight Witnesses apparently saw the plates "soon after" the Three Witnesses had had their experience, sometime in early July after the translation was finished. Joseph and these members of the extended Whitmer

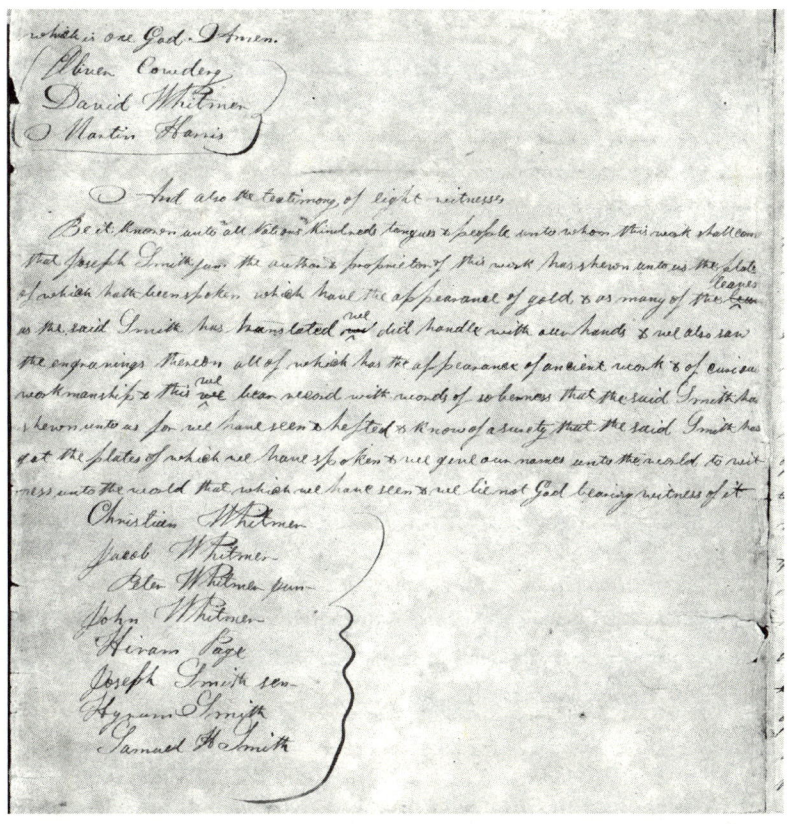

*List of Eight Witnesses, Book of Mormon printer's manuscript. Copied by Oliver Cowdery, Church History Library.*

family traveled to the Smith home in Manchester, where they were joined by Hyrum, Samuel, and Joseph Smith Sr. Lucy Smith related later that the eight men "repaired to a little grove where it was customary for the family to offer up their secret prayers." She went on to explain that "those eight witnesses recorded in the Book of Mormon looked upon the plates and handled them." After they were shown the plates and later that evening, they "held a meeting, in which all the witnesses bore testimony to the facts."[59] Though few extant documents from the Eight Witnesses describe their experience, most of the accounts are consistent with Lucy Smith's history.[60]

One of the Eight Witnesses, John Whitmer, reported that he had both seen and handled the plates, but also claimed that the plates were shown to the men in two different groups of four. He explained that Joseph "handed

❖ FROM DARKNESS UNTO LIGHT

[the plates] uncovered into our hands, and we turned the leaves sufficient to satisfy us." Testifying specifically to the physical nature of the plates, Whitmer was asked whether they were made of a material substance, which he replied, "Yes, and as you know gold is a heavy metal, they were very heavy . . . So far as I recollect, 8 by 6 or 7 inches . . . [the leaves were] just so thick, that characters could be engraven on both sides.[and they were bound] in three rings, each one in the shape of a D." Whitmer also gave a very unique description of the experience. He explained: "Joseph Showed the plates to us, we were four persons, present in the room, and at another time he showed them to four persons more." He said this happened "in Joseph Smith's house," by which he must have meant the Smith family log home in Manchester.[61] If Whitmer's account is accurate, it is possible that the other four may have seen the plates in the grove near their house as Lucy Smith described. The Eight Witnesses, unlike the Three Witnesses, testified strictly to the physical existence of the plates, focusing on their own tactile senses as they lifted and leafed through them.

From the accounts of the Three and Eight Witnesses, along with those given by others who interacted in some way with the plates, a fairly complete description of them can be made. They apparently weighed somewhere between forty and sixty pounds.[62] The shape of the plates was reported as being between six and seven inches wide and around eight inches long.[63] They were also four to six inches thick, with two-thirds of the plates being sealed, most likely by one solid piece of metal that covered the whole two-thirds of the plates.[64] The plates that were not bound together were apparently "thin leaves of gold" about the thickness of tin or "about as thick as parchment."[65] Both the sealed portion and the loose-leaf portion were bound together by three rings in the shape of a capital *D*.[66]

The witnesses to the Book of Mormon apparently shared their experience often. Luke Johnson stated that at a 25 October 1831 conference, "the eleven witnesses to the Book of Mormon, with uplifted hands, bore their solemn testimony to the truth of that book, as did also the Prophet Joseph."[67] The witnesses were also often questioned in personal settings. John Corrill, for example, wrote, "After getting acquainted with them, I was unable to impeach their testimony, and consequently thought that it was as consistent to give credit to them as to credit the writings of the New Testament, when I had never seen the authors nor the original copy."[68]

*Replica of the gold plates. Photo by Gerrit J. Dirkmaat.*

While these men repeatedly shared their experiences with the gold plates in public and private, most people learned their testimonies of them as they read them in the back of the 1830 edition of the Book of Mormon. The two collections of statements from the Three and Eight Witnesses were drafted using different language and emphasis. Though the Three Witnesses' written testimony was partially taken from the text of the Book of Mormon, the Eight Witnesses' statement read much more like an affidavit. It referred to Joseph Smith as "the Said Smith" to distance them from him as if the statement were free from bias. It stated, "[Joseph Smith] has shewn unto us the plates of which hath been spoken, which have the appearance of gold; and as many of the leaves as the said Smith has translated, we did handle with our hands; and we also saw the engravings thereon, all of which has the appearance of ancient work." They declared: "we have seen and hefted . . . the plates." These men testified that Joseph Smith was in fact in possession of gold plates that had what appeared to be ancient characters on them. The Three Witnesses testified with even more power that not only did the plates exist, but that "an angel of God came down from heaven" with the plates to show them. Beyond their existence and even this divine manifestation of their reality, perhaps the most powerful declaration came from the angel, who validated the text that Joseph had dictated over the past several months. The angel declared "that [the plates had] been translated by the gift and power of God."[69]

❖ FROM DARKNESS UNTO LIGHT

## Notes

1. Oliver Cowdery likely paid the first $64 of Joseph's house on 5 April 1829, which he had recently been paid for his services as a teacher in Palmyra. He had recently collected $65.50 and likely made a payment in Lyons for $13, in addition to his travel expenses. See Agreement with Isaac Hale, 6 April 1829, Historical Introduction, in *JSP*, D1:29.
2. The payment was made on 27 April 1829. See Agreement with Isaac Hale, 6 April 1829, in *JSP*, D1:32; Joseph Knight Jr., Autobiographical Sketch, 1.
3. Knight Sr., History.
4. D&C 12.
5. Revelation, May 1829–A [D&C 12], *JSP*, D1:53–55.
6. Joseph Smith, History, vol. A-1, 21.
7. Joseph Smith, History, vol. A-1, 21; Lucy Mack Smith, History, 1845, [151]; "Mormonism," *Kansas City Daily Journal*, 5 June 1881, 1.
8. "Mormonism," *Kansas City Daily Journal*, 5 June 1881, 1.
9. Joseph Smith, History, vol. A-1, 21.
10. See *Kansas City Daily Journal*, Journal, 5 June 1881; *Deseret News*, 25 March 1884; and *Deseret News*, 16 November 1878.
11. *Deseret Evening News*, 16 November 1878.
12. Lucy Mack Smith, History, 1844–45, book 8, [10]. "His answer was that he should give himself no trouble about but hasten her to waterloo and after he arrived a[t] Mr. Whitmore's house if he would repair immediately to the garden he would receive the plates from the hand of an angel to whose charge they must be committed for their safety."
13. *Deseret Evening News*, 16 November 1878.
14. Joseph Smith, History, vol. A-1, 22. Original spelling has been preserved throughout the chapter.
15. See Joseph Smith, History, vol. A-1, 22 and 23.
16. Revelation, March 1829 [D&C 5], in *JSP*, D1:17.
17. Revelation, April 1829–A [D&C 6], in *JSP*, D1:35.
18. Revelation, Spring 1829 [D&C 10], in *JSP*, D1:43.
19. Revelation, June 1829–A [D&C 14], in *JSP*, D1:68.
20. The revelation stated, "Behold I give unto you, Oliver, and also unto David, that you shall search out the twelve which shall have the desires of which I have spoken; and by their desires and their works, you shall know them: And when you have

156

found them you shall show these things unto them And you shall fall down and worship the Father in my name: And you must preach unto the world, saying, you must repent and be baptized in the name of Jesus Christ: For all men must repent and be baptized; and not only men, but women and children, which have arriven to the years of accountability." See Revelation, June 1829–B [D&C 18], in *JSP*, D1:73.

21. See Moroni 2–3.
22. The term "disciple" was likely used to distinguish the American disciples from the Twelve Apostles in Jerusalem. However, the terms apparently refer to comparable offices. In February of 1835, Joseph and Oliver convened a meeting to select twelve Apostles and it was there that Cowdery explained that D&C 18, given in June 1829, called him and Whitmer to choose the twelve "apostles." The 1835 edition of the Doctrine and Covenants also refers to the "disciples" in D&C 18 as "apostles." Minute Book 1, 14 February 1835; Quorum of the Twelve Apostles, Record, 14 February 1835. David Whitmer later claimed that they had already begun choosing the Twelve Apostles in 1829, which may be possible, but they soon thereafter did not recognize whomever they called as disciples. Oliver Cowdery explained at a Church conference on 26 October 1831 that they would choose the Twelve. Minute Book 2, 25–26 October 1831. In 1835 Cowdery also explained that "our minds have been on a constant stretch to find who these Twelve were." Minute Book 1, 14 and 21 February 1835.
23. Revelation, June 1829–B [D&C 18], in *JSP*, D1:70.
24. See Revelation, Articles and Covenants, circa April 1830 [D&C 20], in *JSP*, D1:116; "Articles of the Church of Christ," June 1829, in *JSP*, D1:367.
25. The text of the revelation indicated that this occurred just before or just after the translation was finished in the last few days of June. "Report of Elders Orson Pratt and Joseph F. Smith," *Deseret News,* 27 November 1878, [2]; "Mormonism," *Kansas City Daily Journal*, 5 June 1881, 1. David Whitmer later recounted that their subsequent experience with the plates occurred "shortly before the completion of the translation when there were but few pages left." Cannon, Journal, 27 February 1844. The text stated that Joseph Smith "has translated them even that part which I have commanded him," which indicated that the translation was likely finished.
26. Joseph Smith, History, vol. A-1, 24.
27. He reported that the "heavenly messenger" who delivered the gold plates into his custody in 1827 had charged him to carefully preserve them. Joseph Smith, History, vol. A-1, 8.

28. Revelation, March 1829 [D&C 5], in *JSP*, D1:12.
29. Revelation, March 1829 [D&C 5], in *JSP*, D1:12.
30. Revelation, March 1829 [D&C 5], in *JSP*, D1:12.
31. Revelation, April 1829–A [D&C 6], in *JSP*, D1:34.
32. Revelation, February 1829 [D&C 4], in *JSP*, D1:9; Revelation, May 1829–A [D&C 11], in *JSP*, D1:50.
33. D&C 5:11.
34. Revelation, June 1829–A [D&C 14], in *JSP*, D1:66.
35. Book of Mormon, 1830 ed., 110 [2 Nephi 27:12]. The men were convinced that they were intended to be the Three Witnesses for good reason. One passage of the Book of Mormon stated: "unto three shall they [the plates] be shown by the power of God; wherefore they shall know of a surety that these things are true." Book of Mormon, 1830 ed., 548 (Ether 5:3). A second passage re-emphasized that there would be Three Witnesses by stating, "Wherefore, at that day when the book shall be delivered unto the man of whom I have spoken, the book shall be hid from the eyes of the world, that the eyes of none shall behold it save it be that three witnesses shall behold it, by the power of God, besides him to whom the book shall be delivered; and they shall testify to the truth of the book and the things therein." Book of Mormon, 1830 ed., 110 (2 Nephi 27:12).
36. Joseph Smith, History, vol. A-1, 23.
37. Revelation, June 1829–E [D&C 17], in *JSP*, D1:84.
38. Lucy Mack Smith recalled that after the translation was finished, Joseph Smith "dispatched a messenger to Mr. Smith . . . request[ing] that Mr. Smith and myself should come immediately." Lucy then went on to explain that she was in Fayette when they saw the plates, insinuating that Joseph Smith had already finished the translation. Lucy Mack Smith, History, 1844–1845, book 8, [10]. On the other hand, Joseph Smith's 1839 history and a recollection by David Whitmer stated that the translation was completed after Joseph Smith's parents arrived and after the Three Witnesses viewed the plates. Joseph Smith, History, vol. A-1, 28; Cannon, Journal, 27 February 1844. Whitmer stated, "It was about 11. A. M." on a Sunday, possibly indicating the date was 28 June, the last Sunday of June 1829, in Stevenson, Journal, 15:5, 22 December 1877.
39. Lucy Mack Smith, History, 1844–1845, book 8, [11].
40. Joseph Smith, History, vol. A-1, 24.
41. Joseph Smith, History, vol. A-1, 25; see also McLellin, Journal, June–August 1831.
42. Joseph Smith, History, vol. A-1, 25.

43. *David Whitmer Interviews*, ed. Lyndon Cook, 40. David Whitmer explained decades later to Orson Pratt and Joseph F. Smith that he had signed the statement along with the other two witnesses, demonstrating there was an original document that is no longer extant. In the 1860s, Orson Pratt asked David Whitmer "if he and the other witnesses did or did not sign the testimony themselves," to which Whitmer replied that "each signed his own name." "Report of Elders Orson Pratt and Joseph F. Smith," *Deseret News*, 16 November 1878.

44. Joseph Smith, History, vol. A-1, 25. Even though Joseph Smith and Harris had a separate experience from Joseph Smith, Cowdery, and Whitmer, and even though Whitmer later described the experience in more detail than this document included, each of the witnesses was willing to sign the statement.

45. This experience was not the first or the only divine manifestation. Joseph Smith's 1832 history explained that both Martin Harris and Oliver Cowdery had previously experienced visionary experiences. Harris was convinced by the Lord that Joseph Smith's angelic visit was real and "the Lord appeared unto him in a vision and shewed unto him his marvelous work . . . and said the Lard had shown him that he must go to new York City <with> some of the characters." The 1832 history further recorded that the "Lord appeared unto a young man by the name of Oliver Cowd[e]ry and shewed unto him the plates in a vision and also the truth of the work and what the Lord was about to do through me his unworthy Servant." Joseph Smith, History, circa Summer 1832, in *JSP*, H1:16. Harris described the visitation as a religious visionary experience, rather than focusing on the physical nature of the plates in accounts he reportedly gave decades later. These accounts have sometimes been viewed as partially contradictory to his earliest statement that was published in the back of the Book of Mormon in 1830. John H. Gilbert, "Memorandum, made by John H. Gilbert Esq, Sept. 8th, 1892, Palmyra N.Y.," 5, Palmyra King's Daughters Free Library, Palmyra, NY; John A. Clark to Dear Brethren, 31 August 1840, *Episcopal Recorder*, 12 September 1840, 98. See also Stephen Burnett to Lyman E. Johnson, 15 April 1838, Joseph Smith, Letterbook, 2:64–66, Church History Library; Anthony Metcalf, *Ten Years before the Mast* (Malad City, ID: n.p., 1888), 70. See also Dan Vogel, *Early Mormon Documents* (Salt Lake City: Signature Books, 2003), 193. In any case, in his earliest account of the experience Harris testified that he had "seen the engravings which are upon the plates; and they [had] been shewn unto us by the power of God, and not of man . . . an angel of God came down from heaven, and he brought and laid before our eyes, that we beheld and saw the plates, and the engravings thereon." Book of Mormon, 1830 ed., 589.

❖ FROM DARKNESS UNTO LIGHT

46. Book of Mormon, 1830 ed., 548 (Ether 5:2). The portion of the original Book of Mormon manuscript containing these lines has been lost, but in the 1830 printed version quoted here the mention of the two groups is separated by a semicolon. The printer's manuscript, however, does not include the semicolon, and Royal Skousen has concluded that a period, rather than no punctuation or a semicolon, was likely intended. Royal Skousen, *The Book of Mormon: The Earliest Text* (New Haven, CT: Yale University Press, 2009), 685.
47. Book of Mormon, 1830 ed., 110 (2 Nephi 27:12–13).
48. Book of Mormon, 1830 ed., 110 (2 Nephi 27:12–13).
49. Book of Mormon, 1830 ed., 548 (Ether 5:2).
50. Even though Emma Smith and Lucy Mack Smith were important contributors and supports of the translation, it is possible that they were not selected because of nineteenth-century prejudices against women as legal witnesses.
51. 18 January 1798–27 November 1835.
52. 2 February 1800–21 April 1856.
53. 27 September 1809–22 September 1836.
54. 27 August 1802–11 July 1878.
55. 1800–12 August 1852.
56. 12 July 1771–14 September 1840.
57. 9 February 1800–27 June 1844.
58. 13 March 1808–30 July 1844.
59. Lucy Mack Smith, History, 1853, [141]. According to this account, "Joseph had been instructed that the plates would be carried there [to the grove] by one of the ancient Nephites," but the witnesses themselves reported only that they were shown the plates by Joseph Smith.
60. See Richard Anderson, *Investigating the Book of Mormon Witnesses* (Salt Lake City: Deseret Book, 1981).
61. *Deseret News*, 6 August 1878.
62. Martin Harris explained that they weighed forty to sixty pounds. Martin Harris, interview, *Iowa State Register*, August 1870. Harris believed they were heavy enough that they must have been either "lead or gold." Tiffany, "Mormonism," August 1859, 168–69. Joseph's younger brother believed they were around sixty pounds when he lifted them. William Smith, *William Smith on Mormonism*, 1883, 12. He also explained, "They were much heavier than a stone, and very much heavier than wood." William Smith, interview with E. C. Briggs, *Deseret Evening News*, 4 October 1884, 644. Emma explained that she "moved them from place

to place on the table." "Last Testimony of Sister Emma," *Saints' Herald*, 1 October 1879. Joseph's sister Catherine lifted them and found that they were "very heavy." J. B. Bell, interview with H. S. Salisbury, LDS Church History Library. Cornelius Blatchly apparently heard that the plates weighed around thirty pounds. "The New Bible," *Gospel Luminary*, 10 December 1829.

63. See Joseph Smith, *Times and Seasons*, 1 March 1842, 707; Tiffany, "Mormonisn," August 1859, 165; Martin Harris, interview, *Iowa State Register*, August 1870; David Whitmer, interview, *Chicago Tribune*, 24 January 1888; Orson Pratt, *An Interesting Account*, 13.

64. Orson Pratt explained in his popular pamphlet that the plates were "near six inches in thickness, a part of which was sealed. Orson Pratt, *An Interesting Account*, 13. Martin Harris described the plates, remembering that they were altogether about four inches thick." Tiffany, "Mormonism," August 1859, 165. David Whitmer stated, "What there was sealed appeared as solid to my view as wood." See David Whitmer, interview, *Chicago Tribune*, 24 January 1888; *Deseret Evening News*, 16 August 1878; Orson Pratt, in *Journal of Discourses*, 3:347, 13 April 1856. Orson Pratt explained that about "two-thirds were sealed up, and Joseph was commanded not to break the seal; that part of the record was hid up. The plates which were sealed contained an account of those things shewn unto the brother of Jared."

65. See Tiffany, "Mormonism," August 1859, 165; *Iowa State Register*, August 1870; *Kansas City Daily Journal*, 5 June 1881; Pratt, *An Interesting Account*, 13; *Saints' Herald*, 4 October 1884 and 1 October 1879.

66. See Orson Pratt, in *Journal of Discourses*, 19:211–12, 9 December 1877; David Whitmer, interview with Edward Stevenson, Diary, 22–23 December 1877; *Kansas City Daily Journal*, 5 June 1881, 1; *Chicago Tribune*, 24 January 1888.

67. *Deseret News*, 26 May 1858.

68. John Corrill, History, 1839, 11.

69. Book of Mormon, 1830 ed., [589].

*Joseph Smith and Martin Harris negotiating with E. B. Grandin to print the Book of Mormon. Watercolor by Anthony Sweat.*

# 9

## Negotiating with Printers

As the translation neared its completion in the summer of 1829, Joseph Smith's herculean effort to translate the gold plates was about to give way to another major difficulty: how would the Book of Mormon be printed and distributed to the world? The weight of this responsibility was likely made more pressing as Smith dictated the translation to Oliver of the portion of the Book of Mormon now known as 2 Nephi, chapter 3. In these passages, Joseph in Egypt prophetically speaks about Joseph Smith's latter-day revelatory calling and especially his role in bringing forth the teachings contained in the gold plates to the world:

> But a seer will I raise up out of the fruit of thy loins; and unto him will I give power to bring forth my word unto the seed of thy loins—and not to the bringing forth my word only, saith the Lord, but to the convincing them of my word, which shall have already gone forth among them.[1]

The greatest difficulty of the endeavor was clearly the prohibitive costs involved in producing thousands of copies of a lengthy book. Lacking any substantial assets of his own, Smith naturally turned to his friend Martin

❖ FROM DARKNESS UNTO LIGHT

Harris as a resource. According to Charles Anthon's later account of his meeting with Harris, by mid-1828 Harris was already promising to use his own money and property to finance the publication. Harris was not simply a believer; he had served as Smith's principal scribe during part of 1828, until his loss of the manuscript pages of the book.[2]

While Cowdery and Smith were engaged in the translation in April and May, Harris was back in Palmyra, possibly preparing to help Joseph apply for a copyright for the Book of Mormon and investigating printers who might be willing to publish the book. Likely responding to the difficult experience of having the first manuscript pages, which contained the book of Lehi, stolen from Harris in 1828, Smith was more cautious about the remaining text and this caution led him to attempt to secure an official copyright. A copyrighted book was protected from unauthorized distribution or sale, offering the author the ability to control the sale and printing of the text, while also protecting the printer by securing the text from other printers.[3] Not only would a copyright protect the book from those who sought to steal the text and publish it elsewhere, but it would also give potential printers confidence that if they agreed to take part of their pay in expected proceeds from the book, the text could not be published elsewhere by other printers and thus cut into potential sales.

One of the five steps required for Joseph Smith to obtain a copyright was to provide a printed copy of the title page of the Book of Mormon to the clerk of the Northern District Court of New York, located in Utica, around 120 miles away from Palmyra.[4] While it is known that Smith complied with this requirement (a copy of the title page of the Book of Mormon was filed by the court on 11 June 1829), the production of this initial title page is still shrouded in mystery.[5] It is not known who printed the page, in what town, or even who submitted the page to the court. The journey from Palmyra to Utica, where the court was located, was a six-or seven-day round trip, totaling over 240 miles.[6] Because it was probably filed in Utica on 11 June, it was likely printed at least a week earlier unless a local printer in Utica performed the service. It is likely that during the month of May, someone (possibly Martin Harris) was researching copyright law and preparing to have the title page printed for the court in order to obtain a copyright for the Book of Mormon. Details of the copyright law were well known before the title page was printed because the title page

164

included the phrase that Joseph Smith was the "author and proprietor,"[7] which was the phrase used in the copyright law and in the copyright form. Given the time needed to ascertain the requirements and have the title page printed, much of this work was likely undertaken by Harris while Joseph Smith was still in Harmony or Fayette.

## E. B. Grandin of the *Wayne Sentinel*

In any case, by early June, and possibly before, Martin Harris had a manuscript copy of the title page in his possession and was using it in his negotiations with printers in and around Palmyra.[8] He met with Palmyra printer Egbert B. Grandin, the editor of the *Wayne Sentinel* newspaper and owner of a print shop. It may have been Grandin who actually printed the title page for the copyright application. The eventual typesetter of the Book of Mormon, John Gilbert, later explained that Grandin first met Harris in early June and that Grandin employed Gilbert to estimate the cost to publish the Book of Mormon.

It is likely that this was the first time that the sheer magnitude of the cost was fully comprehended by Martin Harris or Joseph Smith. Grandin's terms, $3,000 to produce the desired five thousand copies of high quality books, was nearly the value of Harris's entire farm. To put the cost in perspective, Joseph had purchased his fourteen-acre, already cultivated farm with accompanying house, in Harmony for only $200. The Book of Mormon cost, by comparison, was fifteen times that of his home and farm. Day laborers in New York often worked for a dollar per day, making the cost of the Book of Mormon printing at least ten times the amount Joseph Smith could have made digging wells for an entire year.[9]

Despite the cost, Harris still tried to persuade Grandin to undertake the printing of the book, but Grandin was skeptical and refused. The reasons for his refusal are difficult to determine with certainty. Grandin's own view of the book was reflected in the 26 June 1829 issue of his paper, in which he editorialized of the gold plates and the Book of Mormon: "Most people entertain an idea that the whole matter is the result of a gross imposition, and a grosser superstition. It is pretended that it will be published as soon as the translation is completed."[10] Given Grandin's skepticism in late June that the book would be published at all, he likely was not seriously considering performing the task himself at that time. Pomeroy Tucker, one of Grandin's business partners, later explained that Grandin's motives for rejecting the proposal to publish the book were altruistic in nature, motivated by his concern over the financial ruin it would bring upon Martin Harris. Tucker said that as soon as Harris proposed to mortgage his farm to pay for the printing of the Book of Mormon, "Grandin at once advised them against the supposed folly of the enterprise." But Grandin's opposition to the plan apparently went much further than a simple refusal. According to Tucker, once Grandin found he could not personally persuade Harris to give up on the idea of paying for the printing of the Book of Mormon, he began a campaign among Harris's neighbors and friends to deter Harris. With their help he "sought to influence [Harris] to desist and withdraw" his financial support. Undaunted by this unified opposition, Harris "resisted with determination" all efforts to persuade him to abandon Smith and the printing endeavor. For Grandin's part, "after repeated interviews and much parleying on the subject" he still gave a final negative answer and thereafter refused "to give it further consideration."[11]

## Jonathan A. Hadley of the *Palmyra Freeman*

Rebuffed by Grandin, who not only refused to help with printing but aggressively sought to derail the entire project, Joseph and Martin appear to have next solicited the aid of Jonathan A. Hadley, editor of another Palmyra newspaper, the *Palmyra Freeman*. Hadley was somewhat of a child protégé in the printing community. Four years younger than Joseph Smith, Hadley had entered the profession in 1825 at the age of sixteen in Rochester, New York, as an apprentice in the print shop of newspaper editor Thurlow Weed.[12] Sometime in 1828, Hadley left for Palmyra and commenced working on the *Freeman*. That small paper had commenced in March 1828 under the editor D. D. Stephenson, and at some point after July 1828 Hadley became the sole editor.[13] Like his mentor Thurlow Weed, Hadley was a dedicated critic of Masonry and allotted the majority of his paper to anti-Masonic rhetoric and articles, including an ongoing battle with the pro-Masonry paper the Rochester *Craftsman*. Barely twenty years old in the summer of 1829, Hadley was nevertheless apparently approached by Joseph Smith with the same proposal: a massive print run of a lengthy book. It is likely that Smith approached Hadley because the latter repeatedly advertised his abilities and facilities, including his acquisition of "a new and choice assortment of Job Type." Hadley advertised that his print shop could execute "all kinds of Job Printing, such as Pamphlets, Hand-Bills, Cards, Labels, &C. &C. in the neatest style." Perhaps the most attractive feature of the advertisement, however, was its promise to perform the work "as expeditiously and reasonable as at any office . . . west of the Capital."[14] Speed and cost were two concerns clearly on Joseph's mind as summer wore on and the realities of the staggering price of the endeavor came into full relief.

*J. A. Hadley advertisement for job printing.*

Hadley's immediate reaction to Smith's proposal can only be speculated, but his publication later that summer of a scornful diatribe against the impending publication of the Book of Mormon suggests that Hadley had extensive, very detailed discussions with Joseph Smith or one of his closest associates. In fact, Hadley's negative article on "the Gold Bible" contains the earliest surviving account of many of the foundational events in Joseph's retrieval and translation of the plates, all of which Hadley indicated were told him by Joseph himself. Hadley explained to his readers that the claim surrounding the Book of Mormon was that in the fall of 1827 Joseph Smith had been "visited in a dream by the spirit of the Almighty, and informed that in a certain hill in that town, was deposited this Golden Bible, containing an ancient record of a divine nature and origin." Hadley further related, "After having been thrice thus visited, as he [Joseph] states, he proceeded to the spot" and "the Bible was found, together with a huge pair of Spectacles!"[15]

After proceeding to explain to his readers that Smith was not allowed to let anyone look at the plates, Hadley gave the earliest surviving description of the plates. In that description, the dimensions of the plates as outlined by Hadley are almost identical to those later sent by Joseph Smith to newspaper editor John Wentworth in his famous 1842 letter. Hadley wrote that "the leaves of the Bible were plates of gold, about eight inches long, six wide,

167

and one eighth of an inch thick, on which were engraved characters or hieroglyphics."¹⁶ More than just the dimensions, Hadley gave the earliest published account of the translation process, stating that "by placing the Spectacles in a hat, and looking into it, Smith could (he said so, at least,) interpret these characters." Hadley was also familiar with Martin Harris's trip to the East with characters from the plates, and even that Dr. Samuel Mitchell was one of the scholars visited.¹⁷

Despite the obvious contempt he held for the story of the gold plates by August 1829, it is very likely that Hadley was the principal reason Smith and Harris traveled the considerable distance to Rochester in search of a printer rather than in the much more convenient surrounding communities. Hadley likely told Joseph that, despite the expansive printing skills he advertised, he had no experience in book printing or binding. But the master he apprenticed under in Rochester, Thurlow Weed, would be a better candidate. Given the connection between Hadley and Weed, the possibility that Smith just happened to approach both men by chance seems remote. Hadley's referral of Weed also helps explain why, by Weed's account at least, Smith and Harris came to him first rather than other printers in Rochester that were more famous and experienced.

## Thurlow Weed of the *Anti-Masonic Enquirer*

Likely arriving in Rochester sometime in July, Joseph Smith and Martin Harris went to Thurlow Weed and tried to persuade him to accept the work. Weed was the irascible editor of Rochester's *Anti-Masonic Enquirer*. While he would eventually become one of the most powerful leaders in the national Whig and then Republican Parties, in 1829 Weed's political machinations were still confined primarily to the state level. He had served in the New York state legislature in 1825 and had only recently garnered national attention. He had indicted the Masonic order for the widely publicized, suspicious 1826 disappearance or death of William Morgan, a man who had threatened to write an exposé of the secrets of the fraternity.¹⁸ Weed was one of the catalyzing influences in the birth of a new political party dedicated to eliminating the political and economic power of Freemasonry.¹⁹ In 1828 Weed had traveled through several counties in the central, southern portion of the state, attempting to organize local

*Thurlow Weed. Library of Congress Prints and Photographs Division.*

branches of the Anti-Masonic Party.[20] Like his acolyte Jonathan Hadley, Weed was embroiled in a very public, ongoing feud with the rival Rochester paper, the *Craftsman,* which defended Masonry against Weed's barrage of attacks.[21] Just a few months after his meeting with Joseph Smith, Weed would again return to the New York state assembly, but his political power

❖ FROM DARKNESS UNTO LIGHT

would always come chiefly from his publications and his party organizing abilities. Those talents would eventually elevate him to the status of primary backer for the great William Seward and a force to be reckoned with even by President Abraham Lincoln.

Of the negotiations, only Weed's reminiscent accounts remain. At the time he gave them, Weed was a key player in first the Whig Party and then the Republican Party. When he gave his first known account of the interview with Joseph Smith, in 1845, the Whig Party was still reeling from the defeat of Henry Clay in the 1844 election, an election in which many Whigs blamed the Mormons and Joseph Smith for the loss of Illinois to the Democrats. Joseph had initially supported and then denounced Clay when the latter refused to publicly support the Mormons' petition to get their lands back in Missouri. Similarly, Weed's 1858 statement on the negotiations came after the Republican Party had staked out a decidedly anti-Mormon presidential platform for the 1856 election, denouncing the "twin relics of barbarism, slavery and polygamy."[22] Therefore, much of Weed's denigration of Joseph Smith and Martin Harris, as well as his reported conversations with them, was likely influenced by the national currency anti-Mormonism held at the time he published these accounts rather than relating a verbatim account of the negotiations or Weed's initial reaction to the proposal to print the Book of Mormon. In any case, in Weed's various accounts of the negotiation, he provided several different reasons why he refused to publish the Book of Mormon, ranging from a lack of book publishing facilities to an outright castigation of Joseph Smith as a fraud.

In his 1845 account of the meeting, after referring to Mormonism as a "delusion" and a "mental disease," Weed explained of Joseph Smith and Martin Harris: "Harris mortgaged his Farm to raise the money required for the temporal support of the Prophet, and printing of the 'Book of Mormon.' The Prophet and his Convert (Smith and Harris) came to Rochester and offered us the honor of being their Printer . . . but as we were only in the newspaper line, we contented ourselves with reading a chapter of what seemed such wretched and incoherent stupidity, that we wondered how 'Joe' had contrived to make the first fool with it."[23] In his account given in 1854, Weed further elaborated on his reasons for refusing to publish the book: "Disgusted with what we deemed a 'weak invention' and not caring to strip Harris of his hard earnings, the proposition was declined."[24] Like Grandin had before him, Weed reportedly advised Harris "not to mortgage his Farm and beggar his family" over the publication of the Book of Mormon.[25]

The most fascinating of Weed's accounts of the negotiations between himself and Joseph Smith is found in Weed's posthumously published autobiography. In it, Weed explained that the first person who visited him concerning the publication of the Book of Mormon was Joseph Smith, whom he described as a "stout, round, smooth-faced young man, between twenty-five and thirty." Joseph explained to him that the book he wanted to publish resulted from a divine vision he had received. Most striking in this account, Weed reported that after Joseph's initial explanation of the book, he apparently demonstrated for the incredulous editor how the book was translated. Joseph "placed what he called a 'tablet' in his hat, from which he read a chapter of the 'Book of Mormon.'" If the desired effect of this demonstration was to convince Weed of the power of God behind the work, Weed was apparently not softened. He claimed that Joseph succeeded in only reaffirming his opinion that Joseph was "either crazed or a very shallow imposter."[26]

Two days after that first meeting during which Weed "declined to become a publisher," Joseph Smith returned to his office, this time accompanied by Martin Harris. Whatever Weed's later attempts to distance himself from any involvement in Mormonism, which was by then politically toxic on a national level, this second visit suggests that despite Weed's later pretensions, his primary concern was over whether or not Joseph Smith could pay him for the work. Apparently concluding that Weed's hesitancy to accept the job rested on principles of profit rather than morality, Harris assured the young Anti-Mason that he would "become security for the expense of printing." Nevertheless, Weed again demurred, and "the manuscript was then taken to another printing office across the street."[27]

## Elihu Marshall of the *Rochester Album*

The "other" printing office was owned by Elihu Marshall, the editor of the *Rochester Album* newspaper. Marshall was perhaps the most well-known printer in Rochester or western New York for that matter. In 1819,

Marshall published a spelling book "designed for the use of common schools." Widely advertised and used, Marshall's book was praised by great and influential men, such as former presidential candidate and New York governor DeWitt Clinton, Chief Justice of the Supreme Court John Marshall, and former president of the United States and founding father John Adams.[28] In October 1825, Marshall founded the *Rochester Album* with the help of two associates and by February 1827 had become the sole proprietor of a printing house at the "Exchange St. Bookstore." Among the multifaceted printing services Marshall advertised was "all orders for Book or Job Printing."[29] In June 1829, Marshall further promoted his enlarged printing establishment and great variety and sizes of type the office had on hand, as well a promise that his prices would "be as reasonable as those of any other establishment in the country."[30]

It is unclear why Joseph and Martin particularly sought out Marshall to publish the Book of Mormon. It is possible that his fame preceded him. In fact, as a schoolteacher, it is very likely that Oliver Cowdery was well acquainted with Marshall's spelling book and perhaps used it in his instruction. Jonathan A. Hadley, for instance, advertised Marshall's book for sale in his printing office in Palmyra.[31] If Joseph was seeking experience as well as willingness, Marshall's book printing capabilities would have been beyond question.[32]

Perhaps, however, after being flatly rejected by Weed even after offering to pay for the printing up front, Joseph considered Marshall because of his unique religious beliefs in addition to his experience. In early 1829, just a few months before Joseph Smith and Martin Harris arrived in Rochester seeking a willing printer, Marshall had become embroiled in a public controversy involving the recent schism within the Religious Society of Friends, commonly referred to as Quakers. Elias Hicks, a Quaker preacher from Long Island, was at the center of the dispute. Hicks preached a different doctrine of Christ than many Quakers were comfortable with, arguing, as one historian has explained, "that Jesus was not born as the Christ. Instead, he became the Christ, the Son of God, because He had been the only human being ever to live in perfect obedience to the Divine Light that was within Him."[33] Hicks also rejected as great "idolatry" the Protestant practice of viewing "the Scriptures as the only rule of faith and practice."[34]

Marshall publicly supported the actions of "Hicksite" Quakers and derided those of the "orthodox" Quakers who tried to control monthly

Quaker meetings. Marshall was even one of the authors of an 1829 pamphlet, "The Inquisition and Orthodoxy, Contrasted with Christianity and Religious Liberty." In it Marshall defended the "right of private judgment" in religious matters and ridiculed the way in which Christian sects had adopted set creedal beliefs that they used to label other Christians as heterodox at best and heretical at worst. Marshall argued that God accepted righteous men regardless of the "speculative religion or abstract theology" they embraced and was therefore unwilling to "anathematize one, whose life is without reproach merely because he does not entertain [another's] on certain points of belief."[35] This rare public expression of religious tolerance would no doubt have been welcome to Joseph, who reflected in his history that during the final months of the Book of Mormon translation they had been visited by many inquirers "some for the sake of finding the truth, others for the purpose of putting hard questions, and trying to confound us, among the latter class were several learned Priests who generally came for the purpose of disputation."[36]

In any case, whether Joseph Smith and Martin Harris sought out Marshall for his expertise, his tolerant religious views (possibly a combination of both), or simply because Weed had referred them, Marshall certainly was a good candidate for the work.[37] He was more experienced than Grandin and Hadley, and apparently more affable and willing than Weed. Marshall's bookstore even specialized in the "latest and most approved editions in History, Biography, Travels, Voyages, Law, Medicine, Theology, Poetry, Arts and Sciences," a list that could comfortably support selling the Book of Mormon as well. He also owned his own book bindery, a necessary accoutrement once the pages of the book had been printed.

The terms of the negotiation with Marshall are not known, but they likely resembled those discussed with the other printers with the large print run of five thousand copies juxtaposed against Martin Harris's willingness to finance an operation that would have seemed well beyond the realm of the ordinary economic speculation incident to book publishing. Pomeroy Tucker, E. B. Grandin's brother-in-law, later explained that Marshall "gave his terms to Smith and his associates for the execution of their work, and his proffered acceptance of the proposed mode of security."[38]

Joseph Smith must have been relieved, after a several-week-long ordeal, to have finally found a publisher who was willing and able to print the

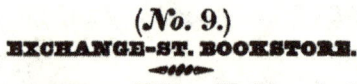

> **(No. 9.)**
> **EXCHANGE-ST. BOOKSTORE.**
>
> **Elihu F. Marshall,**
> *PRINTER,*
> Bookseller and Stationer,
> (Having assumed the late concern of *Marshall & Spalding,*) carries on these branches of business, to wit:
>
> **PRINTING.**
> He will execute, with neatness and despatch, all orders for Book or Job Printing:
> ........SUCH AS........
> CARDS,          SHOW BILLS,
> HANDBILLS,      BLANK RECEIPTS,
> CIRCULARS,      WAY-BILLS,
>         STORAGE RECEIPTS,
>         OR, ANY KIND OF
>         **FANCY,**
> **Plain and Ornamental Printing.**
>
> **BOOKS.**
> He has also on hand, or will procure, at short notice, Books of the latest and most approved editions, in
> History,      Voyages,      Theology,
> Biography,    Law,          Poetry, Arts,
> Travels,      Medicine,     and Sciences;
> TOGETHER WITH A GENERAL ASSORTMENT OF
> **CLASSICAL AND SCHOOL BOOKS,**
> As well as Sabbath School Books.
> *STATIONARY,* of various qualities and prices, to suit purchasers, such as PAPER, of different kinds, *Blank Books, Justices' Blanks, Deeds, Mortgages, Bonds,* Pocket Books, Pencils, Pens, Quills, Penknives, &c. &c.
> ☞ BOOK-BINDING is also carried on, in its various branches: *Paper ruled* to order.
> Rochester, 20th of 2d mo. 1827.

Directory for the Village of Rochester . . . from 1812 to 1827, *96.*

book. Still, Rochester was nearly twenty-five miles away from Palmyra, and publishing the Book of Mormon there introduced a host of logistical problems. Because Joseph wanted to maintain a tight control of the pages of the manuscript, no doubt a result of the earlier fiasco involving Martin Harris, someone would have to board in Rochester throughout the time it took to make a printer's copy of the book, set the type, and print the hundreds of pages. The potential cost of such an arrangement, especially for men who were already short on funds, was daunting. Rather than signing a contract with the willing and able Marshall, the decision was made to again return to the shop of E. B. Grandin back in Palmyra. Joseph Smith hoped to leverage Grandin into accepting the job, given Marshall's willingness to print the book with Harris's funding.

## Renegotiating with Grandin

Returning to Palmyra with Marshall's offer to print the Book of Mormon already assured, they "renewed their request to Mr. Grandin, assuring him that the printing was to be done at any rate." Although Grandin had gone out of his way to stop Harris from supporting the publication of the Book of Mormon, "it was upon this state of facts and view of the case, that Mr. Grandin, after some further hesitation, reconsidered his policy of refusal, and finally entered into a contract for the desired printing and

## NEGOTIATING WITH PRINTERS ❖

binding."[39] However, the reluctant Grandin agreed to do the job only if "his terms were accepted." And they were steep indeed. Grandin demanded the payment up front before he would begin the work, unlike the more usual method of sharing in the proceeds from a book's sale to cover the costs. The $3,000 he demanded in order to produce five thousand copies of the book revealed that he either had not ever really cared about Harris's financial well-being or had stopped caring in a fit of speculation or frustration. Under those terms, Grandin could have potentially profited well over $1,000, after paying for his materials, space, and labor.[40] One popular manual for calculating the cost of printing listed that on a book the size of the Book of Mormon, a printer should calculate a 12 percent profit margin in his negotiations. Grandin's terms, by comparison, allowed for a profit margin of more than 33 percent! It is not known how favorably Marshall's previous offer compared with Grandin's; perhaps both men sensed a desperation from Joseph Smith that allowed them to inflate the price. In any case, Joseph was left with little choice other than to accept Grandin's terms, unless he wanted to travel back and forth between Palmyra and Rochester to work with Marshall, a situation that could have easily allowed for further problems associated with controlling the text of the manuscript once it was in the hands of Marshall.[41] While it is not known definitively when the men settled on terms with Grandin, by 11 August 1829, Jonathan Hadley reported in his paper that the Book of Mormon was "soon to be put to press" in Palmyra rather than in Rochester.

However, despite having struck the deal, the printing operations did not begin immediately as Joseph had hoped. Martin Harris, who had for over a year and half professed to Joseph Smith and others that he would front the money for the publication of the book, was now left with the difficult task of turning his words into actions. The exorbitant sum would require him to mortgage all of the property he owned, and this too in the face of incessant criticism that the venture was only to end in abject failure. Men who knew the industry like E. B. Grandin and Thurlow Weed assured Harris that he was throwing his money away, and, closest to home, Harris's wife, Lucy, was mortified that Martin would endanger their personal well-being in pursuit of the fantastical claims made by Joseph Smith—claims that she had once believed.

175

## Notes

1. 2 Nephi 3:11.
2. After his arrival in Harmony in early April 1829, Oliver Cowdery became the primary scribe for the remainder of the translation. Smith and Cowdery translated the plates day after day for two months, until discontent about the translation in Harmony caused them to move in early June to Peter Whitmer Sr.'s house in Fayette, New York, to complete the project. Smith, History, vol. A-1, 13; Smith, History, circa Summer 1832, in *JSP*, H1:16; Lucy Mack Smith, History, draft, book 8, [1]. Smith recommenced translating soon after he arrived. See David Whitmer interviews in *Kansas City Journal*, 1 June 1881, in Zenas Gurley Collection, Church History Library. John and Christian Whitmer served as scribes along with Oliver Cowdery. *Chicago Times*, 14 October 1881; Joseph Smith, History, vol. A-1, 22.
3. See David Finkelstein and Alistair McCleery, *An Introduction to Book History* (New York: Routledge, 2005), especially chapter 4. See also Richard Peters, ed., "An Act for the Encouragement of Learning, by Securing the Copies of Maps, Charts, and Books, to the Authors and Proprietors of Such Copies, during the Times Therein Mentioned" [May 31, 1790], 1st Cong., 2nd sess., ch. 15, in *The Public Statutes at Large of the United States* (Boston: Charles C. Little and James Brown), 1:124.
4. Peters, "Act for the Encouragement of Learning," 1:124. See Wadsworth, "Copyright Laws and the 1830 Book of Mormon," 80–81.
5. As noted, in early to mid-June 1829, Joseph Smith petitioned a number of printers in the Palmyra and Rochester area to publish the Book of Mormon, yet the type used to print the title page found at the Library of Congress has not been matched to any of those print establishments' types. Though this does not rule out the possibility that one of the printers in the area printed the title page, it opens the possibility that it was printed in Utica. Nevertheless, even though the type does not match, Egbert B. Grandin's press, printing the *Wayne Sentinel*, had motive to print it.
6. Joseph Smith does not appear to have been absent from the Palmyra/Fayette areas during the month of June. Given his schedule of activities, including upwards of twenty days of translation, print negotiations, travel between Fayette, Palmyra, and Rochester, and the dictation of five revelations in Fayette and Manchester, it is very unlikely he personally went to Utica.
7. The copyright record or application stated that it was done in conformity to an act of Congress that stated: "An act for the encouragement of learning, by securing

the copies of Maps, Charts, and Books, to the authors and proprietors of such copies, during the times therein mentioned."

8. Orsamus Turner, a printer in Palmyra in the early 1820s and later a historian, wrote that Harris was displaying the title page during his negotiations. Turner, *History of the Pioneer Settlement of Phelps and Gorham's Purchase and Morris' Reserve* (Rochester, NY: Erastus Darrow, 1851), 215.

9. Recollections of John H. Gilbert [Regarding printing the Book of Mormon], 8 September 1892, Palmyra, New York, typescript, Brigham Young University; Stanley Lebergott, "Wage Trends, 1800–1900," in *Trends in the American Economy in the Nineteenth Century* (National Bureau of Economic Research, 1960), 457.

10. *Wayne Sentinel*, 26 June 1829.

11. Pomeroy Tucker, "Mormonism and Joe Smith—The Book of Mormon or Golden Bible," *Wayne Democratic Press*, 26 May 1858.

12. "Jonathan A. Hadley—The Pioneer Editor of Watertown," *Proceedings of the Wisconsin Editorial Association* (Madison, WI: Atwood & Culver, 1870), 24–25.

13. "Married," *Rochester Album*, 15 July 1828.

14. "Job Printing," *Palmyra Freeman*, 7 July 1829.

15. "Golden Bible," *Palmyra Freeman*, 11 August 1829.

16. "Golden Bible," *Palmyra Freeman*, 11 August 1829. The 1842 letter to Wentworth gives this description of the plates: "These records were engraven on plates which had the appearance of gold, each plate was six inches wide and eight inches long and not quite so thick as common tin." "Church History," *Times and Seasons*, 1 March 1842.

17. "Golden Bible," *Palmyra Freeman*, 11 August 1829.

18. "Morgan," *Pennsylvania Gazette*, 27 October 1827; "Morgan, Morgan, Morgan," *Olive Branch*, 15 September 1827; "Highly Important," *Republican Compiler*, 27 October 1827.

19. *Louisville Public Advertiser*, 11 October 1828, reprinted from the *New York American*.

20. Thurlow Weed and Harriet Weed, *Life of Thurlow Weed, Including His Autobiography and a Memoir* (Boston: Houghton Mufflin, 1883), 341–42.

21. See, for example, "Anti-Masonic Inquirer," *Craftsman* (Rochester), 7 July 1829.

22. "The Three Platforms," *Boston Daily Atlas*, 8 August 1856.

23. "A Letter From Joe Smith's Widow," *Albany Evening Journal*, 10 December 1845.

24. "Recent Progress of the Mormons," *Albany Evening Journal*, 31 July 1854.

25. "Prospect of Peace with Utah," *Albany Evening Journal*, 19 May 1858.

26. Weed and Weed, *Life of Thurlow Weed*, 341–42.
27. "Recent Progress of the Mormons," *Albany Evening Journal*, 31 July 1854.
28. *Providence Patriot*, 12 July 1820, reprinted from the *Saratoga Sentinel*; *New-Hampshire Statesman*, 17 March 1823.
29. *Directory for the Village of Rochester: Containing the Names, Residence and Occupations of All Male Inhabitants Over Fifteen Years of Age, in Said Village, on the First of January, 1827. To Which is Added, a Sketch of the History of the Village, from 1812 to 1827* (Rochester, NY: Elisha Ely, 1827), 96.
30. "Book and Job Printing," *Craftsman*, 6 June 1829.
31. "Marshall's and Webster's Spelling Books," *Palmyra Freeman*, 11 August 1829.
32. See 1840 Census of Rochester, Monroe County, New York, 312. One history explained that "Elihu Marshall was a plain and ornamental printer and bookbinder, and the quality both of the printing and binding still in existence verifies all that Mr. Marshall claimed in 1827." William F. Peck, *Semicentennial History of Rochester*, 260, 646.
33. Thomas D. Hamm, *The Quakers in America* (New York: Columbia University Press, 2003), 40.
34. Elias Hicks to Phebe Willis, 23 September 1820, in *Letters of Elias Hicks* (New York: Isaac T. Hopper, 1834), 64.
35. Elihu Marshall, *The Inquisition and Orthodoxy: Contrasted with Christianity and Religious Liberty* (Lockport: E. A. Cooley, 1829), 3–4.
36. Joseph Smith, History, vol. A-1, 26.
37. Though his early accounts of the visit do not contain this information, in 1880 Weed said that after he had rejected Smith he had suggested "a friend who was in that business," likely a reference to Marshall. Ellen E. Dickinson, *New Light on Mormonism with Introduction by Thurlow Weed* (New York: Funk and Wagnalls, 1885), 260.
38. Tucker, "Mormonism and Joe Smith."
39. Tucker, "Mormonism and Joe Smith."
40. Thomas Curson Hansard, *Typographia*, 797–98.
41. Though it is impossible to know what Grandin's exact costs were, it can be estimated that they were between $1,700 and $1,900. For example, Grandin would have paid as high as $370 in labor costs if Gilbert had done all the work at $0.25 per 1000 ems (characters), like he claimed, and as low as $200 if the two journeymen Grandin hired in December 1829 set half of the type at a much lower rate for labor. Gilbert remembered Grandin purchasing 500 pounds of small pica type that cost $0.38 a pound,

leaving Grandin with an expense totaling no more than $200 for type. Grandin's journal explained a lawsuit stemming from a note he gave Luther Howard, the binder, promising $298 that he left unpaid that was associated with the Book of Mormon. While paper could be purchased for $4 to $24 per ream, Grandin likely paid closer to the bottom of that range per ream for the size of the Book of Mormon. Paper with dimensions similar to the sheets used in printing the Book of Mormon sold for $4.75 a ream in 1821. The Book of Mormon was created from 37 octavos sheets with 16 pages per octavo for a total of 592 pages. The sheets of paper utilized in the printing were approximately 18 by 30 inches with each sheet containing two octavos. Because the sheets were cut in half and folded into their individual octavos, 2,500 sheets of paper were required per octavo for 5,000 copies of the Book of Mormon. Grandin, therefore, needed approximately 92,500 sheets of paper to print 5,000 copies of the Book of Mormon. With 500 sheets of paper per ream, the printing necessitated 185 reams of paper. At this price, Grandin paid approximately $900 for paper. Nevertheless, even with these variables, Grandin would have profited at least $1,000, with a margin that approached 40 percent in a printing market in which a 15 percent profit margin was considered to be a very high one. See John H. Gilbert Interview, 1877, in Vogel, *EMD* 2:518; John H. Gilbert Interview, September 1888, in Vogel, *EMD* 2:539; John H. Gilbert, Memorandum, 8 September 1892, photocopy, Church History Library. John H. Gilbert Interview, 1893, in Vogel, *EMD* 2:549; "Printing Types, Presses, &c.," *Republican Complier*, 22 September 1829; Theodore Gazlay, *Practical Printers' Assistant*, 127; and Grandin, Journal, 14 December 1831. See also Weeks, *History of Paper Manufacturing in the United States*, 119–20; Theodore Gazlay, *Practical Printers' Assistant*, 122, 137. For a contemporaneous and comparable example with similar figures, see Hansard, *Typographia*, 797–98.

*Martin Harris's farm that he mortgaged to fund the publication of the Book of Mormon. Watercolor by Anthony Sweat.*

# 10

# Paying for the Book of Mormon: Doctrine and Covenants Section 19

Many nineteenth-century printers shouldered the initial costs associated with printing a book and trusted that once a book was published its sales would generate profits for them as well as the author. But Grandin would make no such arrangement with Joseph Smith. He believed not only that Joseph Smith was a religious imposter but that the Book of Mormon he wanted to publish would be a colossal financial failure. Grandin had rebuffed Harris and Smith's initial attempts to employ him as a publisher and as late as 26 June 1829 portrayed his personal disgust for the claims Joseph Smith had made about divine visitations and a sacred calling. While Smith and Harris were still busily engaged trying to find a willing printer, Grandin was publishing an article that derided the gold plates as a "pretended discovery." More important, though, for the financial prospects of the book, Grandin asserted that "most people entertain an idea that the whole matter is the result of gross imposition, and a grosser superstition."[1] Such public misgivings would not likely translate into lucrative sales. Certain that the Book of Mormon could generate no profits through regular sales, Grandin required Joseph Smith and Martin Harris to pay for the entire project up front before he devoted any of his own resources to start the printing.

The costs associated with printing any book, especially one the size of the Book of Mormon, were substantial. Every nineteenth-century printer had to buy hundreds of pounds of metal type for each large book they published, requiring them to spend hundreds of dollars before they could print a single page. In order to print the Book of Mormon to the specifications agreed upon with Joseph Smith, Grandin needed to buy 800 pounds of small pica type. This large initial expenditure was combined with the expense of buying the reams of paper necessary to publish 5,000 copies of a book that would be nearly 600 pages in length. In addition, the printing process would take months, and Grandin would have to employ several workers as typesetters, proofreaders, and binders before the project would be completed. Faced with such costs and his own certainty that every dollar spent on the Book of Mormon publication would be unrecoverable through sales, Grandin was strict and unyielding on the payment. Even after Harris had agreed to pay for the printing process up front, Grandin refused to begin the publication process at all until he actually received the payment from Harris. According to John Gilbert, the typesetter of the book, Grandin would not even make the journey to New York City to purchase the type until he had the payment secured. He was taking no chances on this speculative "Gold Bible" venture.

It is unclear precisely when Joseph Smith struck the deal with Grandin to publish the Book of Mormon. Clearly, by 26 June 1829, Grandin was not only not planning to publish it, but he was mocking the project. Sometime during the weeks that followed, Joseph Smith and Martin Harris had negotiated with at least two other printers

Portrait of Egbert B. Grandin. *Painting by Alonzo Parks, Grandin Press Building, Palmyra, New York.*

in Rochester but had returned to Palmyra with Elihu Marshall's terms and used them to convince Grandin to undertake the project himself. This agreement likely came in late July or early August at the latest, because by 11 August 1829, the plan to publish the Book of Mormon at Grandin's print shop in Palmyra, rather than at Marshall's in Rochester, was already publicly understood.[2] However, despite this late July or early August agreement with Grandin, by the end of August Grandin had still not begun the printing. The reason? Martin Harris had not yet paid him the promised money.

## Delaying the Publication

As early as October 1827, when Lucy Smith went to Martin Harris's home, the Harris family had been offering Joseph Smith some form of financial backing to help translate the gold plates and bring forth the Book of Mormon. In fact, Lucy Harris and her friend had immediately offered to invest money into the project the same day Lucy Smith first spoke to them about the gold plates.[3] Martin Harris had apparently already begun offering his assets to help pay for the printing of the Book of Mormon in February 1828 when he spoke with Charles Anthon in New York City.[4]

Harris found little support from his friends, family, and acquaintances. Despite her early eagerness to support the project, by the spring of 1828 his wife, Lucy, had become angry over Joseph Smith's refusal to show her the actual plates and subsequently forbade Martin from paying for any of the costs associated with the translation, let alone the staggering costs of the publication. In fact, likely in response to Lucy's fears that he would sell his property to finance the endeavor, Martin deeded some eighty acres of the farm directly to Lucy, by way of her brother, thus preventing him from selling that land without her consent.[5]

Lucy's resistance to Martin's financial involvement was the rule rather than the exception. All throughout the summer of 1829, Harris was likely told by the printers—E. B. Grandin, Jonathan Hadley, and Thurlow Weed—that the Book of Mormon would not sell. Grandin had doggedly refused to take Martin's money and even tried to convince Harris's friends to help him persuade Martin to give up his support for the project. By August, Martin Harris must have realized that the $3,000 price tag to print the Book of Mormon would require him to give up most of his assets.

183

Though he had been a part of the translation process, writing the words Joseph spoke as he read them from the seer stones and even being shown the gold plates by an angel of God, when faced with the realities of losing his wealth, Harris's will faltered. Perhaps the condescending words from men like Thurlow Weed and Charles Anthon echoed in his ears. Each had assured him that the enterprise was doomed to failure. Even if the work really was from God, if the public refused to buy the book, Harris would be financially ruined. To make matters worse, around the same time, Lucy had reportedly gathered witnesses to testify against Joseph Smith in a trial alleging that Smith had knowingly committed fraud by claiming the gold plates existed.[6] Lucy Harris had apparently gathered the testimony of three local residents, who were each willing to testify that Joseph Smith had admitted to them that the gold plates did not exist and that he had concocted the whole story to fraudulently rob Martin of his money. These witnesses asserted on the stand that Smith never had possession of the gold plates.[7] Refuting their allegations, Martin Harris took the stand and testified that Smith had not defrauded him and that Harris had only "put $50 into his [Joseph's] hands . . . for the purpose of doing the work of the Lord." Harris reportedly concluded his testimony with a warning that echoed the revelation he had received in March 1829: "As to the plates of which he professes to have . . . if you gentlemen do not believe it but continue to resist the truth it one day [will] be the means of damning your souls."[8]

Despite this courageous public display of support, Harris apparently balked at fulfilling his promise to pay for the printing of the Book of Mormon. Grandin's brother-in-law, who was working in his print shop, later recalled that "Harris became for a time in some degree staggered in his confidence; but nothing could be done in the way of printing without his aid."[9] Exactly how long Harris hesitated or whether he expressed his financial concerns to Joseph Smith directly is not known, but sometime that summer Joseph Smith dictated a revelation for Martin Harris. That revelation (D&C 19) not only revealed much about the nature of Christ and God's punishment, but also expressly commanded Martin Harris to pay for the Book of Mormon and even told him how to raise the funds.

The revelation forcefully commanded Harris in the voice of the Lord to "repent: repent, lest I smite you by the rod of my mouth, and by my wrath, and by my anger, and your sufferings be sore: How sore you know not!

PAYING FOR THE BOOK OF MORMON ❖

How exquisite you know not! Yea, how hard to bear you know not!" In particular, the revelation commanded Harris, "thou shalt not covet thine own property, but impart it freely to the printing of the book of Mormon." This revelation not only instructed Harris to pay for the printing but explained precisely how Harris was to "pay the printers debt." He was told to "Impart a portion of thy property; Yea, even a part of thy lands and all save the support of thy family."[10]

## Martin Harris's Mortgage

On 25 August 1829, Harris did precisely what the revelation had commanded. Harris mortgaged all of the property to which he still held legal rights, 151 acres, to Egbert B. Grandin to the amount of $3,000. By paying for the printing in the form of a mortgage on his property, Harris had greater flexibility than if he had paid for the printing outright in cash. Although the mortgage gave Grandin legal ownership of his farm, Harris was still able to occupy the property and even farm the land over the course of the next eighteen months until the entire balance of the note came due.

The mortgage contained a provision which allowed Harris to reclaim his land and fulfill the debt if he paid Grandin $3,000 in cash within the allotted eighteen months. Additionally, if the property sold for more than $3,000 while it was mortgaged to Grandin, Harris would be legally entitled to the excess money.[11] On the other hand, if Harris defaulted on the mortgage by not paying Grandin in full by February 1831, Grandin would own Harris's land outright, allowing Grandin to keep or sell the property as he wished. Most importantly for Grandin,

*Martin Harris, Utah State Historical Society.*

185

❖ FROM DARKNESS UNTO LIGHT

the mortgage could be easily sold to other interested speculators for ready cash. This process of a creditor selling a mortgage to another party, something many Americans are familiar with in the twenty-first century, was called assigning.

Grandin readily understood the cash value of Martin Harris's mortgage as a salable commodity. Months before he began negotiating with Harris, his newspaper (the *Wayne Sentinel*) had frequently printed details concerning the sale and assignment of mortgages. His subscribers often advertised that they were selling a mortgage or that they had purchased one and wanted to sell it to someone else as an assignee. In 1829, Grandin also printed numerous accounts of individuals defaulting on their mortgages for the benefit of investors. He even printed several public announcements of a mortgage for his brother, Philip, who owned the building Grandin's press was located in.[12] Individuals in Palmyra, as they did elsewhere in upstate New York, frequently bought and sold mortgages in a speculative attempt to make money. Palmyra residents were well aware that if they mortgaged their land, their mortgage could be sold to someone else.

For Grandin, receiving his payment in the form of Harris's mortgaged land gave him the flexibility of a readily salable asset and the potential that he could in turn sell the mortgage to someone else for more than the $3,000. His right to "assign" or sell the mortgage assured him that he did not have to wait eighteen months for Harris to sell his farm to obtain the money.[13] In any case, within eighteen months Grandin would have either the cash from Harris paying off the mortgage, the cash from an assignee buying the mortgage, or Harris's valuable, well-cultivated land. In each of these scenarios, Grandin stood to profit handsomely from his agreement to publish the Book of Mormon. Harris's mortgage essentially paid for the cost of printing before the first page came off the press; it gave Grandin the confidence to invest his own money in the cost of the type, paper, and labor for the project.[14] With Harris's mortgage firmly in hand, Grandin finally began the printing process, certain of his own profit regardless of the success or failure of the book.

Grandin likely never intended to live on Harris's property. Grandin was not a farmer and invested instead in things that aided his growing printing enterprise, such as his new printing press and Luther Howard's bindery on the second floor of his print shop. In any case, in October 1830, four months before the $3,000 payment was due, Grandin assigned the mortgage to Thomas Rogers II, a wealthy Palmyra resident and an extended family member, for $2,000.[15] In April 1831, Rogers sold Harris's property to Thomas Lakey for $3,000, who in turn sold the property only two years later for $3,300, demonstrating that these men were likely only interested in the property as a short-term investment.[16] The fact that Grandin eventually sold Harris's mortgage for cash suggests strongly that he had always intended to sell the mortgage.

In any case, whatever Grandin's original intentions with Harris's mortgage were, the mortgage constituted the full payment from Joseph Smith to Grandin for the publication of the Book of Mormon. When Harris signed the mortgage with Grandin on 25 August 1829, nothing more was required in order to pay Grandin. Harris had heeded the revelation delivered to him through Joseph Smith, ceased wavering over the financial implications for the time being, and demonstrated himself to be fully committed to the cause of the Book of Mormon, even to the point of financial ruin.

Although the weight of evidence demonstrates that the Book of Mormon was paid for up front by the means of Martin Harris's mortgage to Grandin following his receipt of Doctrine and Covenants 19, for decades confusion has surrounded the way in which the Book of Mormon was financed and Grandin's expectations of Smith during the publication process.

## Historical Confusion about the Agreement

This confusion about the payment for the Book of Mormon comes from two main sources: Lucy Mack Smith's reminiscent account of this period of Joseph Smith's life written fifteen years later, and the misdating of Doctrine and Covenants 19 in the Book of Commandments and the Doctrine and Covenants. In her account, Lucy Mack Smith recalled that her sons vigorously worked to pay for the Book of Mormon throughout that fall and winter. She also claimed that Grandin eventually became concerned over whether or not he would be paid and threatened to halt the entire publication process even though he had already printed nearly half of the pages.[17] She blamed Grandin's alleged stoppage of the work on a forthcoming boycott of the sales of the book that had been announced by the local Palmyra residents. In her account, only Joseph Smith's personal intercession with Grandin persuaded the printer to resume the work despite the public animosity.[18]

❖ FROM DARKNESS UNTO LIGHT

However, Lucy's claims appear to have very little substance. First, while Joseph and Hyrum may have been laboring throughout those months in order to raise money, it certainly could not have been their intention to pay for the entire printing of the Book of Mormon before the publication was finished by the means of their meager wages. In fact, it would have required both of them to work for nearly a decade to pay the $3,000 balance on the printing. Additionally, it is highly unlikely that Grandin, who had initially refused to print the book precisely because he thought it was a public farce, would be surprised or dissuaded from doing so because of a boycott organized in Palmyra. The print run of 5,000 copies made the boycott of the book in such a small hamlet as Palmyra essentially inconsequential to the eventual profits to be garnered from sales. Even if a local boycott bothered him, what could halting the publication at the midway point have profited him? Was not a decreased number of sales still preferable to no sales at all and hundreds of dollars wasted on ink, labor, type, and paper? Clearly Grandin was not relying on Palmyra sales to recoup his investment. Furthermore, if Grandin really believed that his profits were in danger because of the boycott, and the possession of a mortgage guaranteeing the payment from Harris was not enough to reassure him, it seems doubtful at best that the penniless Joseph Smith could have persuaded him otherwise. Also, rather than halting the publication that winter as Lucy Smith claimed, Grandin hired two journeymen to finish the second half of the printing in January 1830, a decision demonstrating that he was continuing to invest in the project as late as that time.[19] Given these factors, Lucy's claim that Grandin was relying on sales from the Book of Mormon to obtain his own payment is simply untenable. Grandin had already been paid up front before he began.

Nevertheless, once Lucy's account was published it soon came to dominate the story of the Book of Mormon publication told by others. David Whitmer, for instance, wrote in 1887 that "When the Book of Mormon was in the hands of the printer, more money was needed to finish the printing of it. We were waiting on Martin Harris who was doing his best to sell a part of his farm, in order to raise the necessary funds." However, by all accounts, Whitmer was not present in Palmyra during either the negotiations over or the actual printing of the Book of Mormon. Whitmer's claim is also not supported by the historical evidence. By the time the book "was in the hands of the printer," Martin Harris no longer possessed any lands that he had a legal right to sell. How then could Grandin have expected him to obtain additional funds while Grandin was in possession via the mortgage of all of Harris's property? Grandin's typesetter for the project, John Gilbert, aggressively corrected Whitmer's claim.[20] Gilbert was adamant that Harris "had given security for the full amount agreed upon for printing, before the work was commenced, and there was no delay because of financial embarrassment." Gilbert was apparently angry over Whitmer's mistake. In an interview, Gilbert unabashedly exclaimed that "David Whitmer had made statements in the book which were not true. He represented that they were short of means and that they wanted to sell the manuscript, which was not so, as the pay was all arranged for before the printing was commenced."[21] Demonstrating Gilbert's point, the printing commenced almost directly after Harris mortgaged his property to Grandin on 25 August 1829. Gilbert stated that once the mortgage was signed over to Grandin, "As quick as Mr. Grandin got his type and got things all ready to commence the work, Hyrum Smith brought to the office 24 pages of manuscript on foolscap paper" and the printing process began.[22]

Other historical evidence further demonstrates that Grandin was in no way relying on the potential sales of the Book of Mormon as even part of the payment. Because most printers were paid partially through the sales of the books that they printed, they usually had a financial interest in advertising and promoting the books. But unlike most printers who worked with authors in the 1830s, Grandin took no noticeable steps to ensure that the Book of Mormon sold well. In fact, it appears that Grandin even passively encouraged others who were deriding the verity of the Book of Mormon. For instance, there is no evidence he was alarmed by the activities of Abner Cole, who was using his print shop and press to print illegal excerpts of the pages of the Book of Mormon in January 1830 in his newspaper, the *Reflector*.[23] This would have potentially affected the sale of the books and hence potentially affected whether Grandin was paid in a timely manner, if he had been relying on sales of the books for payment.

This breach of copyright was also not the last time that Grandin's press was used to ridicule the Book of Mormon. Cole printed portions of the Book of Mormon in January 1830 until Joseph Smith and others

❖ FROM DARKNESS UNTO LIGHT

*Grandin Press. Photo by Brent R. Nordgren.*

confronted him. Possibly after arbitration, the unauthorized printing stopped, but Cole continued to deride the Book of Mormon in his newspaper printed on Grandin's press by publishing mock chapters of an excerpt he called "The Book of Pukei" (this name was meant to mimic the book of Nephi in the Book of Mormon). The "Book of Pukei" publications further lampooned the content of the Book of Mormon. In April 1830, when the book was finally finished and available for sale, Cole was still deriding the Book of Mormon in the *Reflector*, and Grandin continued to allow Cole to use his press to make such public denunciations. Grandin's ambivalent attitude toward Cole further demonstrates that, contrary to Lucy Smith's later claims, Grandin did not expect to be paid for the Book of Mormon through the sales of the completed books. Grandin had already been paid by Harris's mortgage and thus looked upon the difficulties surrounding Cole with apathy.

## Misdating Doctrine and Covenants 19

The other major factor in the misconception about the payment for the publication of the Book of Mormon stems from the misdating of Doctrine and Covenants 19, which commanded Harris to "impart" of his lands to

*[handwritten note at top: D&C was originally misdated as Aug 1830 instead of Aug 1829]*

pay for the printing of the book. Although Harris mortgaged his property in August 1829 in order to fulfill the commandments in that revelation, the earliest printed versions of Doctrine and Covenants 19 dated the revelation to 1830. The Book of Commandments, for example, dated it as 1830.[24] However, an 1830 dating would have meant that Harris was asked to "impart a portion" of his land after he had already distributed the rights to "all" of his land. After 25 August 1829, Harris did not have legal rights to any additional land, making it impossible for him to "impart" further another portion of his property in 1830. Moreover, the editors of the Book of Commandments included parentheses around the date, a practice they used throughout the book to indicate that they had inserted a character or date that was either not included in the manuscript copy or that had been subsequently changed.[25] The editors of the 1835 Doctrine and Covenants discarded the use of parenthetical notations such as this in every instance except the 1830 date of this revelation, likely reflecting their continued reservations about this date.[26]

This 1830 date published in the Doctrine and Covenants subsequently influenced those who compiled later histories and accounts of this early era of Joseph Smith's history. For instance, Joseph Knight Sr.'s reminiscence and Joseph Smith's 1838 history took the 1830 date at face value. Knight related a story in which he gave Joseph Smith a ride in his horse-drawn wagon from Harmony to Manchester in late March 1830. Approaching their destination, they saw Martin Harris crossing the road carrying some copies of the newly published Book of Mormon. Knight reported that Harris "came to us and after Compliments he says The Books will not sell for no Body wants them." He further wrote, "Says he [Martin] I want a Commandment [revelation from God] Why says Joseph, fullfill what you have got. But, says he, I must have a Commandment." Knight stated that the next morning Harris persisted in his call for a revelation and claimed that Smith and Cowdery received a revelation later that day for Harris, though it is unclear whether Knight was actually there when that revelation was supposed to have been given. Using his copy of the Doctrine & Covenants as his guide, Knight mistakenly assigned this "1830" revelation (D&C 19) to that event, even giving the page number from the Doctrine and Covenants, as though Joseph Smith were reacting to Harris's request for a revelation when he gave it. Because he provided page numbers from the Doctrine and Covenants in this manner only two other times in his history, both times reporting events for which he was apparently not present, it can be reasonably assumed that he was also not present when this revelation was dictated. If he was not present for the dictated revelation, he may simply have used the dating in the Doctrine and Covenants as a guide without knowing whether Smith had actually acquiesced to Harris's request for a new revelation in March 1830.[27]

Joseph Smith's later history that was compiled by several scribes further demonstrates that there may have been some confusion about the revelation as the result of the date published in the 1835 Doctrine and Covenants. The history copied the revelation directly from the Doctrine and Covenants, including the 1830 date in the parentheses, but placed it in an 1829 historical context. The revelation was inserted into the chronological narrative after the negotiations with E. B. Grandin to print the Book of Mormon in June 1829, suggesting that Smith and his scribes were aware of the fact that the revelation was given in the summer of 1829 at the same time as the negotiations rather than after the book was already published.[28] The compilers of the history likely copied in all of the revelations from the Doctrine and Covenants verbatim, including the assigned dates, but relied more heavily on Joseph Smith for the historical context in which to place them.

In addition to all of the evidences that Doctrine and Covenants 19 was given in the summer of 1829 to convince a wavering Martin Harris to mortgage his property, the recent discovery of the Book of Commandments and Revelations (BCR) further confirms an 1829 date. The BCR contains the earliest handwritten copy of the revelation. Unfortunately, only the second half of the revelation survives in the book. The date, which is usually found with the title of the revelation, is therefore missing from the manuscript. Nevertheless, when John Whitmer created the index for the revelation book, he dated the revelation as an 1829 document. The index included dates for all of the revelations and in every case the date in the index matched the date given on the first page of the revelation. The index also listed the revelations in chronological order according to when they were dictated and placed Harris's revelation between two others that were dated 1829.[29]

In March 2013, as a result of the research done by the Joseph Smith Papers Project, the date of the revelation was changed in newest edition of the scriptures. No longer maintaining the previously published error of March 1830, the date now reflects the strong likelihood that it was received in the summer of 1829.

Although Martin Harris had for years pledged to pay for the printing of the Book of Mormon, the reception of Doctrine and Covenants 19 demonstrates that he had for a time hesitated to actually fulfill his commitment. Heeding the commandment given from God, Harris mortgaged his property and the printing of the Book of Mormon began. Over the months that followed, several other difficulties would impede the process of the work, and Harris himself would again falter in his total financial commitment to the endeavor before the first books would be available for sale in March 1830.

## Notes

1. The *Wayne Sentinel*, 26 June 1829.
2. "Golden Bible," *Palmyra Freeman*, 11 August 1829. Jonathan Hadley explained in his 11 August article that Joseph had formed an agreement with E. B. Grandin by the time he published his newspaper that day.
3. Lucy Smith wrote that Martin's wife "commenced urging me to receive a considerable amount of money which she had at her own command a kind of private purse which her husband permitted her to keep." Lucy Mack Smith, History, 1845, book 6, [4–7].
4. See Tiffany, "Mormonism," August 1859, 168–70; and Erin Jennings, "Charles Anthon—The Man Behind the Letters," *John Whitmer Historical Association Journal* 32, no. 2 (Fall/Winter 2012): 171–87. See also chapter 5, herein.
5. Martin Harris, Indenture to Peter Harris, Wayne Co., NY, 29 November 1825, Mortgage Records, US and Canada Record Collection, Family History Library.
6. Though the timing is unclear and no record of the proceedings remains, Harris apparently returned to his home about the same time the legal proceedings occurred in Lyons, the county seat of Wayne County, New York.
7. Lucy Mack Smith wrote that the first witness claimed the box in which Joseph Smith kept the plates was filled with sand and that Joseph Smith told him it was to deceive, the second witness claimed Joseph Smith said the box was filled with lead, and the third witness declared that the box was empty. See Lucy Mack Smith, History, 1844–1845, book 8, [6–7]. The first witness was likely Peter Ingersoll,

❖ FROM DARKNESS UNTO LIGHT

who had been a Smith family friend. In 1833, Ingersoll swore in an affidavit that Joseph Smith had told him his "frock" allegedly containing the plates was filled with sand. See Howe, *Mormonism Unvailed*, 235–36.

8. Lucy Mack Smith, History, 1844–1845, book 8, [7]. Compare Martin Harris's reported court testimony to the following warning from the revelation: "Now if this Generation do hardon their hearts against my words Behold I deliver them up unto Satan . . . & Behold the Sword of Justice doth hang above their heads & if they persist in the hardness of ther hearts the time cometh that it must fall upon them."

9. Pomeroy Tucker, *Origin, Rise, and Progress of Mormonism*, 51.

10. Revelation, circa summer 1829 [D&C 19], in *JSP*, D1:85.

11. In 1830, the legal scholar James Kent wrote, "A MORTGAGE is the conveyance of an estate, by way of pledge, for the security of debt, and to become void of payment of it. The legal ownership is vested in the creditor, but in equity the mortgagor remains the actual owner, until he is debarred by his own default, or by judicial decree." James Kent, *Commentaries on American Law* (New York: O. Halsted, 1830), 4:129.

12. See *Wayne Sentinel*, 2 January 1829, 1, which described the legal proceedings of an assignee, Judah Colt, for a mortgage that he purchased and later sold; *Wayne Sentinel*, 27 February 1829, 1, which described the legal proceedings of joint investment of three assignees for Elihu Granger's mortgage; *Wayne Sentinel*, 24 April 1829, 1, Philip Grandin, his brother who he had originally rented his printing house from, had purchased a mortgage and was apparently trying to collect after the owner had defaulted; *Wayne Sentinel*, 21 August 1829, 1; *Wayne Sentinel*, 28 August 1829, 1; and *Wayne Sentinel*, 18 September 1829, 1, Philip Grandin, assignee.

13. The mortgage agreement did not require Harris to make any payments.

14. Foundries generally allowed buyers up to six months of credit for purchases, and he could have purchased paper on loan, but typesetters were generally paid weekly, making it doubtful that he could have produced the Book of Mormon before most of the costs were incurred. (For an example, see the advertisement for a Cincinnati type foundry in the *Sandusky Clarion*, 26 December 1829.) It appears that type foundries assumed their type would be bought on credit. *New-Hampshire Statesman and Concord Register*, 19 September 1829.

15. Wayne County New York, *Book of Deeds*, 5:363.

16. Grandin sold the mortgage for $2,000 to his great uncle-in-law Thomas Rogers II. As stated, above 12 percent of the cost was the usual amount for printers to

194

charge for profit, making it likely that even though he sold the mortgage for $1,000 less than he could have received, he still probably made a fair return on the printing. When Harris's property was eventually sold, Rogers collected the full $3,000 from the buyer, Thomas Lakey. It is unknown why Grandin sold the mortgage just four months before he could have collected the full $3,000. Though Grandin may have sold the mortgage out of desperation, he may have also sold it as part of larger deal with Rogers to make additional money or to invest in an additional project. Grandin continued to build his printing business by buying Luther Howard's bindery, for example. He also recorded in his journal that he had been sued for unpaid debts, such as when Luther Howard sued him for the money he owed him for binding the Book of Mormon. See E. B. Grandin, Journal, 14 December 1832.

17. She wrote: "The men who were appointed to do this errand, fulfilled their mission to the letter, and urged upon Mr. Grandin the necessity of his putting a stop to the printing, as the Smiths had lost all their property, and consequently would be unable to pay him for his work, except by the sale of the books." Anderson, *Lucy's Book*, 476; see also footnote 272; Lucy Mack Smith, History, book 9, 3, 4, 11.

18. Though Joseph and Oliver apparently attempted to sell the books in bulk or wholesale even before the printing was finished, there are no indications that the money generated by the sale of the books was originally intended to pay for Harris's mortgage. However, on 16 January 1830, Joseph Smith signed an agreement that allowed Harris to sell the books until he recovered the entire cost of the mortgage. The money that individuals paid for the copies of the Book of Mormon eventually reimbursed Harris, though he did not originally intend to have the cost of his property refunded. When Grandin's *Wayne Sentinel* first advertised the book on 26 March 1830, it stated that it would be sold for both retail and wholesale prices. Joseph may have been trying to sell the books wholesale to Josiah Stowel in October 1829 before they were printed, because he stated in a letter to Cowdery that "Mr. Stowell has a prospect of getting five or six hundred dollars he does not know certain that he can get it but he is a going to try and if he can get the money he wants to pay it in immediately for books." Letter to Oliver Cowdery, 22 October 1829, in *JSP*, D1:97; see Agreement with Martin Harris, 16 January 1830, in *JSP*, D1:104–8.

19. Recollections of John H. Gilbert [Regarding printing Book of Mormon], 8 September 1892, Palmyra, NY, typescript, BYU.

20. "Mormon Leaders at Their Mecca," *New York Herald*, 25 June 1893, 12.

FROM DARKNESS UNTO LIGHT

21. Kate B. Carter, comp., *Our Pioneer Heritage* (Salt Lake City: Daughters of Utah Pioneers, 1967), 10:294.
22. John H. Gilbert to James T. Cobb, 10 February 1879, in the Theodore A. Schroeder Papers, Rare Books and Manuscripts Division, New York Public Library. There were no type foundries in the Palmyra area. If Grandin purchased his type in New York City and did not travel there to get it until after the 25 August 1829 agreement was signed with Harris giving him payment, then it is unlikely that Grandin returned before September. See Letter from Oliver Cowdery, 6 November 1829, in *JSP*, D1:98.
23. Oliver Cowdery, 28 December 1829, in *JSP*, D1:102.
24. Book of Commandments, 39.
25. Joseph Smith, who dictated the revelation, and Martin Harris, who the revelation addressed, were not part of the team of editors who added the date to the Book of Commandments. The primary editors were Oliver Cowdery, John Whitmer, and William W. Phelps. Cowdery may have been there when the revelation was given, and the evidence for his presence is found in Joseph Knight Sr.'s reminiscent account. Knight relied heavily upon the 1835 Doctrine and Covenants as a guide to his history. While Knight did not reference other sources in his account, he did reference the Doctrine and Covenants, even providing readers a page number where they could find this revelation in that volume. Knight's reliance on the Doctrine and Covenants as a guide may have influenced his interpretation and dating of the featured revelation.
26. Doctrine and Covenants, 1835 ed., 174. For example, because only given names were usually recorded in earlier copies, the editors added the initial of each person's surname in parentheses—like "Joseph (K.)." The Doctrine and Covenants began using parenthetical statements more conventionally and included full surnames—like "Joseph Knight"—yet of all the headings for each revelation, only the featured revelation included parentheses around the date of the revelation.
27. Knight Sr., History, 6. "Now in the Spring of 1830 I went with my Team and took Joseph out to Manchester to his Father. When we was on our way he told me that there must be a Church formed But did not tell when. Now when we got near to his fathers we saw a man some Eighty Rods Before us run acros the street with a Bundle in his hand. 'There,' says Joseph, 'there is Martin going a Cros the road with some thing in his hand.' Says I, 'how Could you know him so far? Says he, 'I Believe it is him,' and when we Came up it was Martin with a Bunch of morman Books. He Came to us and after Compliments he says, 'The Books will

not sell for no Body wants them. Joseph says, 'I think they will sell well.' Says he, 'I want a Commandment.' 'Why,' says Joseph, 'fullfill what you have got.' 'But,' says he, 'I must have a Commandment.' Joseph put him off. But he insisted three or four times he must have a Commandment." Original spelling has been preserved throughout the chapter.

28. Joseph Smith, History, vol. A-1, 34.
29. The date for the revelation that followed section 19 was copied incorrectly, but it was later changed to 6 April 1830. See Revelation, 6 April 1830 [D&C 21], in *JSP*, D1:126–30.

*Joseph Smith and Martin Harris reviewing the bound Book of Mormon. Watercolor by Anthony Sweat.*

# 11

# THE PUBLICATION OF THE BOOK OF MORMON

*[handwritten note: Oliver Cowdery and Hyrum Smith supervised the printing of the Book of Mormon]*

*[handwritten note: while Cowdery did the bulk of the copying Hyrum Smith and one other (not identified) person also helped]*

The actual printing of the Book of Mormon was primarily facilitated by Oliver Cowdery and Hyrum Smith. In the summer of 1829, Cowdery had begun creating a complete copy of the Book of Mormon manuscript.[1] This copied manuscript, often referred to as the printer's manuscript, was intended for use by Grandin's print shop as they typeset the book. The men were taking no chances that some nefarious person might get ahold of the original manuscript and steal it as had happened with the "book of Lehi" that Martin Harris had borrowed in 1828. Along with making a copy of the manuscript, the men took further steps to maintain a tight control on the text. They provided Grandin's typesetter, John Gilbert, with only a few of the pages at a time so there would be less of a chance for anyone to steal the text. *[handwritten note: Type Setter John Gilbert]* The care they took to protect the manuscript reflected their fear that others might take steps to harm or steal the work. Despite this concern, in a demonstration of the trust he had in Cowdery and his brother, Joseph Smith left Palmyra to return to his home in Harmony only weeks after the printing began. In his absence he communicated with Oliver Cowdery through a series of letters, the earliest surviving correspondence penned by Joseph Smith.

❖ FROM DARKNESS UNTO LIGHT

## The Printed Pages of the Book of Mormon

Though it is not known precisely why Joseph Smith left at such a crucial time in the printing of the Book of Mormon, he reported in a letter to Oliver Cowdery on 22 October 1829 that one of the reasons he left Palmyra was to spread the news about the Book of Mormon. He explained that his trip was "prosperous" and that people had been requesting copies of the Book of Mormon. Joseph wrote that "we shall be glad to have truth prevail[.] there begins to be a great call for our books in this country[.] the mind of the people are very much excited when they find that there is a copy right obtained and that there is really books about to be printed." Though it is unknown if those he spoke with actually prepaid for books, Josiah Stowell, Smith's previous employer, offered to buy five or six hundred dollars' worth. Such a request to buy books in bulk also indicated that Smith was trying to pre-sell the books while he was gone. Cowdery wrote back to Joseph that "we rejoice to hear that you are well and we also rejoice to hear that you have a prospect of obtaining Some money."[2] There were numerous merchants and booksellers in New York and Pennsylvania that may have been interested in purchasing copies of the Book of Mormon, but it seems that Joseph and his colleagues were particularly interested in using the book to attract converts.

According to one local editor, Joseph Smith and the other believers had already begun to "preach the doctrines contained in the GOLD BIBLE."[3] In fact, they began using the early printed sheets of the book in their proselyting efforts. William Hyde reported that his family was given loose pages of the printed Book of Mormon by their neighbor, Warren A. Cowdery, who had obtained them from his brother Oliver. Those pages were the first step in the conversion of the Hyde family.[4] In another instance, Thomas B. Marsh, who was a Methodist from Charlestown, Massachusetts, visited Martin Harris, Oliver Cowdery, and others during that fall and took interest in the Book of Mormon. Marsh explained that in the summer of 1829 he "thought the Spirit required [him] to make a journey West." He and a colleague departed from their hometowns seeking religious enlightenment as they traveled, though they apparently did not have any specific purpose guiding where they went; according to Marsh, they were directed by the Spirit. They eventually ended up in Livingston County, New York, just south of Rochester in a small town called Lima, where they stayed for approximately three months. On their way back to Massachusetts they stopped in Palmyra and learned

200

# THE PUBLICATION OF THE BOOK OF MORMON ❖

that the Book of Mormon was in the process of being published there. They also met Martin Harris, who took them to meet Oliver Cowdery, apparently then at Grandin's print shop in the center of town. Marsh explained that Cowdery "gave [him] all the information concerning the Book [he] wanted" and sent him home with the first sixteen printed pages of it.[5] Marsh was sincerely interested in the Book of Mormon and what Cowdery had told him about it, even writing back to Cowdery a few weeks later that he had shared the news of the Book of Mormon with others in Massachusetts.[6] Marsh continued to correspond with Cowdery and eventually moved to Palmyra in September 1830 and was baptized a member of the Church.[7]

Pomeroy Tucker, E. B. Grandin's brother-in-law, reflected back on this period and remembered that there were a variety of people from the surrounding area who were the "pioneer Mormon disciples." He remembered the names of a few dozen people from Palmyra, Macedon, Brighton, Pultneyville, Fayette, Farmington, and Manchester who had embraced Joseph Smith's teachings as early as the fall of 1829.[8] Local newspapers reported the efforts of these believers to evangelize outside of Palmyra. One wrote that "some few evenings since, a man in the town of Mendon," just east of Rochester, was preaching from the "GOLD BIBLE," though the paper quickly pointed out this preacher had been unsuccessful.[9] Like Marsh, others were also given early sheets containing the printed Book of Mormon pages and took them hundreds of miles away from Palmyra to show them to people they knew. On a boat ride up the Erie Canal on his way to Canada, one early believer, Solomon Chamberlain, listened as a woman on the boat excitedly described the "Gold Bible" to other passengers. Chamberlain remembered, "when she mentioned gold Bible, I felt a shock of the power of God go from head to foot, I said to myself, I shall soon find why I have been led in this singular manner." Getting off at the Palmyra dock, he walked through town and down to Manchester, where the Smith's farm was located. Chamberlain found Hyrum Smith pacing back and forth when he opened the door to the small log house. Before anyone could speak, he began telling them that all "Churches and Denominations on the earth had become corrupt" and that God "would shortly rise up a Church, that would never be confounded nor brought down and be like unto the Apostolic Church." Astonished by his preaching, Hyrum, Joseph Sr., and some of the Whitmers gathered around Chamberlain and for "2 days . . . they instructed [Chamberlain], in the manuscripts of the Book of Mormon."

They then led him back up to Grandin's shop in Palmyra, where they gave him sixty-four pages of the Book of Mormon to take with him on his journey to Canada. Chamberlain remembered, "I preached all that I knew concerning Mormonism, to all both high and low, rich and poor."[10]

In addition to giving some of the early printed pages of the Book of Mormon, the small group of believers also distributed copies of the book's title page as an advertisement to encourage people to buy the book. Even before the book was printed, therefore, portions of it reached fairly prominent persons in New York, some of whom commented on the Book of Mormon publicly.

Perhaps one of the most interesting inquirers was Dr. Cornelius Blatchly, a radical Quaker advocate for social reform and egalitarianism and a supporter of the growing Anti-Masonic movement.[11] Blatchly had carried on a correspondence with radical Quaker Elias Hicks in the mid-1820s and had gained national attention in 1825 by way of a letter he had sent to former president Thomas Jefferson, extolling the virtues of Robert Owens's communal-living ideologies. Jefferson's gracious but ultimately unsupportive response was published in several newspapers.[12] By November of 1829, Blatchly had essentially abandoned organized religion and declared himself "a devout follower of no man, woman, party, or church."[13] However, in the latter part of 1829, Blatchly became interested in the stories of the Book of Mormon because "Copies of the title page, and other means, have been taken to sell next year this wonderful translation." He had recently received a copy of the title page himself and decided to request more information from "those concerned in, and witnesses to the facts and circumstances." He wrote a letter directly to Martin Harris to find out more about the story surrounding the Book of Mormon and the gold plates. He particularly wanted to know if the book "could be substantiated by indisputable evidences and witnesses" on the basis that those "who take such means to make and sell their books to a wondering community, ought to afford incontrovertible truths."[14]

Dealing with some of the first critical questions from outside the area about the authenticity of the Book of Mormon, Oliver Cowdery replied to Blatchly's letter. Blatchly had opened his inquiry by asking why Joseph Smith had been listed as the "author" on the title page of the work if it was actually just a translation of an ancient text. The title page stated

"BY JOSEPH SMITH, JUNIOR, AUTHOR AND PROPRIETOR," but this phrase originated from the legal dictum of Joseph's printed copyright, which was also printed with the Book of Mormon. Cowdery replied to Blatchly that "Joseph Smith Jr., certainly was the writer of the work, called the book of Mormon, which was written in ancient Egyptian characters,—which was a dead record to us until translated" by Joseph Smith. Cowdery added, "And he, by a gift from God, has translated it into our language." Blatchly did not accept this explanation and expressed in a newspaper article the belief that if Joseph was not the originator of the writing found on the gold plates that Joseph was not the author. This semantic argument with Cowdery over the meaning of the word "author" was really aimed at demonstrating Blatchly's contempt for the idea that Joseph Smith in fact had an ancient record and had been given the power to translate it into English.

However, Blatchly's skepticism went beyond mere semantics. He maintained, in an argument that would be echoed for centuries, that if the record really did exist, Joseph Smith needed only to show it to others to prove its physical reality and hence its religious import. He reasoned: "It appears, therefore, a very unreasonable thing to deprive mankind of good, sufficient and incontrovertible testimony." Dismissing fears over the safety of the plates, Blatchly wrote that "such an ancient, curious, and most precious golden relic of primitive ages, I should judge, would be estimable beyond conception, and would be preserved, with the greatest care by good or wise beholders, from any violence or rudeness." Cowdery replied by explaining that it was a commandment from the Lord that Joseph Smith could not show the gold plates to others, but also that the Lord had allowed a few, including himself, to see the plates. Cowdery also sent him a description of the plates and testified of his experience when he saw them. He told Blatchly that he had been "far from any inhabitants, in a remote field,[15] at the time we saw the record, of which it has been spoken, brought and laid before us, by an angel, arrayed in glorious light, [who] ascend [descended I suppose][16] out of the midst of heaven."[17]

Although Blatchly believed that all inquiry into the authenticity of the Book of Mormon could be answered merely by allowing others to see the plates, both the angel that had delivered Joseph the plates and the revelations he had received informed Joseph otherwise. In response to a similar request to see the plates by Martin Harris in March 1829, one of Joseph's revelations had declared that "if they will not believe my words [found in the Book of Mormon] they would not believe my servants [Joseph Smith] if it were possible he could show them [the gold plates]."[18] In the revelation, the voice of the Lord explained that the miraculous nature of the translation and Joseph Smith's otherwise unexplainable production of the text of the Book of Mormon should be enough evidence for an honest seeker of truth to know the gold plates were real. Furthermore, the revelation also taught Harris that the claim that people would believe if only they saw the plates rested upon unsound logic. Believing was not a matter of logic but of faith. Even if Joseph Smith could show the gold plates openly to all who inquired, it would not have convinced them to believe, even though men like Blatchly claimed they would if shown.

As the text of the Book of Mormon itself declares, only seers could translate the records described in the Book of Mormon. They were carefully protected and passed down from prophet to prophet along with seer stone interpreters to enable King Mosiah, for example, to translate the twenty-four gold plates created by the brother of Jared.[19] Additionally, once the records of the ancient American prophets were compiled and abridged by Mormon and Moroni, they declared that no one could read the "reformed Egyptian" they used to write on the gold plates. The Book of Mormon explained that seer stones had been "prepared from the beginning, and were handed down from generation to generation, for the purpose of interpreting languages." It also explained that they had "been kept and preserved by the hand of the Lord . . . and whosoever has these things is called seer."[20] The reality of the gold plates, in other words, could only be known by examining the translated text—not the characters or the plates. Essentially, nullifying Blatchly's insistence that all who believed in the gold plates were being duped if they did not see them with their own eyes, the text of the Book of Mormon had already explained that even if one were able to examine the inscriptions on the plates they would not be able to understand them. In fact, Joseph Smith and Martin Harris knew firsthand that the most learned of scholars could not decipher the characters on the plates at all. How then could viewing the plates themselves have convinced those scholars, or anyone, that Smith's translation was accurate? In fact, bereft as they were of the ability to read the characters, a secular study of the plates would have likely created more questions about Joseph Smith's translation, ultimately leading readers to judge its contents on secular rather than religious grounds. Nonetheless, Blatchly was not convinced.[21]

A few months later, Blatchly again published a criticism of the Book of Mormon. This time, perhaps in response to Cowdery's insistence that God would not permit the viewing of the gold plates by inquirers to facilitate belief, Blatchly assailed the text of the Book of Mormon itself. Sometime in early to mid-February 1830, Blatchly had obtained one of the sixteen-page gatherings of the forthcoming book. Precisely who gave Blatchly the printed pages is unknown. It is possible that Oliver Cowdery sent the pages as part of their correspondence with one another. However, this possibility is not supported by any corroborating evidence. For instance, if Cowdery had sent the pages, why did Blatchly not reference another communication from Cowdery in his condemnatory article? More likely is that Jonathan Hadley, the editor of the *Palmyra Freeman*, had obtained some of the pages and sent them to Blatchly. Throughout Blatchly's February commentary on the gold plates, he quoted extensively from Hadley's article on the "Gold Bible" from the *Freeman*. Blatchly's support of the working class had led him to support the antiestablishment, Anti-Masonic movement, and Hadley denounced masonry with a zeal paralleled by few. It is also possible that Elias Hicks, the famous Quaker radical, obtained either the Book of Mormon pages or information about the plates when he was preaching in Palmyra in early September 1829.[22] In any case, Blatchly must have had some Palmyra-area contact that not only sent him the pages but told him the plates weighed a mere thirty pounds, information not found in any other published accounts.[23]

Blatchly attacked what he saw as subpar writing in the Book of Mormon. He mocked the repetitious use of phrases such as "and it came to pass" and "yea." He further assailed sentences that seemed to use poor grammar and word choice. Ultimately, he condemned the book and cautioned the readers of his article, "These facts are given to caution people not to spend their money uselessly for a book that is more probable a hoax—or a money-making speculation—or an enthusiastic delusion, than a revelation of facts by the Almighty."[24]

While Blatchly's public assault on the veracity of the Book of Mormon presaged the general criticisms that would be leveled by most commentators once the book was published, a greater threat to the book came from much closer to home, in fact from within the printing office in Palmyra itself. Despite the caution and care taken by these men to protect the Book of Mormon text and shepherd it through the publication process from outside interlopers or a sticky-fingered pressman, problems arose from a complication that none of them had ever anticipated. One Sunday afternoon Hyrum Smith was troubled by a feeling of uneasiness. He told Oliver "that his peculiar feelings led him to believe that something was going wrong at the printing office." Because it was the Sabbath, the men debated about whether or not it would be appropriate to travel into town to the printing office to see for themselves what was going on. Exasperated, Hyrum finally said, "I shall not stop to consider the matter any longer for I am going [and] you may suit yourself about the matter but I will not suffer such uneasiness any longer without knowing the cause." Persuaded, Cowdery joined him and they made their way to E. B. Grandin's printing house. When they arrived, they were astonished to find another man using the press to produce his own paper. But their real alarm came when they glanced down at the sheets the man was printing and found he was printing portions of the Book of Mormon in his paper. This man was Abner Cole.

## Abner Cole's Unauthorized Printing of the Book of Mormon

At roughly the same time the printing of the Book of Mormon began in September, Abner Cole had also begun publishing his newspaper, the *Reflector*, on nights and weekends. Cole printed his paper using the exact same press that was used throughout the week to print the Book of Mormon, under the pseudonym "Obadiah Dogberry."[25] Cole had worked as a lawyer and even a local judge before he began publishing his paper, and his quick and biting wit marked his satirical publications. No sooner did Cole start his newspaper than he immediately began deriding the Book of Mormon. He wrote on 2 September 1829, "The Golden Bible, by Joseph Smith Junior, author and proprietor, is now in press and will shortly appear. Priestcraft is short lived!"[26] This first notice suggested that Cole was in fact reading the information from the title page of the Book of Mormon. The title page, with the designation of Joseph Smith as "author and proprietor," would not have

## THE PUBLICATION OF THE BOOK OF MORMON

> *Abner Cole uses Grandin's press at night and on the weekends to publish his paper "The Reflector" which includes extracts from the Book of Mormon*

been printed yet in Grandin's print shop by the time Cole set the type on his paper, but it had been published by both the *Wayne Sentinel* and the *Palmyra Freeman* in June and August respectively. His knowledge of it showed that he had more than just a passing interest in the story of Joseph Smith and the gold plates. Throughout the first few months of his paper's existence, Cole had access to the earliest proof sheets of the Book of Mormon as they hung drying in Grandin's print shop or stacked on the floor awaiting the eventual

*Abner Cole's* Reflector, *September 4, 1830.*

207

❖ FROM DARKNESS UNTO LIGHT

binding. Unbeknownst to Hyrum Smith or Oliver Cowdery, Cole had begun reading through these earliest printed pages and began incorporating ideas and phrases from the pages in an effort to humorously mock the entire "Gold Bible" project. For instance, just days after the first pages of the Book of Mormon came off the press, Cole wrote that once the Book of Mormon was printed, "Great and marvelous things will 'come to pass' about those days," deriding the oft-repeated phrase in the book.[27] In the first chapter of 1 Nephi that Cole was likely reading, forty-one of the forty-nine paragraphs began with some form of the phrase "and it came to pass," an opportunity for insult that Cole could not pass up, even though his readers could not themselves have recognized the phrases from the as-yet-unpublished Book of Mormon. At any rate, at this early stage, Cole was willing to exploit the copyrighted content as soon as the pages came off the press in order to sell his newspaper.

Cole's vitriolic reaction to the Book of Mormon and his attempt to profit from sardonically commenting on it reflected the influence Joseph Smith's claim to possess and to have translated ancient golden plates was having on the community even before it was published. In fact, Cole's commentaries on the content of the Book of Mormon in his paper demonstrated that he had a greater understanding of the project than just access to the already printed pages would allow.[28] Cole may have heard about some of the topics within the pages of the Book of Mormon from his interaction with Martin Harris or others who were helping Joseph to print the book and who had access to the Book of Mormon manuscript. As early as 23 September 1829, Cole mentioned a place called the "New Jerusalem" that was described as a gathering place in the last days for believers as part of the Book of Mormon's description of Christ's post-Resurrection ministry. That particular account from the Book of Mormon was not printed on Grandin's press until months later, demonstrating that Cole knew about it from another source by September when he printed his article.[29] Though Joseph Smith and other Church leaders would discuss the concept of the New Jerusalem at length in September and October of 1830 and eventually dedicate Independence, Missouri, as the gathering place in the summer of 1831, Cole's understanding of the concept demonstrates that believers were highlighting the coming New Jerusalem prophesied of in the unpublished Book of Mormon manuscript by the summer and fall of 1829.[30]

Cole's understanding also reflected an early belief that the Book of Mormon and Joseph Smith's preaching would have particular impact on the American Indians and that the believers planned to build temples. On 7 October 1829 Cole sarcastically wrote that "The 'New Jerusalem-Reflector'[31] states that the building of the TEMPLE OF NEPHI is to be commenced about the beginning of the first year of the Millennium. Thousands are already flocking to the standard of Joseph the Prophet. The Book of Mormon is expected to astonish the natives!!"[32] One year later, in September 1830, Oliver Cowdery was commanded by a revelation to go preach to the American Indians, and he was told to establish a church among them, where "The City shall be built."[33] Once his missionary companions were chosen, he signed a missionary covenant that declared he would "rear up a pillar as a witness where the Temple of God shall be built, in the glorious New Jerusalem."[34]

Cole's understanding of Book of Mormon doctrines and ideas seems to have come from a mixture of plagiarism and hearsay. Aside from occasional conversations he may have had with local believers or with those that had spoken to believers, Cole's greatest source of information appears to have been the pages of the Book of Mormon that had already been printed and were being stored in Grandin's printing office awaiting binding. For instance, his 7 October reference to the "TEMPLE OF NEPHI" likely came from reading the completed third gathering of the book. Those pages stated, "And I Nephi did build a temple; and I did construct it after the manner of the temple of Solomon."[35]

Cole had gone to great lengths to denigrate Joseph Smith. He had perused Charles Buck's *Theological Dictionary* to find other heretics from the religious past to compare to Joseph Smith in order to deride his claims as a revelator that had brought forth new scripture beyond the Bible. In one publication, Cole made the stark contrast between accepted forms of American Christianity and the ideas Joseph Smith was preaching. He compared Mormonism to Islam, a religion that was not only distinctly non-Christian, but one that was widely regarded by most Americans as being practiced by those in a lower state of civilization, often with distinctly racial overtones. He played upon his own readers' xenophobia and exclaimed that "The 'Gold Bible' is fast gaining credit; the *rapid spread* of Islamism was *no touch* to it." Cole attempted to slow the spread of interest in the Book of Mormon by severing its connection to Christianity and the Bible through his sarcastic commentary. He insinuated that regardless of its popularity, it should be seen by Christians as having as much relevance and sanctity as the Koran. In the same issue of the paper he also compared "the pretensions of Jo Smith Jr." with early modern Christian dissenters. Copying from Buck's dictionary, he asked whether Joseph was like "Egidus Cantor, and . . . William of Hendenison, a Carmelite Monk" from Flanders and Brussels in the early sixteenth century. According to Buck, "They pretended to be honoured with celestial visions; denied that any could arrive at a perfect knowledge of the Holy Scriptures without the extraordinary succors of a divine illumination, and declared the approach of a new revelation from heaven, more perfect than the Gospel of Christ."[36]

By the fall of 1828, Cole had also apparently heard about the revelation that commanded Oliver Cowdery and David Whitmer in June 1829 to call twelve disciples, in the same manner as Christ had appointed disciples in his American ministry described in the Book of Mormon.[37] Cole declared in late September, "The number of Gold Bible Apostles is said to be complete. Jo Smith, Jr. is about to assign to each, a mission to the *heathen*."[38] His mistaken claim that they had actually called twelve disciples may have come as a result of proselyting by the early believers. Cole disdainfully reported that "a man in the town of Mendon, had a loud call to go and preach the doctrines contained in the Gold Bible, under heavy denunciations."[39]

Nevertheless, despite his recurring interest in the "Gold Bible," all of Cole's previous rhetoric against Joseph Smith and his mockery of the Book of Mormon text and the revelations had apparently gone unnoticed by Oliver Cowdery and Hyrum Smith prior to the Sunday evening sometime that winter when Hyrum had felt his uneasy feeling about the printing. On 9 December 1829, Cole had written that the Book of Mormon would "not be ready for delivery for some months to come" but emphasized that many of his readers had encouraged him to begin printing samples of the book.[40] Having already mimicked some of the phrases found in the Book of Mormon, Cole planned on selecting portions of the manuscript to include in his newspaper. Though their proximity suggests that Oliver Cowdery and Hyrum Smith could have easily had access to Cole's paper, they apparently had not read it, and they even seemed surprised that Cole

## THE PUBLICATION OF THE BOOK OF MORMON

was publishing a paper in the print shop at all. They were certainly stunned to learn of Cole's intentions to unlawfully publish parts of the Book of Mormon. Even though Oliver Cowdery corresponded with Joseph Smith during that fall and winter about the progress and problems facing the publication work, Cowdery never mentioned Cole as a problem. Even after Cole had announced his intentions to publish portions of the book, Cowdery's 28 December 1829 letter said nothing to Joseph about Cole's threats.[41] Until they confronted Cole that Sunday evening, Hyrum Smith and Oliver Cowdery were apparently unaware that Cole was publishing portions of the book.

Outraged at Cole's "unfair and dishonest course," Hyrum Smith said to him, "What right have you to print the book of Mormon in this way. Do you not know that we have received a copy right?" An indignant Cole retorted, "It is none of your business sir, I have hired the press and I will print what I please so help yourself." Undeterred, Hyrum insisted to Cole, "I forbid you printing any more of that book in your paper for that is sacred and you must stop it. An enraged Cole dropped whatever pretenses to gentlemanly conduct he had been conveying and barked at Hyrum, "I don't care a dam [*sic*] for what you say Mr. Smith I'm determined that damned Gold bible is going into my paper." The argument escalated and apparently continued for quite some time before Hyrum and Cowdery finally gave up the fight and returned home, determined to inform Joseph Smith of Cole's unauthorized printing of the text.[42]

Joseph Smith Sr. almost immediately set out for Harmony to inform his son of Cole's refusal to halt his printing of text from the Book of Mormon. The idea that the sacred words of the Book of Mormon were being printed amidst biting sarcasm and derision in the *Reflector* apparently bothered Joseph Smith greatly. He and his father returned from Harmony without any delay despite a powerful winter storm that had moved into the area. Lucy Smith remembered that they returned on the next Sunday and that it was "one of the most blustering cold and disagreable [nights] that I ever experinced But they breasted the storm all day long and when they arrived there they were nearly stiffened with the cold." Taking just enough time to warm himself from the cold, Joseph again set out into the weather that same night, this time for the printing office and his impending confrontation with Cole.

❖ FROM DARKNESS UNTO LIGHT

Entering the office, Joseph attempted at first to be congenial with Cole, saluting him and commenting on his hard work. Cole, who likely had been anticipating a confrontation with Joseph Smith since his argument with Oliver Cowdery and Hyrum Smith the week before, responded with a cold pleasantry of his own. Taking up one of Cole's completed papers and seeing for himself the plagiarized text, Joseph declared to the onetime lawyer, "that book and the right [of] publishing it belongs to me and I forbid you [from] meddling [with] it in the least degree." The surly Cole had grown tired of the challenge to his printing and "threw off his coat and rolling up his sleeves came towards" Joseph Smith in an apparent attempt to settle the matter violently. Cole came at Joseph "in a great rage and roaring out at the top of his voice 'do you want to fight sir? Do you want to fight?'" he asserted he would publish whatever he wanted and again yelled, "if you want to fight just come on—"[43]

According to Lucy Smith, Joseph remained calm and said, "Now Mr. Cole you had better keep your coat for it's cold and I am not going to fight nor anything of that sort but you have got to stop printing my book sir I assure you for I know my rights and shall maintain them." The time and effort Joseph had taken to obtain a copyright for the book made him feel that he had every legal advantage over Cole in the dispute. Cole, on the other hand, perhaps sensing the weakness of his legal case, still wanted to resort to his physical arguments to win the dispute. He angrily demanded of Joseph, "if you think you are the best man just take off your coat try it." Joseph Smith, however, would not be goaded into a fight. He instead replied, "there is Law—and you will find that out if you did not know it before but I shall not fight you for that would do no good and there is another way of disposing of the affair that will answer my purpose better than fighting." Lucy recounted that following his assertion of copyright privilege, Joseph was eventually able to persuade Cole to submit to an arbitration of the dispute. It is not known exactly what that arbitration entailed, who performed it, or when it was conducted.[44] In any case, Cole continued to publish segments of the Book of Mormon for at least two more issues of his paper, but he finally ceased after the 21 January issue.

*[Handwritten note at top: The original price for a copy of the Book of Mormon was $1.75. Selling all 5,000 copies should return $8,750]*

THE PUBLICATION OF THE BOOK OF MORMON ❖

## Martin Harris and the Canadian Copyright of the Book of Mormon

Likely at the same time Joseph Smith was in Palmyra to confront Abner Cole, he also had an important meeting with Martin Harris, the financier of the Book of Mormon publication. Although Harris had done precisely what the revelation [D&C 19] had commanded him the previous summer, he clearly had concerns over the money he had paid in the form of the mortgage on his farm. It is unclear whether or not Joseph Smith had ever intended that Harris should receive some compensation in return when the books began to sell, but the revelation indicated that Harris's contribution was a gift rather than a loan. It is possible that Harris became concerned reading Joseph Smith's letter to Oliver Cowdery in October 1829. In it, Smith explained that he was attempting to sell copies of the Book of Mormon in bulk to Josiah Stowell.[45] Harris undoubtedly was cognizant of the fact that the sale of the Book of Mormon could generate over $8,000, since the price of the Book of Mormon had been set at $1.75 by revelation, making it an expensive book in 1830.[46] At that price, if they sold all 5,000 copies of the book, they would have collected $8,750; even after Joseph Smith later reduced the price to $1.25 per book,[47] they would have collected no less than $6,250 if they sold all of the books.[48] In any case, the Abner Cole affair had demonstrated the unforeseen circumstances that might arise that could damage their ability to sell the book. Had Cole proceeded with his publication unabated, the local residents would have seen no need to purchase the entire book to satisfy what was at this point a curiosity that was at least three years in the making. The proceeds from the book were intended to help defray the costs of establishing a new church, but by January, Martin Harris wanted to guarantee he received a portion of the sales. On 16 January 1830, Smith signed an agreement with Harris allowing Harris "equal privilege" to sell copies of the Book of Mormon until he had been reimbursed for the value of his property.[49] Therefore, though it was not part of the original agreement, after 16 January, Harris was guaranteed the ability to sell copies of the Book of Mormon until he had made back his $3,000.

213

❖ FROM DARKNESS UNTO LIGHT

Soon after Smith signed the agreement with Harris, he received another revelation that commanded him and others to obtain a Canadian copyright for the Book of Mormon.[50] Like the American copyright Smith had obtained in June 1829, a Canadian copyright would help protect the Book of Mormon from those who sought to illegally reprint it in the British dominion in Canada. The ability to control the text of the Book of Mormon and the potential sales of it had by then been threatened twice: once in the summer of 1828 and again in January of 1830 when Abner Cole printed excerpts of the Book of Mormon in the *Reflector*.[51] It seems that whatever the impetus was for the signed January agreement with Martin Harris, it had caused Harris to fall once again out of favor. Perhaps because that agreement potentially siphoned off nearly half of the intended proceeds from the sales of the Book of Mormon that were otherwise intended to help create a church, Joseph Smith was displeased in Martin Harris's apparent lack of commitment and faith. Apparently unannounced to Harris,[52] Smith dictated the copyright revelation, which described a covenant between God and those who "assist" him who had "done that which is pleasing in my sight, yea even all save Martin only."[53] The revelation made it clear that the Book of Mormon was to be distributed not just in the local Palmyra area and urged the men to "be dilligent in Securing the Copy right of my work upon all the face of the Earth of which is known by you unto my Servent Joseph." Specifically, it instructed them to travel to Kingston, Canada, and "sell a copyright" obtained there. Because a popular book was usually reprinted in other countries without authorization at any rate in absence of international copyright laws, selling the rights to the Book of Mormon in Canada not only hastened the printing and distribution of the book in that part of the British Empire, but it provided more funds needed to help found the Church. Nevertheless, the revelation hinged the success of the mission to Canada on the righteousness of those they would encounter there. It declared, "if the People harden not their hearts against the enticeings of my spirit & my word" they would be able to sell the copyright. In fact, their response to the Book of Mormon would be to "their condemnation or their salvation."

In response to the revelation, Oliver Cowdery and Hiram Page traveled to Kingston but discovered that there was little interest in the Book of Mormon and that they could not easily obtain a copyright.[54] A local resident apparently informed them that they were more likely to secure

# THE PUBLICATION OF THE BOOK OF MORMON ❖

a copyright if they traveled to York,[55] but rather than proceed more than 160 miles further to the capital, they returned to New York and reported to Joseph Smith at the home of Peter Whitmer Sr. in Fayette Township.[56]

## The Publication Is Completed

This failure to sell the copyright in Canada notwithstanding, the spring of 1830 was time of great optimism and excitement for Joseph Smith and those who believed in his revelations. After years of hard work and anticipation, numerous fiscal trials, and various difficulties with disbelieving antagonists, the words anciently etched onto the gold plates by Nephite prophets would finally be available for all to read. By late March 1830, Luther Howard, who owned the bindery on the second floor of Grandin's three-story shop, had started binding the printed pages of Book of Mormon. The third floor of the shop, where Grandin printed the book, was apparently covered with stacks of paper that composed the content of the 5,000 books. Using a pulley system, Grandin lowered the pages to the second floor, where they were bound by Howard. Then the completed books were lowered to the first floor, where they could be sold and distributed.

Even the selling of the books was fraught with controversy and antagonism, however. Lucy Mack Smith recalled that "the inhabitants of the surrounding country . . . gathered their forces together, far and near, and organizing themselves into a committee of the whole, they resolved, as before, never to purchase one of our books."[57] In the face of this local boycott, Martin Harris was not at first able to sell

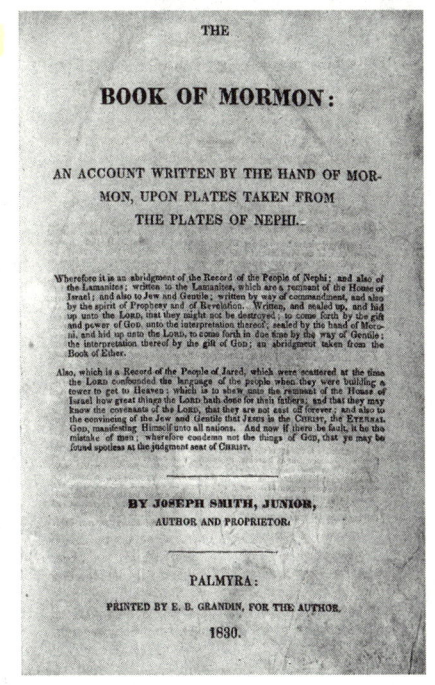

*John Moyle's 1830 copy of the Book of Mormon, Church History Library.*

215

*First edition Book of Mormon. © Intellectual Reserve, Inc.*

the books as readily as he had anticipated. Harris knew that if he were to make back his money, the books needed to sell.[58] In a panic, Harris told Smith, "The Books will not sell for no Body wants them."[59]

But that initial local boycott of the Book of Mormon would give way to hundreds who read it and joined themselves to the newly formed Church as a result of its teachings. Many would have experiences like Rachel Ridgeway Grant, who initially rejected the Mormon message in the face of serious opposition from her pastor but later remarked that reading the Book of Mormon was the turning point. After obtaining a copy, she explained, "I read nearly all night in the Book of Mormon, and felt that it was true, and then I got the spirit of gathering" and moved to live with the rest of the Saints.[60]

Jared Carter had a similar experience. Leaving his home in January 1831 for what he thought would be a business trip of several weeks, Carter first heard about the Book of Mormon from a man opposed to the idea of it in Lisle, Broome County, New York. Despite this negative introduction to the Book of Mormon, Carter explained in his journal that it "caused much astonishment to fill my mind." He obtained a copy of the Book of Mormon and began to read it himself. He explained that "after reading a while in the book of mormon and praying earnestly to the Lord that he would show me the truth of the Book I became immediately convinced that it was a revelation of God." Carter abandoned his previous business plans and went to join himself to the Church.[61]

# THE PUBLICATION OF THE BOOK OF MORMON

Parley P. Pratt eloquently testified of the power of the words of the Book of Mormon. Intrigued by stories of it, he explained what happened when he finally got his hands on a copy: "I opened it with eagerness, and read its title page. I then read the testimony of several witnesses in relation to the manner of its being found and translated. After this I commenced its contents by course. I read all day; eating was a burden, I had no desire for food; sleep was a burden when the night came, for I preferred reading to sleep." Pratt's study of the book led to a spiritual awakening in him. He explained, "As I read, the spirit of the Lord was upon me, and I knew and comprehended that the book was true, as plainly and manifestly as a man comprehends and knows that he exists. My joy was now full, as it were, and I rejoiced sufficiently to more than pay me for all the sorrows, sacrifices and toils of my life."[62]

Parley P. Pratt, *Engraving by George Q. Cannon and Sons*, © Intellectual Reserve, Inc.

In the first days after the publication was finished, Martin Harris may have found few interested in purchasing the Book of Mormon. But the word spread rapidly, and hundreds soon obtained copies of the book and joined the newly founded Church of Christ that would eventually come to be known as The Church of Jesus Christ of Latter-day Saints. By November 1830, Oliver Cowdery and his missionary companions had baptized dozens in the Kirtland, Ohio, area, and Cowdery wrote back to Joseph Smith, "There is considerable call here for books. I wish you would send five hundred immediately here."[63] In fact, less than a year after Harris had bemoaned the fact that the books would not sell, Joseph Smith sent a letter to Martin from the new headquarters of the Church in Kirtland and told him, "it is nec[e]ssary for you to come here as soon as you can . . . [and] bring or cause to be brought all the books, as the work is here breaking forth on the east west north and south."[64]

❖ FROM DARKNESS UNTO LIGHT

# Notes

1. While Cowdery produced most of the copied manuscript, Hyrum Smith and at least one other unidentified scribe also aided in the process. See Skousen, *The Printer's Manuscript of the Book of Mormon*, 1:9.
2. Letter from Oliver Cowdery, 6 November 1829, in *JSP*, D1:98. Original spelling has been preserved throughout the chapter.
3. "Selected Items," *Reflector*, 23 September 1829.
4. Private Journal of William Hyde, Church History Library.
5. T. B. Marsh, "1, Historians Office, Histories of the Twelve," ca. 1858–1880, Church History Library.
6. Letter from Oliver Cowdery, 6 November 1829, in *JSP*, D1:100.
7. Marsh, "1, Historians Office, Histories of the Twelve." See Revelation, September 1830–F [D&C 31], in *JSP*, D1:193.
8. Pomeroy Tucker, *Origins, Rise, and Progress of Mormonism* (1867), 37. However, not all who heard about the Book of Mormon or read its pages joined the movement. Tucker also wrote about George Crane of Macedon, who was "a Quaker of intelligence, property, and high respectability." After being handed pages of the Book of Mormon to read, Crane rebuked Joseph Smith, "denouncing them as in a high degree blasphemous and wicked."
9. "Selected Items," *Reflector*, 23 September 1829.
10. See Larry C. Porter, "Solomon Chamberlain—Early Missionary," *BYU Studies* 12, no. 3 (Spring 1972): 314–17.
11. Blatchly was also a prominent physician. He had only months earlier published an article, "Two Cases of Ascaris Lumbricoides," *New York Medical and Physical Journal* 6, no. 1 (1827): 209.
12. Thomas Jefferson to Mr. [Cornelius Camden] Blatchly, 22 October 1824, *Aurora and Franklin Gazette*, 24 September 1825.
13. Sean Wilentz, *Chants Democratic: New York City and the Rise of the American Working Class, 1788–1850* (Oxford: Oxford University Press, 2004), 158.
14. "The New Bible," *Gospel Luminary*, 10 December 1829.
15. This is the earliest account known that describes where the Three Witnesses' vision of the gold plates occurred. It, however, explains that it occurred in a field rather than the woods. "The New Bible," *Gospel Luminary*, 10 December 1829.
16. The insertions here are Blatchly's.
17. "The New Bible," *Gospel Luminary*, 10 December 1829.

18. Revelation, March 1829 [D&C 5], in *JSP*, D1:17.
19. Mosiah 28:17.
20. Mosiah 28:13–16.
21. "The New Bible," *Gospel Luminary*, 10 December 1829.
22. Elias Hicks, *Journal of the Life and Religious Labours of Elias Hicks*, 5th ed. (New York: Isaac T. Hopper, 1832), 433.
23. "The New Bible," *Gospel Luminary*, 10 December 1829.
24. "Caution Against the Golden Bible," *New-York Telescope*, 20 February 1830.
25. By fall of 1829, Smith's possession and translation of the plates were well known in the region. In June 1829 the *Wayne Sentinel* reported on the rumors surrounding the translation of the "Golden Bible" and explained that "most people entertain an idea that the whole matter is the result of a gross imposition and a grosser superstition. It is pretended that it will be published as soon as the translation is completed." Jonathan Hadley of the *Palmyra Freeman* also reported that by early August 1829 Joseph Smith's translation of the plates was "generally known and spoken of as the 'Golden Bible.'" The *Freeman* incredulously reported Joseph Smith's claims: "Now it appears not a little strange that there should have been deposited in this western world, and in the secluded town of Manchester, too, a record of this description: and still more so, that a person like this Smith (very illiterate) should have been gifted by inspiration to find and interpret it." Newspapers as far away as Ohio reprinted this denunciation of the "Golden Bible." News Item, *Wayne Sentinel*, 26 June 1829, [3], italics in original; "Golden Bible," *Palmyra Freeman*, 11 August 1829, [2], italics in original; see also, for example, "Golden Bible," *Niagara Courier* (Lockport, NY), 27 August 1829, [2]; "Golden Bible," *Rochester Advertiser and Telegraph*, 31 August 1829, [2]; "Golden Bible," *Painesville Telegraph*, 22 September 1829, [3]; "Golden Bible," *Salem Gazette*, 2 October 1829, [1].
26. *Reflector*, 3 September 1829.
27. *Reflector*, 16 September 1829.
28. When the Book of Mormon was printed, it was done on sixteen-page sheets, front and back, totaling thirty-two pages in each signature. But Cole did not have access to most of the Book of Mormon until months after Grandin began printing it, because each of the pages was printed 5,000 times before the typesetter would move on to the following pages.
29. "Selected Items," *Reflector*, 23 September 1829. Cole wrote, "We understand that Abraham Chaddock intends to build the first house in Harris' New-Jerusalem."

❖ FROM DARKNESS UNTO LIGHT

30. Revelation, September 1830–A [D&C 29], in *JSP*, D1:177.
31. Likely a tongue-in-cheek insult directed at rival Jonathan Hadley's *Palmyra Freeman* that had just recently published its own lengthy attacks on Joseph Smith. Not only was Hadley a competitor, but Cole disapproved of the anti-Masonic bent to Hadley's *Freeman*.
32. *Reflector*, 7 October 1829.
33. September 1829–B [D&C 28], in *JSP*, D1:184.
34. Covenant of Oliver Cowdery and Others, 17 October 1830, in *JSP*, D1:204.
35. 2 Nephi 5:16.
36. Charles Buck, *Theological Dictionary*, 1823, 354.
37. Revelation, June 1829–C [D&C 18], in *JSP*, D1:75.
38. "Selected Items," *Reflector*, 23 September 1829.
39. *Reflector*, 23 September 1829. Compare Tucker, *Origins, Rise, and Progress of Mormonism*, 80.
40. "Gold Bible," *Reflector*, 9 December 1829, [1].
41. Letter from Oliver Cowdery, 28 December 1829, in *JSP*, D1:101.
42. Lucy Mack Smith, History, 1844–1845, book 9, [9–10].
43. Lucy Mack Smith, History, 1844–1845, book 9, [12–13].
44. It is difficult to determine exactly when Hyrum's and Joseph's confrontations with Cole respectively happened, but given Lucy Smith's account of the terrible cold weather that Joseph Smith endured to return home, the initial confrontation with Hyrum likely occurred on 3 January 1830 and the second with Joseph Smith on 10 January 1830. In any case, by 16 January Joseph Smith was in Palmyra to conclude an agreement with Martin Harris concerning the proceeds of the sales of the forthcoming books. See Letter from Oliver Cowdery, 28 December 1829, in *JSP*, D1:101.
45. In March 1830 as the binder finished the books, Grandin advertised in the *Wayne Sentinel* that he was selling the book retail and wholesale. *Wayne Sentinel*, 26 March 1830.
46. Howe, *Mormonism Unvailed*, 252.
47. Agreement with Martin Harris, 16 January 1830.
48. Of course, by the time the lower rate had been instituted, many books had already been sold.
49. A printer's apprentice in Palmyra, Orsamus Turner, who apparently saw the agreement, wrote that it was "signed by the Prophet Joseph himself, and witnessed by Oliver Cowdery, and secures to Martin Harris one half of the proceeds of the sale

of the Gold Bible until he was fully reimbursed." Turner, *History of the Pioneer Settlement of Phelps*, 216.

50. Though the only copy of this revelation (in the Book of Commandments and Revelations) is simply dated 1830—and placed between two April 1830 revelations—David Whitmer helped narrow the dating when he recalled that the revelation was dictated in January 1830 and that Cowdery and Page crossed Lake Ontario on the ice to reach Kingston, which only would have been possible that winter between January and early March. See Traughber, "False Prophecies," J. L. Traughber Collection, J. Willard Marriott Library, University of Utah, Salt Lake City. They could not have left before the Martin Harris agreement on 16 January because it had been an unusually warm winter and Lake Ontario was not frozen until at least 15 January. The following newspapers gave the weather and indicated when the lake was frozen enough to walk on: Kingston Bay froze on 9 January 1830. On 15 January the Hudson froze. On 18 January 1830 the Erie Canal was "free from ice." On 19 January 1830 in Albany there were thunder showers. By 29 January 1830 "the Hudson [was] locked with ice down below the Highlands." They also could not have walked back on the ice after mid-March. By 13 March the ice had thinned enough that it was questionable whether one could travel across it. By 20 March it was recorded that "we have had for the last two days a rapid thaw; the slighting, however, as yet has not been much affected.—the mometer this day rose to 60." *Kingston Chronicle*, 9 January 1830, 2; "From Albany," *New-York Spectator*, 15 January 1830, 1; "Erie Canal," *Louisville Public Advertiser*, 18 January 1830, 3; *New-York Spectator*, 19 January 1830, 3; "The Weather," *Kingston Chronicle*, 13 March 1830, 3; "The Weather," *Kingston Chronicle*, 20 February 1830, 2.

51. "From the Book of Mormon," *Reflector*, 2 January 1830, 1; "Gold Bible," *Reflector*, 13 January 1830, 17; "Book of Mormon," *Reflector*, 22 January 1830, 27–28; Lucy Mack Smith, History, 1844–1845, book 9, [9–10]; and Wadsworth, "Copyright Laws and the 1830 Book of Mormon," 89–91.

52. Hiram Page, Fishing River, MO, to William E. McLellin, 2 February 1848, typescript, Letters and Documents Copied from Originals in the Office of the Church Historian, Reorganized Church, Church History Library. "In a sly manor so as to keep Martin Haris from drawing a share of the money."

53. David Whitmer later recalled that Hyrum Smith suggested to Joseph that they could make money by selling the publication rights for the Book of Mormon in Upper Canada. Hiram Page later recalled that they assembled at the Manchester

221

home of Joseph Smith Sr. to obtain a revelation that would tell them whether they should travel to Canada to sell the rights of the Book of Mormon to printers. Whitmer, *Address to All Believers*, 31; Hiram Page, Fishing River, MO, to William E. McLellin, 2 February 1848, typescript, Letters and Documents Copied from Originals in the Office of the Church Historian, Reorganized Church, Church History Library.

54. Regardless of the fact that Canada did not have binding laws pertaining to copyrighted materials, the British copyright law also did not provide actual protection for its North American subjects, leaving very little protection for any books printed in the Canadian provinces. The 1709 Statute of Anne technically provided copyright protection for British subjects of the "four provinces" of Canada, but technical rules found with the laws required the authors of such works to physically register the copyrighted material with Stationers Hall in London. *8 Anne c. 19* (enacted in 1710); see also *41 Geo. III, c. 107* (1801); and *54 Geo. III, c. 156* (1814). A 1747 ruling by the British Court of Sessions determined that "no Action lies upon the Statute, except for such books as have been entered at Stationers Hall." From 1814 to 1835 no author or printer registered any books from the Canadian provinces, and in part because of the lack of enforcement, even if they had registered their books it would have offered them little or no protection for the imprints they made and sold in North America. See *Books and Pamphlets Published in Canada*, 15–39; Fleming and others, *History of the Book in Canada*, 1:352; Ehat, "'Securing' the Prophet's Copyright in the Book of Mormon," 4–70. Ultimately, Canada had not enacted its own copyright laws until years later, and British copyright protection was only effective in England. Lower Canada created copyright laws in 1832, but copyrights could not be enforced until 1841, when provincial legislatures enacted local statutes. See Vogel, *Early Mormon Documents*, 5:259n11; Fleming et al., *History of the Book in Canada*, 1:352, 456n35; *An Act for the protection of Copy Rights in this Province*, S. Prov. C. 1841 (4 & 5 Vict.), c. 61; and *An Act for the Protection of Copy Rights*, S.L.C. 1832, c. 53. Therefore, the only copyright that was available in Canada to Joseph Smith and his colleagues was under British common law and would have only been enforceable in England. See Revelation, circa Early 1830, in *JSP*, D1:108.

55. Hiram Page, Fishing River, MO, to William E. McLellin, 2 February 1848, typescript, letters and documents copied from originals in the Office of the Church Historian, Reorganized Church, Church History Library.

56. More than half a century later David Whitmer, in an attempt to demonstrate that Joseph Smith had become a fallen prophet shortly after the translation of the Book of Mormon was complete, questioned the legitimacy of the revelation because of the failure of Cowdery and Page to secure and sell a copyright in Canada. He claimed that in November of 1831, at a council held to consider printing the revelations, Whitmer confronted Smith regarding his intentions for the copyright revelation, at which time Smith repudiated it as a "false" revelation. While convenient for Whitmer, this late reminiscence would not explain why John Whitmer copied it into the Book of Commandments and Revelations only a few months earlier if Joseph Smith already believed it to be a "false" revelation. For his part, Hiram Page, one of the men that had actually walked to Canada because of the revelation, left no indication that he had bitter feelings about the revelation. Nevertheless, along with one other revelation copied into the Book of Commandments and Revelations, this revelation to go to Canada was not published in the 1833 Book of Commandments even though it showed all of the prepublication editing marks of the other revelations. Traughber, "False Prophecies," J. L. Traughber Collection, J. Willard Marriott Library, University of Utah, Salt Lake City, UT; David Whitmer, *Address to All Believers*, 31.
57. Lucy Mack Smith, History, book 9. Lucy Mack Smith, *Biographical Sketches*, 142. Lucy Mack Smith recalled that "half of the price for the printing was to be paid by Martin Harris, and the residue by my two sons, Joseph and Hyrum." Though she dated the agreement to the summer of 1829, her statement indicates that Harris's "equal privilege" may have given him the right to sell half the books.
58. On 26 March it was announced that the Book of Mormon was for sale at the Palmyra Book Store. *Wayne Sentinel*, 26 March 1830.
59. Knight, Reminiscence, 6–7.
60. *Young Woman's Journal* 16–17 (1905–6): 551.
61. Jared Carter, Journal, MS 1441, Church History Library, 2.
62. Parley P. Pratt, ed., *Autobiography of Parley P. Pratt* (Salt Lake City: Deseret Book, 1985), 22.
63. Oliver Cowdery to Joseph Smith, 12 November 1830, in *JSP*, D1:213.
64. Joseph Smith to Martin Harris, 22 February 1831, in *JSP*, D1:262–63.

*Joseph Smith with seer stone and hat. Watercolor by Anthony Sweat.*

# 12

# Conclusion

Only days after the Book of Mormon was first available for sale in Grandin's shop, Joseph Smith, along with other believers, formally founded the Church of Christ on 6 April 1830. Soon after the meeting began, Joseph and Oliver ordained each other to be the first and second elders of the Church respectively, to which those in attendance gave their common consent. At that meeting, Oliver Cowdery was instructed by a revelation given through Joseph Smith to lay his hands upon Joseph's head and ordain him to be "a seer & translator & prophet, an Apostle of Jesus Christ, an Elder of the Church."[1]

However, only a few months later, Joseph Smith found his seership challenged. It started in the summer of 1830 when he received a letter from Cowdery, who was then in Fayette. Rather than being a pleasant communication from his scribe and friend, the letter ordered Joseph Smith to make a change to the revelatory text now known as Doctrine and Covenants 20, which had just been adopted as the Articles and Covenants of the Church in a conference held a few weeks earlier. Cowdery had taken great issue with a requirement in the Articles and Covenants concerning baptism that he felt differed from teachings found in the Book of Mormon. He audaciously wrote, "I command you in the name of God to erase those words, that no priestcraft be amongst us." Ironically, Joseph Smith's seership, his role as prophet and leader of the Church, was being challenged on the basis of the words found in the Book of Mormon that he, through his role as a seer, had produced. Cowdery held that the words dictated by Joseph Smith during the translation were somehow closer to divine truth than the ones revealed by Joseph afterward. Stunned by the tone and content of the letter, Joseph immediately made the two-day journey to Fayette to persuade Cowdery of his error. When he arrived, he was shocked to learn that all of the Whitmer family also believed that Joseph had made an error in the revelation. Cowdery and the Whitmers seemed at first entirely unwilling to listen to Joseph. Joseph Smith's history explained that it was "not without both labor and perseverance" that he "could prevail with any of them to reason calmly on the subject." The heated discussion continued until finally Joseph convinced Christian Whitmer that his revelation clarified rather than contradicted the Book of Mormon. With Christian on his side, Joseph convinced Cowdery and the Whitmer family "that they had been in error, and that the sentence in dispute was in accordance of the rest of the commandment."[2]

Only weeks after this controversy seemed settled, another arose in Fayette among the Whitmers and Oliver Cowdery. Hiram Page, one of the eleven witnesses of the gold plates, had begun to record his own revelations that contradicted things taught by Joseph Smith. Joseph Smith's history explained that Page had "got in his possession, a certain stone, by which he had obtained . . . revelations, concerning the upbuilding of Zion, the order of the Church, etc., all of which were entirely at variance with the order of God's house, as laid down in the new Testament, as well as in our late revelations."[3] One early member explained that Page had "found a smooth stone, upon which there appeared to be a writing, which when transcribed upon paper, disappeared from the stone, and another impression appeared in its place. This when copied, vanished as the former had done, and so it continued alternately appearing and disappearing; in the meanwhile, he continued to write, until he had written over considerable paper. It . . . was received as an authentic document by most of the Mormonites, till [Joseph] Smith . . . discovered it to be a Satanic fraud."[4] According to Newel Knight, an elder of the Church, Page "had quite a roll of papers full of these revelations, and many in the church were led astray by them. Even Oliver Cowdery and the Whitmer family had given heed to them."[5]

# CONCLUSION

This whole matter of these revelations and Joseph Smith's sole authority as the prophet was the topic of a conference of the Church held in late September 1830. Encountering widespread support for Page's revelations in the days before the conference, Joseph thought it "best to enquire of the Lord concerning so important a matter," and he dictated a revelation specifically directing that "no one shall be appointed to Receive commandments & Revelations in the Church, excepting my Servant Joseph." It also refuted Page's revelations and told Cowdery to "take thy Brother Hyram Between him & thee alone & tell him that those things which he hath written from that Stone are not of me & that Satan deceiveth him for Behold those things have not been appointed unto him Neither shall any thing be appointed unto any of this Church contrary to the Church Articles & Covenants for all things must be done in order & by Common consent in the Church." Joseph never accused Page of intentionally writing false revelations in an attempt to pass them off as divine; rather, Page had received his revelations from a supernatural power producing words on his seer stone, a power that the revelation denounced as satanic. Directly addressing Cowdery's continued resistance to Joseph's leadership, the revelation declared, "Thou shalt not command him which is at thy head & at the head of the Church for I have given him the keys of the mysteries of the Revelations which are sealed until I shall appoint unto him another in his stead."[6]

At the conference meeting that followed, the membership of the Church reaffirmed Joseph's leadership, and he was "appointed by the voice of the Conference to receive and write Revelations & Commandments for this Church." Newel Knight remembered that "after considerable investigation and discussion, brother Page and all the church present renounced the stone, and the revelations connected with it, much to our joy and satisfaction."[7] By September 1830, the membership of the new Church reaffirmed that Joseph Smith was the man authorized to receive revelations for it. In dozens of subsequent revelations over the next decade, Joseph delivered the word of the Lord to members of the Church. Those revelations unfolded the doctrine of Christ to the believers, rebuked the wicked and the unrighteous, and comforted the downtrodden.

Joseph's prophetic calling was demonstrated not only in the revelations he received throughout the rest of his life but also in his revision or translation of the Bible, the revealed text of the Book of Moses, and the Book of Abraham, and the countless discourses and sermons he delivered to the men and women of the Church. Even those who joined the Church years after Joseph had translated the Book of Mormon and received his earliest revelations recognized him as God's chosen seer. In early 1842, Wilford Woodruff marveled in his journal at the power and calling of the Prophet Joseph Smith. He wrote, "Truly the Lord has raised up Joseph the Seer of the seed of Abraham out of the loins of ancient Joseph, & is now clothing him with mighty power & wisdom & knowledge. . . . The Lord is Blessing Joseph with Power to reveal the mysteries of the kingdom of God; to translate through the urim & Thummim Ancient records & Hyeroglyphics as old as Abraham or Adam, which causes our hearts to burn within us while we behold their glorious truths opened unto us." For faithful believers like Woodruff, Joseph's seership was real and extended far beyond the words of the translated Book of Mormon. Woodruff further related in the pages of his journal a pronouncement of Joseph Smith's calling that millions after him would embrace as they accepted the Book of Mormon, Joseph's revelations, and the church Joseph Smith founded:

> My Soul has been much edifyed of late from time to time in hearing Joseph the Seer convers about the mysteries of the Kingdom of God. Truly GOD is with him & is making him mighty in wisdom & knowledge & I am convinced for myself that none of the Prophets Seers or Revelators of the Earth have ever accomplished a greater work than will be accomplished in the Last days through the mercy of God By JOSEPH THE SEER.[8]

## Notes

1. Revelation, 6 April 1830 [D&C 21], in *JSP*, D1:129.
2. Joseph Smith, History, vol. A-1, 49–50.
3. Joseph Smith, History, vol. A-1, 52–53.
4. Ezra Booth, "Mormonism—Nos. VIII–IX," *Ohio Star*, 8 December 1831.
5. Newel Knight, History, 171–72.
6. Minutes, 26 September 1830, in *JSP*, D1:185–86. Original spelling has been preserved throughout the chapter.
7. Newell Knight, History, 171–72.
8. Kenney, ed., *Wilford Woodruff's Journal*, 2:155.

# Appendix

---❖---

# By the Gift and Power of Art

### Anthony Sweat
Anthony Sweat is an assistant professor of Church
history and doctrine at Brigham Young University.

*How far has Fine Art, in all or any ages of the world, been conducive to the religious life?*
*—John Ruskin,* Modern Painters, *1856* [1]

Being a Brigham Young University religion professor and a part-time professionally trained artist[2] is a bit like being a full-time police officer and a weekend race-car driver. At times the two labors are mutually reinforcing, and at others they are completely at odds. As a teacher of Latter-day Saint history and doctrine, it is extremely beneficial to have visual art represent and bring understanding to our history, and as an artist it is invaluable to have meaningful history to illustrate and provide context to messages in a piece of art. Many of the world's most iconic pieces of art, such as Michelangelo's *Pietà* or Jacque-Louis David's *Death of Marat*, are visual representations of historical events. However, true art and true history rarely, if ever, fully combine.[3] They are intertwined entities (history needs to be visually represented, and artists need meaningful history to create impactful images), but their connection more often creates difficult knots instead of well-tied bows that serve both art and history. These knots often result because the aims of history and the aims of art are not aligned,

❖ FROM DARKNESS UNTO LIGHT

often pulling in entirely different directions. History wants facts; art wants meaning. History wants to validate sources; art wants to evoke emotion. History is more substance; art is more style. History wants accuracy; art wants aesthetics. The two disciples often love, yet hate, one another as they strive to serve their different masters. This discord has never been more apparent to me than in my recent experience of painting the feature image of the translation of the Book of Mormon, *By the Gift and Power of God*, and illustrating the subsequent chapter headings for *From Darkness unto Light*. Using images of the translation of the Book of Mormon as the primary example, this appendix attempts to briefly illuminate why this discord between art and history exists and the roles that art and scholarly sources play in our understanding of historical events.

## The Language of Art

Often an inherent misunderstanding exists between artists and historians partly because the two disciplines speak different native languages. The language of history is facts and sources (and the interpretive merits of those facts and sources), and the language of art comprises symbolic representations in line, value, color, texture, form, space, shape, and so forth (and the interpretive merits of those symbols). The tension lies in that historians, scholars, and teachers often want paintings that are historically accurate because images often shape our perceptions of history as much as, or perhaps more than, many of the scholarly works about history. A great example of how works of art shape our historical memory would be to ask, "How did George Washington cross the Delaware?" What comes to mind? Probably Emanuel Leutze's famous *Washington Crossing the Delaware* (1851), with Washington standing heroically toward the front of a rowboat in daylight. However, historically the boat is probably wrong, the weather is off, the flag is anachronistic, and the pose is just downright unrealistic (try standing in a rowboat like that and it will probably capsize). Thus, when paintings carry apparent egregious historical errors, manipulations, or complete fabrications, there are some who bristle and wonder why the artist didn't paint it more accurately, wishing that painters and sculptors and the like wouldn't engage in revisionist history by distorting reality.[4]

# BY THE GIFT AND POWER OF ART

Washington Crossing the Delaware. *By Emanuel Leutze. Historically, this painting is most likely not a correct rendition of how Washington actually crossed the Delaware. The boat is probably wrong, the weather is off, the flag is anachronistic, and the pose is just downright unrealistic.*

However, artists often have little to no intent of communicating historical factuality when they produce a work. Artists want to communicate an idea, and they want to use whatever medium or principle and element of art that it takes to communicate that idea to their viewers. In doing research on this topic, I interviewed a handful of well-known and talented Latter-day Saint artists and asked them various questions regarding the responsibility of an artist to paint historical reality. Almost unanimously, they said the artist carries no responsibility to do so. When I asked this question of prominent LDS artist Walter Rane, who has painted many Church history–related paintings, he said:

> I don't think an artist has any responsibility to be historically accurate. If I am doing a painting I can do whatever I want. I can look at a sunset and paint it blue instead of red if I want to express something. I don't feel like as an artist I have a responsibility to be historically accurate unless someone has commissioned me. Art is self-expression. Art is communication. That's what art is. If I'm trying to express something that is important to me I'll do whatever I want. If it means

putting Christ in contemporary clothing or whatever, if it's important to the message I'm trying to make then I'll do it.[5]

Thus, for example, one of the greatest biblical painters and illustrators of all time, Rembrandt, set many of his biblical paintings in quaint seventeenth-century Dutch settings and dress perhaps because it communicated biblical ideas in ways familiar to his audience, but far from historical reality. I was once conversing with a group of Muslim religious educators from Saudi Arabia when they visited a local LDS seminary. One of them pointed to perhaps our most oft-printed LDS image—Del Parson's portrait of Christ in a red robe titled *The Lord Jesus Christ*—and he asked me who that person in the portrait was. "Jesus," I told them. They all broke out in spontaneous laughter. "You think that is what Jesus looks like? An American mountain man?" they said humorously. "What do you think he looks like?" I asked in return. "Us!" they said in unison. And perhaps they are right. But whether Jesus looks American or Swedish or Saudi Arabian or African American, all that matters to an artist is the message that comes through to the audience receiving that image.[6]

The Lord Jesus Christ. *By Del Parson.* © Intellectual Reserve, Inc. Whether Jesus looks American or Swedish or Saudi Arabian or African American, all that matters to an artist is the message that comes through to the audience receiving that image.

In an interview I conducted with Del Parson, he had a similar attitude of feeling over facts: "When I'm painting the Savior I am going for emotion more than anything else. When they [the viewers] see the painting, they see the Savior. I did the best I could [to create the painting] with what I had. I got some material and wrapped it around a model and painted it. The last thing I was worried about was whether the robe was at the right level at the neck. The whole thing I was worried about was 'Can they feel the Savior?'"[7] Artist J. Kirk

Richards, when speaking with me about painting the First Vision, said, "I've had people talk about what the 'correct' clothing is [of the First Vision] and so on and so forth. In reality, I don't care. I want it to feel what we feel when we think about the First Vision. And a lot of times historical details detract from getting that feeling across. So, very low on my list of considerations is historical detail. Sorry, historians. Don't hate me. . . . I'm usually trying to present the principle of a spiritual truth rather than a historical truth."[8]

Thus, because art and artists' first language is usually meaning and message, it is not necessary for an artist to be bilingual and able to fluently speak the language of history. Paradoxically, a piece of art can and often does communicate "truth" without being historically true, as countless images over the years have exemplified.[9] David Morgan, Duke professor of religion and art, says that the meaning of "truth" in art is therefore "ambivalent . . . whose meanings range from 'credible,' to 'accurate,' and 'correct' to 'faithful' and 'loyal.' In each case, *true* designates not the image as much as the proactive contribution of the 'eye of faith.'"[10]

However, while art and artists are often credited with making historical, and particularly religious, ideas come alive and plainer to understand,[11] an inherent problem enters when the language of religious art becomes translated into the language of history by its viewer. What we see becomes what we believe, and often, therefore, what we think we *know* about facts and details of history. And when we learn religious facts and history (from scholars or historians) that contradict what we think we know (through artistic renderings), a state of cognitive dissonance—and in the case of religious art, spiritual dissonance—can often be the result. The translation of the Book of Mormon is perhaps the most pertinent and pressing example of this problem today in the LDS mind.

## Artistic Renderings of the Book of Mormon Translation

In the fall semester of 2013 in one of my Doctrine and Covenants courses at Brigham Young University, we were studying about the translation of the Book of Mormon (D&C sections 6–9). I showed and discussed with my class many of the sources found in *From Darkness unto Light* about Joseph translating the Book of Mormon using the seer stone(s) placed in a hat to presumably eliminate light. We had a great discussion and learning experience together. Later that day I received the following e-mail from a student:

> I just wanted to thank you for today's lesson about Joseph Smith and the translation process. A little over a year ago, I started spending a lot of time with my friend [name omitted] who had recently left the Church and was pretty much convinced of atheism. He had researched some things about Joseph Smith and would tell me all about it. . . . When he would tell me about these things, my first instinct was to deny it and say, "No that can't be true; that's not what the illustrations of the translation look like and I've never been taught that at church.". . . This time in my life turned out to be a huge trial of my faith.[12]

Of particular importance to this article is her phrase "That can't be true; that's not what the illustrations of the translation look like." This student (and many others) had formed her historical knowledge of the translation through representations in religious art. Many of us do the same.[13] Regarding the translation of the Book of Mormon, this becomes particularly problematic because none of the currently used Church images of the translation of the Book of Mormon are consistent with the historical record.

Over the past year, my research assistant, Jordan Hadley, and I have documented and analyzed all of the paintings of the translation of the Book of Mormon that have ever been published in the Church's *Ensign* magazine since its inception in 1971 through March of 2014. This provided us with the last forty-three years of published representations of the translation of the Book of Mormon in one of the Church's official magazines. In all, the *Ensign* has depicted the translation of the Book of Mormon over fifty-five times the past forty-three years, repeatedly using seventeen different images. The most oft-used image is Del Parson's *Joseph Smith Translating the Book of Mormon* (also printed in the *Gospel Art Book* and *Preach My Gospel*), used a total of fourteen times since January of 1997.[14] All of the *Ensign* images are inconsistent with aspects of documented Church history of the translation process of the Book of Mormon. For example, in *each* of the seventeen *Ensign* images, Joseph Smith is shown looking into *open* plates (not closed or wrapped or

BY THE GIFT AND POWER OF ART

Joseph Smith Translating the Book of Mormon. *By Del Parson.* © *Intellectual Reserve, Inc. All of the* Ensign *images are inconsistent with aspects of documented Church history of the translation process of the Book of Mormon. Only one painting in the past forty-three years depicts Joseph Smith using the Urim and Thummim.*

absent plates). In eleven of the images, Joseph Smith has his finger on the open plates, usually in a studious pose, as though he is translating individual characters through intellectual interpretive effort, and not through revelatory means through the Urim and Thummim. Only one painting[15] in the past forty-three years depicts Joseph Smith using the Urim and

235

❖ FROM DARKNESS UNTO LIGHT

Thummim, an image that was used only twice (once in November of 1988, and once in February of 1989). Most tellingly, none of the images ever printed in the history of the *Ensign* (or recent Church videos, such as *Joseph Smith, Prophet of the Restoration*) depicts the translation process of the Book of Mormon as having taken place by placing a seer stone or the Nephite interpreters in a hat. Is there any wonder, then, that there is confusion in the minds and hearts of believing persons when they learn through repeated scholarly sources (including this work, and recently the "Book of Mormon Translation" article on lds.org's topic page[16] and *The Joseph Smith Papers*[17]) that the Book of Mormon was apparently translated through seer stones placed in a hat to obscure light and that the plates were often concealed under a cloth or not in the room and not by opening the plates with his finger on them and studying it out?

## Unpainted Translation Images

A logical question emerges upon analyzing the published images of the translation: Why don't the renderings of the translation reflect the seer-stone(s)-in-a-hat process if that is how it happened based upon multiple historical sources? I cannot answer that question, as only those who have commissioned, created, and published the past artistic images can give an informed response. The language of art is a factor, however. When I asked Walter Rane about creating an image of the translation with Joseph looking into a hat, he surprised me by telling me that the Church had actually talked to him a few times in the past about producing an image like that but that the projects fell by the wayside as other matters became more pressing. Note how Walter refers to the language of art as to why he never created the image:

> At least twice I have been approached by the Church to do that scene [Joseph translating using the hat]. I get into it. When I do the drawings I think, "This is going to look really strange to people." Culturally from our vantage point 200 years later it just looks odd. It probably won't communicate what the Church wants to communicate. Instead of a person being inspired to translate ancient records it will just be, "What's going on there?" It will divert people's attention. In both of those cases I remember being interested and intrigued when the commission was changed (often they [the Church] will just throw

out ideas that disappear, not deliberately) but I thought just maybe I should still do it [the image of Joseph translating using the hat]. But some things just don't work visually. It's true of a lot of stories in the scriptures. That's why we see some of the same things being done over and over and not others; some just don't work visually.[18]

In my interview with J. Kirk Richards, when I asked him how he would approach the translation of the Book of Mormon image, he said to me, "It would be hard for me to paint a painting with Joseph with his head in a hat. We would have no sense of the vision of what is happening inside."[19] Thus great and gifted artists like Walter Rane and J. Kirk Richards and others, who do know the history and have considered creating translation paintings with Joseph using the hat, have not created an image to reflect that history because it doesn't translate well in the language of art. Their point of view as artists is perfectly valid: If the image doesn't communicate the proper message, even if it is historically accurate, then the art doesn't work and has failed to speak properly in its native tongue.

As an artist, I can sympathize with Walter and Kirk. Many of my own sketches for this book project didn't look right or feel right in terms of the marvelous work and wonder of the Book of Mormon. I joked that some of my sketches with Joseph in the hat should have been called "The Sick of Joseph" because he looks like he is vomiting into the hat. When multiple people unfamiliar with our history saw my sketches, they asked me if Joseph was ill. It didn't communicate anything about inspiration, visions, revelations, miracles, translation, or the like—just stomach sickness. For past artists (or *Ensign* art directors) who may have known about the historical documents of the translation, it may simply be that choosing to depict Joseph with his finger in open plates with a pensive look was more visually appealing and communicative than the historical reality of what the translation may have looked like. It is easy for critics to assume a coordinate cover-up or historical rewrite when looking at the images,[20] but the unjuicy reality may have more to do with a preference for speaking artistic language that is "truer" in its communication, even if the depicted events contain historical error.

However, when my colleagues Michael MacKay and Gerrit Dirkmaat introduced me to their manuscript, notwithstanding the tension between the language of art and the language of history (and in spite of my artistic shortcomings when compared to more qualified artists), I felt impressed that it was time to try and provide a faithful, well-executed artistic image (as many of the existing images of translating using the hat are either deliberately pejorative or devoid of much artistic merit) of the translation of the Book of Mormon that better reflected historical reality.

## The Painting *By the Gift and Power of God*

Toeing a difficult line, my image of the translation attempts to be based upon factual reality yet also employ the principles and elements that create good art. I wanted the image to be edifying for a believer and sufficiently accurate for a scholar. In terms of historical accuracy, the image is set from actual interior photographs taken in the replica Whitmer home on location in Fayette, New York, where Joseph and Oliver finished the translation of the Book of Mormon. There is not a sheet between them, and the plates lie wrapped in a linen cloth, as Emma Smith explained they often lay. Both Joseph and Oliver were young at this time (twenty-three and twenty-two years old, respectively, in June of 1829), and I wanted their youth reflected accurately in the image. The clothing is time-period specific, but alas, I didn't research it in too much detail. (I am sure there is a clothing expert somewhere saying, "They didn't wear that type or color of two-toned vest!") The chair Joseph is sitting on is straight out of my front room. I did look at photos of top hats from the time period, and I painted the top hat white to try to be accurate to Martin Harris's description of the "old white hat" Joseph used, but it may not be exactly right (perhaps the brim is too wide or the bottom too deep; I don't know). The model for Oliver Cowdery was a BYU student who providentially passed by as I was shooting photographs and just "looked' like Oliver Cowdery to me (similar hairline and facial features to some of the historical Oliver Cowdery photos), but not exactly. I used my body to model for Joseph's (naturally, some inconsistencies there). Joseph's face was an amalgamation of profiles from the death mask and some of the features off the actor of the movie *Plates of Gold*, who has a great, youthful Joseph look to him. But, really, what did Joseph look like when he was twenty-four? Aside from stylized Sutcliffe Maudsley drawings done later in Joseph's life, his historical image is difficult to pin down and we don't know.[21]

BY THE GIFT AND POWER OF ART ❖

By the Gift and Power of God. *By Anthony Sweat.*

Although my attempt tried to include basic historical accuracy, most notably Joseph's face is *not* "buried" in the hat, as some translation sources claimed. Why? This is the question of my image I get most often from people who are familiar with the historical explanations of the translation. There are three reasons I chose not to bury his face in the hat: (1) Simply put, it didn't work visually for this composition. I wanted an unfamiliar viewer to immediately recognize that it was Joseph Smith, and having his face in the hat made this difficult for many of the people with whom I ran by preliminary sketches. Without knowing the historical background, they didn't know who or what this image depicted. (2) Returning to the language of art, I wanted to communicate the message of inspiration in this image. The human face carries a lot of subtle emotion, and by covering Joseph's face in the hat, it was difficult to portray things such as prayer, pondering, focus, reverence, and revelation. A hat obscured all of those ideas visually. By showing his face, I could more easily portray inspiration elements in Joseph—the studying it out in your mind and heart and the revelatory gift of a seer—yet still have the image be set in historical reality (as opposed to a figurative or abstracted composition). (3) Last, his face outside the hat still reflects historical reality. Logically, Joseph had to put his face into, and pull his face back from the hat. I imagine the moment depicted in my painting as Joseph getting ready to go into the hat to see—starting the process of revelation. He almost looks like he is getting ready to tip forward, and the anticipation of that moment makes the viewer want to put his face into the hat, visually measuring Joseph's face and looking into the opening of the brim and fitting the two together. With this composition, your mind can imagine what Joseph is *about* to do—the revelatory mode he is moving into and the gift he is starting to exercise at this moment. Having the face out of the hat helped to provide a more interactive and purposeful viewing experience.

Speaking of viewing experience, any well-composed piece of art uses artistic devices to move the eye of the viewer in certain orders, directions, and places. I tried to do the same in this image. When you initially look at the image, odds are that you will look first at the hat. I placed it centrally in the painting for that reason, and used the brightest white to pull the eye there. I wanted the viewer to look at the hat first, to deal with it, think about it, examine it, and process it. Next, the eye moves up to Joseph's face, seeing him move into a revelatory mode and connecting it with the opening in the hat. The viewer then might naturally move to the covered plates on the table, contrary to past visual representations of open plates and sheets. Next, the eye moves to Oliver Cowdery in the background as he sits and scribes "the sound of a voice dictated by the inspiration of heaven"

(Joseph Smith—History 1:71 footnote). Deliberately, the diagonal line of the floor and wall joint coming in from the bottom left of the image, and the vertical line made by where the walls meet, visually pass through Joseph and Oliver and lead the eye to the hat and the plates. Finally, after the viewer examines the hat, Joseph, the plates, and Oliver, I hope his or her eye looks outward into the simpleness of the space. Using artistic devices of light, I intentionally included the window with sun streaming through, illuminating the ground and room to suggest ideas such as light, truth, revelation, and inspiration upon Joseph.

While my painting is a faithful attempt to visually depict the translation of the Book of Mormon in a manner that is more consistent with the historical records than previous translation paintings, it also contains some elements that are purely aesthetic and speak the language of art. Although I tried to accommodate both, the inherent tension between artistic merit and historical reality tugged at me during the creation of this painting. A commentary on one detail in the painting, the lit lantern, is a fitting item and topic upon which to both illustrate and conclude this brief appendix on the language of art and the language of history. After examining the central aspects of the painting—the white hat, Joseph, the plates, and Oliver—ultimately I hope the viewer's eye looks up and sees the black lantern above Joseph and Oliver. Michael MacKay asked me, when he saw the painting in process, why the lantern was lit in the middle of the bright daylight sun in the room. Historical reality? No. Artistic device? Yes. And without explaining, you can already deduce what that illuminated lantern might suggest and symbolize. That's the joy of the language of art, even when it isn't entirely historically accurate.

## Notes

1. John Ruskin, *Modern Painters*, vol. 3 (London: 1898), 61.
2. Anthony Sweat received a bachelor of fine arts in painting and drawing from the University of Utah in 1999.
3. Jacque Louis David's *The Death of Marat* (1793) is a prime example of a historical painting that is not entirely historically accurate. The painting depicts the death of the radical French Revolution journalist Jean-Paul Marat as he was murdered in his bathtub by a French loyalist. However, it is full of historical inconsistencies,

artistic license, and idealizations intended to cause the viewer to sympathize for the martyr and the revolution. The painting was meant as a political piece of art, not a historical re-creation of the actual murder scene.

4. See Corey Kilgannon, "Crossing the Delaware, More Accurately," *New York Times*, December 23, 2011, for an article describing a recent, more historically accurate painting done to try and correct the historical inconsistencies in Leutze's famous painting.

5. Walter Rane, interview with the author, February 7, 2014.

6. A great example of the "feeling" of a Christ-centered painting being more important than the historical reality of it comes from popular LDS artist James Christensen. He tells of an experience when he sat down with LDS Church President Spencer W. Kimball about a painting of Jesus he was working on and asked President Kimball, "If you were going to hang a painting of the Savior in your office, what would you want that picture to look like?" Christensen relates that the prophet "took off his glasses and put his face about a foot away from mine and said, 'I love people; that's my gift. I truly love people. Can you see anything in my eyes that tells you that I love people? In that picture, I would like to see in the Savior's eyes that he truly loves people.'" See James C. Christensen, "That's Not *My* Jesus: An Artist's Personal Perspective on Images of Christ," *BYU Studies* 39, no. 3 (Fall 2000): 11–12.

7. Del Parson, interview with the author, February 7, 2014.

8. J. Kirk Richards, interview with the author, January 24, 2014.

9. One such image, for example, is John Trumbull's 1817 classic *Declaration of Independence*, showing forty-two of the fifty-six signers of the declaration in one room together, although the declaration was signed by different men over multiple days. They were never all together in the same room at the same time signing the document, as the image shows, a fact that caused John Adams to detest the painting. While historically inaccurate, it is an example of a painting being true to an idea, even though it distorts historical truth.

10. David Morgan, *The Sacred Gaze: Religious Visual Culture in Theory and Practice* (Oakland, CA: University of California Press, 2005), 77.

11. Artist and historian Graham Howes summarized this point by stating, "As early as 1005 a local synod at Arras [France] had already proclaimed that 'art teaches the unsettled what they cannot learn from books.' Two centuries later we find Bonaventure defining the visual . . . as an open scripture made visible through painting, for those who were uneducated and could not read." Graham Howes, *The Art of the Sacred* (New York: I. B. Tauris, 2007), 12.

12. Private e-mail with the author, September 18, 2013, quoted with permission.
13. Arnold Friberg's paintings are proof enough of how art becomes fact. Ask most any Mormon to close his or her eyes and imagine Abinadi, and he will be old, shirtless, and in extremely good shape for an aged man. King Noah? Overweight, on a throne. What pets does King Noah have? Leopards. Two of them at that. None of these details are supported in the Book of Mormon text (perhaps that Noah was a wine bibber, but how does that make him overweight?). Yet Friberg's masterful hand has made those images become near historical reality to those who grew up feasting on his Book of Mormon images.
14. *Ensign*, January 1997, 38; August 1997, 11; July 1999, 41; January 2001, 22; February 2001, 47; December 2001, 29; February 2002, 15; October 2004, 55; February 2005, 12; January 2006, 37; October 2006, 40; January 2008, 37; October 2011, 19; December 2012, 9.
15. Gary E. Smith, *Translation of the Book of Mormon*. Interestingly, Gary E. Smith painted a very similar image of the translation of the Book of Mormon that was published in the *Ensign* in December of 1983 on the inside front cover. In that image, Joseph Smith does not have the breastplate or the Urim and Thummim. Gary Smith seemingly redid the painting using essentially the same composition for his November 1988 painting, but in that painting Joseph Smith is wearing the breastplate and seems to be holding a pair of spectacles, or what could be the Urim and Thummim, in his right hand. See *Ensign*, November 1988, 46.
16. https://www.lds.org/topics/book-of-mormon-translation?lang=eng.
17. Michael Hubbard MacKay and others, eds. *The Joseph Smith Papers, Documents, Volume 1: July 1828–June 1831*, introduction, xxix–xxxii.
18. Walter Rane, personal interview with the author, February 7, 2014.
19. J. Kirk Richards, personal interview with the author, January 24, 2014.
20. Two critics wrote, after viewing a historically inaccurate image of the translation of the Book of Mormon in the *Ensign*, "What could be the reason for leaving these items out of a publicity painting except to distance the translation from the ocultic [sic] practices that really characterized the Book of Mormon translation!" See Bill McKeever and Eric Johnson, "A Seer Stone and a Hat—'Translating' the Book of Mormon," Mormonism Research Ministry, retrieved from http://www.mrm.org/translation.
21. See Ephraim Hatch, *Joseph Smith Portraits: A Search for the Prophet's Likeness* (Provo, UT: Religious Studies Center, 1998), 31–45.

# About the Authors

## Michael Hubbard MacKay

Michael Hubbard MacKay received an engineering degree from the US Air Force before receiving a double major in history and political science at Weber State University. He received an MA from the University of York in England, focusing on world history, culture, and the history of science and medicine. His PhD was also awarded by the University of York, where he studied cultural theory, the history of science and medicine, and print culture. He is an assistant professor of Church history and doctrine at Brigham Young University. He was the lead historian and editor on *Documents, Volume 1* of *The Joseph Smith Papers* and a document specialist for *Histories, Volume 1*.

## Gerrit J. Dirkmaat

Gerrit J. Dirkmaat received his PhD in history in 2010 from the University of Colorado. He has worked as a historian and writer for *The Joseph Smith Papers* since 2010 at the LDS Church History Department. He was a volume coeditor of *Documents, Volume 1* and the lead volume editor of *Documents, Volume 3*. He is now an assistant professor of Church history and doctrine at Brigham Young University.

# Acknowledgments

We appreciate the assistance of the Religious Studies Center's full-time publishing staff: Thomas A. Wayment, Devan Jensen, Brent R. Nordgren, and Joany O. Pinegar. We are also grateful for the editing work of Shanna Clayton, Rachel I. Gessel, Rebecca Hamson, Hadley Griggs, Rebekah Weaver, Alison Maeser, and Leah Welker as well as the typesetting and cover design by Madison Swapp. We would like to thank our wives for allowing us to burn the midnight oil to finish this book. We also had many readers, reviewers, and blind reviews that have helped tighten, trim, and focus the content of the book. Most important, we would like to thank Dr. Brent Rogers, who read every word and edited every page and provided insightful feedback, which greatly enhanced the content and structure of the book. Eric Smith also selflessly volunteered to read and edit several chapters, adding his expertise at every turn. We would like to offer special thanks and remembrance to Peter Dirkmaat, who read several drafts of the book and offered suggestions, all while battling the cancer that finally took him from us in February 2015. Others also offered financial support. The Religious Studies Center was indispensable in this regard, especially in hiring artists to produce images.

# Index

Aaronic Priesthood, 132–33
Adair, James, 45
Albany, New York, Marin Harris's trip to, 40–41
American Bible Society Library, 48–49
American Philosophical Society, 44–45, 46
Anthon, Charles, 49–52, 58n49, 70, 75n29, 91
Apostles, Twelve, 157n22
art
    discord between history and, 229–30
    language of, 230–33, 236–37
    learning history from, 233, 243n13
    renderings of Book of Mormon translation, 233–41
*Articles and Covenants of the Church of Christ*, 147, 225–26
*Articles of the Church of Christ*, 147
Atwater, Caleb, 45
baptism
    authority for, 130–34
    contention over, 225–26
    and organization of Church, 145–46
    teachings on, in Book of Mormon, 138–39n49
Barker, Edmund Henry, 50
Beaman, Alvah, 15, 24n72
black snake, Lucy Harris frightened by, 83
Blatchly, Cornelius, 202–5
Book of Commandments and Revelations, 192, 196n25
book of Lehi
    lost manuscript pages of, 93–97, 103n58, 105
    retranslation of, 124
Book of Mormon. *See also* gold plates; publication of Book of Mormon; translation of Book of Mormon
    acceptance of, xi–xii
    American copyright for, 164, 176–77n7, 211–12
    authenticity of, 110
    boycott on, 187–88, 215–16
    Canadian copyright for, 213–15, 221n50, 222n54, 223n56
    chronology of, 124

Book of Mormon (*continued*)
   criticism of, 202–6, 218n8, 219n25
   Harris family and coming forth of, 26–27
   ridiculed by Abner Cole, 189–90
   sale of, 195n18, 200, 213
   teachings on baptism in, 130–32, 134, 138–39n49
   use of, in proselyting efforts, 200–202
   Wilford Woodruff on, ix–x
box for storing gold plates, 7–8, 16, 32. *See also* stone box
boycott on Book of Mormon, 187–88, 215–16
Bradish, Luther, 40–42, 44, 47
breastplate
   Lucy Smith as witness of, 202n27
   role of, in translation of Book of Mormon, 88–89
   spectacles attached to, 63
British copyright law, 222n54
brother of Jared, 64
*By the Gift and Power of God* (Sweat), 238–41
Canadian copyright for Book of Mormon, 213–15, 221n50, 222n54, 223n56
Canandaigua Academy, 40
Carter, Jared, 216
Chamberlain, Solomon, 201–2
Champollion, Jean Francois, 44
Chase, Sally, 136n26
Chase, Willard, 7, 8, 11–12, 136n26
chest for storing gold plates, 7–8, 16, 32

child, Book of Mormon to be translated by, 74n28
Christensen, James, 242n6
Church of Jesus Christ of Latter-day Saints, The
   baptism and membership in, 134
   compared to Islam, 209–10
   contention and controversy in, 225–26
   conversions to, 216–17
   organization of, 145–49, 225
   proselyting efforts of, 200–202
Clark, John, 80, 91
Coe, Truman, 85–86
Cole, Abner, 189–90, 206–12, 220n44
copyright
   American, 164, 176–77n7, 211–12
   British, 222n54
   Canadian, 213–15, 221n50, 222n54
Cowdery, Oliver
   *Articles of the Church of Christ*, 147
   artistic renderings of, 238
   as Book of Commandments editor, 196n25
   as Book of Mormon scribe, 114, 119–20, 125–28, 137n28, 176n2
   and Canadian copyright of Book of Mormon, 214–15, 221n50
   and Cole's unauthorized printing of Book of Mormon, 206, 210–11
   contention with, over baptism, 225–26
   correspondence with Cornelius Blatchly, 202–3

Cowdery, Oliver (*continued*)
  correspondence with David Whitmer, 143
  facilitates printing of Book of Mormon, 199
  and false revelations of Hiram Page, 226–27
  interest of, in gold plates, 112–14
  mission to Native Americans, 209
  proselyting efforts of, 200–201, 217
  relationship with Smith family, 117n25
  revelation for, 120, 146–47
  and revelation regarding baptism, 130–34
  seeks financial support, 141–42
  and seer stone of Joseph Smith, 137n26
  translation ability of, 120–23
  and translation of Book of Mormon, 71
  visionary experiences of, 159n45
  as witness of gold plates and spectacles, 127, 149–51
Crane, George, 218n8
*Death of Marat, The* (David), 241–42n3
*Declaration of Independence* (Trumbull), 242n9
disciples, twelve, 146, 157n22, 210
divining rod, Oliver Cowdery's ability to use, 122
Doctrine and Covenants 19, misdating of, 190–93, 196n25
Dyke, Flanders, 80–81
Edwards, Abraham, 48
Egyptian, reformed, 42, 44, 54n12

*Ensign*, artistic renderings of Book of Mormon translation in, 234–36
First Vision, 1–3
Friberg, Arnold, 243n13
Gazelem, 68, 92, 125
Gilbert, John, 189
gold plates. *See also* Book of Mormon; translation of Book of Mormon
  and antagonism of Lucy Harris, 81–84, 107–9
  Charles Anthon and translation of, 49–52
  David Whitmer as witness of, 159n43
  David Whitmer hears about, 113
  description of, 154, 160–61n62, 64, 167–68, 177n16
  efforts to steal, 7–12, 20–21n29, 22n35, 24n72
  hiding and revealing, 14–16
  Isaac Hale as witness of, 33–34
  language of, 41–44, 54n12
  Lucy Harris as witness of, 28–29
  Martin Harris as witness of, 29–30, 92, 109–10
  and Martin Harris's visit to scholars, 39–40
  Mary Whitmer as witness of, 145
  Oliver Cowdery as witness of, 127
  Oliver Cowdery hears about, 112–14
  and origin of Native Americans, 45–47
  protection of, 21n33, 73n27
  proving authenticity of Book of Mormon with, 203–5
  retrieving, 5–7, 19n19, 20nn21–22, 46–47, 54–55n16

249

gold plates (*continued*)
  role of, in translation of Book of Mormon, 87–88, 123
  rumors surrounding, in Palmyra, 25–26
  Samuel Mitchill and translation of, 47–49
  taken from Joseph Smith, 96–97, 103–4n62
  taken to Harmony, Pennsylvania, 30–34
  taken to Smith home, 12–14
  transcription of characters on, 34–35, 79–81
  and visits of Moroni, 4
  witnesses and antagonists of, 108–9
  witnesses of, 13, 15, 149–55, 158n35
Grandin, E. B.
  and completion of publication, 215
  and confusion regarding payment for printing, 187–89
  and cost of printing Book of Mormon, 181–83
  Martin Harris mortgages property to, 185–87
  negotiation with, to publish Book of Mormon, 165–66, 174–75
  publication costs and profits of, 178–79n41
  sells mortgage of Martin Harris, 195n16
Grant, Rachel Ridgeway, 216
Hadley, Jonathan, xi, 166–68, 205
Hale, Isaac, 33–34, 74n28, 142
Hale, Reuben, 35, 85

Harmony, Pennsylvania, Joseph and Emma move to, 30–34
Harris, Lucy
  antagonism of, 80–84, 107–9
  files lawsuit against Joseph Smith, 107–8, 184
  and lost book of Lehi, 93, 95
  Lucy Mack Smith's depiction of, 25–26
  marital problems of, 102n47
  Martin signs property over to, 98nn14,15
  reaction of, to Book of Mormon, 27
  resistance of, to funding Book of Mormon, 183
  as witness of gold plates, 28–29
Harris, Martin
  and antagonism of Lucy Harris, 107–9
  and Canadian copyright of Book of Mormon, 213–14
  and coming forth of Book of Mormon, 26–28
  finds box in Hill Cumorah, 9
  hesitates in financing Book of Mormon, 183–85
  initiates visits to scholars, 39–40, 55n17
  knowledge of, regarding language of gold plates, 42–44
  and lost book of Lehi, 93–97
  marital problems of, 102n47
  meets with Charles Anthon, 49–52, 75n29
  meets with Samuel Mitchill, 47–49, 57n38
  and misdating of Doctrine and Covenants 19, 191–92, 193

# INDEX

Harris, Martin (*continued*)
   mortgages property to finance Book of Mormon, 185–87
   negotiation with E. B. Grandin, 165–66, 174–75, 182–83
   negotiation with Elihu Marshall, 171–74
   negotiation with Thurlow Weed, 168–71
   proselyting efforts of, 200–201
   and publication of Book of Mormon, 163–64
   reimbursement of, 213
   rift between Joseph Smith and, 105
   and sale of Book of Mormon, 215–16
   as scribe, 89–92, 101nn36,37,40, 110–11
   settles Joseph Smith's debts in Palmyra, 31
   signs property over to Lucy Harris, 98nn14,15
   and transcription of characters on gold plates, 80–81
   and translation of Book of Mormon, 61–62, 66–67, 69–70, 84
   travels to Albany, 40–41
   visionary experiences of, 159n45
   as witness of gold plates, 15, 29–30, 109–10, 149–51
Hicks, Elias, 172
history
   accuracy in artistic representations of, 230–33
   discord between art and, 229–30
   learning, from art, 233, 243n13

Howard, Luther, 215
Howe, Eber D., xi
Humboldt, Alexander von, 46
humility
   of gold plate witnesses, 150–51
   and translation of Book of Mormon, 129–30
Hyde, William, 200
Ingersoll, Peter, 194n7
Islam, LDS Church compared to, 209–10
Israel, Native Americans as descendants of lost tribes of, 45–46
Jared, brother of, 64
Jaredites, record of, 64–65
Jesus Christ
   artistic renderings of, 232, 242n6
   teaches importance of baptism, 132
John the Baptist, 132–33
John the Beloved, 122–23
Kimball, Spencer W., 242n6
Knight, Joseph Sr., 6, 106–7, 141–42, 151–55, 191–92, 196n25
Lawrence, Samuel T., 8–9, 11–12, 16, 22n36, 24n72
lawsuit, filed against Joseph Smith, 107–8, 110, 184, 193–94n7
Lehi, book of
   lost manuscript pages of, 93–97, 103n58, 105
   retranslation of, 124
Liahona, 67
*Lord Jesus Christ, The* (Parson), 232
lost tribes of Israel, Native Americans as descendants of, 45–46
Marsh, Thomas B., 200–201
Marshall, Elihu, 171–74

251

McIntyre, Alexander, 31
Mitchill, Samuel, 47–49,
   57nn38,39,43, 58n49
Mormon, 65
Moroni
   identified as treasure guardian, 84
   and retrieval of gold plates, 5–6,
      19n19, 42, 54–55n16
   and revelation regarding baptism,
      130
   visits of, 3–4, 19nn14,16, 65
mortgage, of Martin Harris, 185–87,
   195nn16,18
Moses, 122
Mosiah, translation device of, 67–68
Mulek, 56–57n36
Native American languages, scholars
   of, 45
Native Americans
   Book of Mormon's impact on, 209
   origins of, 45–47
New Jerusalem, 208

Page, Hiram
   and Canadian copyright of Book
      of Mormon, 214–15, 221n50
   false revelations of, 226–27
   as witness of gold plates, 151–55
Palmyra, New York
   Joseph and Emma leave, 30–34
   Joseph Smith leaves, during Book
      of Mormon printing, 199–200
   religious surge in, 1–2
   rumors surrounding gold plates in,
      25–26
Parson, Del, 232
Pluche, Noel Antoine, 48
Pratt, Parley P., 217

priesthood authority, for baptism,
   130–34
publication of Book of Mormon
   completion of, 215–16
   confusion regarding payment for,
      187–93
   conversions following completion
      of, 216–17
   copyright and, 164–65
   cost of, 165, 178–79n41, 181–82
   criticism following, 202–6
   delay in, 183–85
   financed through Martin Harris's
      mortgage, 185–87
   location of, 176n5
   negotiation with E. B. Grandin,
      165–66, 174–75
   negotiation with Elihu Marshall,
      171–74
   negotiation with Jonathan A.
      Hadley, 166–68
   negotiation with Thurlow Weed,
      168–71
   obstacles to, 163–64
   payment for, 183–84
   precautions taken in, 199
   rumors surrounding, 219n25
   unauthorized, of Abner Cole,
      206–12
Quakers, 172–73
Rafinesque, Samuel, 45
Rane, Walter, 231–32, 236–37
rebaptism, 134
reformed Egyptian, 42, 44, 54n12
Religious Society of Friends, 172–73
repentance
   following loss of manuscript pages,
      96–97, 103–4n62

repentance (*continued*)
  of Martin Harris, 151
  and translation of Book of
    Mormon, 129–30
revelation(s)
  concerning authenticity of Book of
    Mormon, 110
  contention over perceived error in,
    225–26
  for David Whitmer, 146
  false, of Hiram Page, 226–27
  for Joseph Knight Sr., 142
  for Martin Harris, 184–85
  for Oliver Cowdery, 120, 146–47
  Oliver Cowdery possesses spirit of,
    121–22
  received by Joseph Smith, 111–12
  received through Urim and
    Thummim, 96, 150
  regarding baptism, 130–34
  regarding Canadian copyright,
    214, 221n50, 223n56
  regarding translation of Book of
    Mormon, 105–6
Richards, J. Kirk, 232–33, 237
Rogers, Mr., 109, 115–16n15
Ruskin, John, 229
Saunders, Lorenzo, 9
seer stone(s). *See also* spectacles; Urim
    and Thummim
  of Hiram Page, 226–27
  Joseph Smith's use of, 67, 69,
    76n44, 77–78nn45,49
  Lucy Mack Smith as witness of,
    6–7
  Martin Harris replaces, 111
  origin and current location of,
    136–37n26

  origin of, 36n4
  prepared and delivered to Joseph
    Smith, 67–69
  translation of Book of Mormon
    through, xiv, 92, 116n22,
    124–29, 138n37, 233–37
  Wilford Woodruff as witness of, x
sheet, in translation process, 91,
    100–101nn34–36
Smith, Alvin, 8
Smith, Emma
  Joseph Smith apologizes to,
    129–30
  and lost book of Lehi, 93
  moves to Harmony, Pennsylvania,
    30–34
  and protection of gold plates,
    11–12
  and retrieval of gold plates, 6
  as scribe, 85–89, 106, 126,
    137n31
  seen through spectacles, 69
  and transcription of characters on
    gold plates, 35
  as witness of Book of Mormon
    translation, 99n23
  as witness of gold plates, 32
Smith, Ethan, 45–46
Smith, Hyrum
  and Cole's unauthorized printing
    of Book of Mormon, 206,
    210–11, 220n44
  facilitates printing of Book of
    Mormon, 199
  and financing printing of Book of
    Mormon, 188
  protects gold plates, 15
  as witness of gold plates, 151–55

Smith, Joseph Jr.
   antagonism against, 81–84, 107–9
   artistic renderings of, 234–41
   as author of Book of Mormon, 202–4
   and Cole's unauthorized printing of Book of Mormon, 211, 220n44
   contention with, over baptism, 225–26
   criticism of, 209–10
   and false revelations of Hiram Page, 226–27
   finds seer stone, 36n4
   First Vision of, 1–3
   knowledge of, regarding language of gold plates, 42–44
   lawsuit filed against, 107–8, 110, 184, 193–94n7
   and learning to use spectacles, 65–66
   and lost book of Lehi, 93–97
   meets Lucy Harris, 28
   meets Martin Harris, 29–30
   as money digger, 22n45
   moves to Harmony, Pennsylvania, 30–34
   negotiation with E. B. Grandin, 174–75, 182–83
   negotiation with Elihu Marshall, 171–74
   negotiation with Jonathan A. Hadley, 166–68
   negotiation with Thurlow Weed, 168–71
   and organization of Church, 145–49
   during printing of Book of Mormon, 199–200
   prophecy of, on Book of Mormon translation, 74n28
   prophetic calling of, 227–28
   protects gold plates, 7–12, 14–16, 20–21n29, 22n35, 73n27
   retrieves gold plates, 5–7, 12–14, 19n19, 20nn21–22, 21n33, 46–47
   returns to Book of Mormon translation, 105–6
   and revelation regarding baptism, 130–34
   revelations received by, 111–12
   seeks financial support, 141–42
   seeks translator for gold plates, 34
   seer stone prepared and delivered to, 67–69
   and translation process, xiii–xiv, 73n25, 124–26
   use of, of seer stone, 76n44, 77–78nn45,49
   and use of spectacles in Book of Mormon translation, 69–71
   visited by Moroni, 3–4, 19nn14,16
   and worthiness for Book of Mormon translation, 129–30
Smith, Joseph Sr.
   as alleged author of Book of Mormon, 110
   and Cole's unauthorized printing of Book of Mormon, 211–12
   and protection of gold plates, 8–9, 11
   and translation of Book of Mormon, 106
   as witness of gold plates, 151–55

## INDEX

Smith, Katherine, 15
Smith, Lucy Mack
   bias in account of, 25–26
   and confusion regarding payment for Book of Mormon printing, 187–88
   enlists Harrises' help in Book of Mormon translation, 27–28
   and protection of gold plates, 7–8
   as witness of breastplate, 202n27
   as witness of Urim and Thummim, 6–7
Smith, Samuel H.
   baptism of, 134
   as scribe, 106–7, 115n9
   as witness of gold plates, 151–55
Smith, William, 15, 55n17
snake, Lucy Harris frightened by, 83
spectacles. *See also* seer stone(s); Urim and Thummim
   history and description of, 62–65
   learning to use, 65–66
   Martin Harris as witness of, 92
   Oliver Cowdery as witness of, 127
   taken from Joseph Smith, 96–97, 103–4n62
   translation of Book of Mormon through, 67, 69–71, 85–87, 89–90, 99n23, 127–29, 138n37
Statute of Anne (1709), 222n54
stone box
   description of, 5, 20n23
   search for, following retrieval of plates, 9–10
Stowell, Josiah, 6, 13, 195n18, 200
temples, 209
Three Witnesses, 149–51, 158n35

translated beings, 122
translation, ability of, possessed by Oliver Cowdery, 120–23
translation of Book of Mormon
   and antagonism of Lucy Harris, 107–9
   artistic renderings of, 233–41, 243n15
   to be done by young child, 74n28
   chronology of, 124
   completion of, 158n38
   Emma Smith as scribe for, 85–89, 137n31
   financial support for, 106–7, 141–42
   history and description of spectacles, 62–65
   Joseph Smith returns to, 105–6
   and learning to use spectacles, 65–66
   and lost book of Lehi, 93–97, 103n58, 105
   Martin Harris as scribe for, 89–92, 110–11
   obstacles to, 79
   by Oliver Cowdery, 120–23
   Oliver Cowdery as scribe for, 114, 119–20, 126–27, 137n28, 176n2
   opposition to, 110
   preparation for, 61–62
   and proving authenticity through gold plates, 204–5
   revelation regarding, 105–6
   rumors surrounding, 219n25
   by scholars, 66–67
   and seer stone given to Joseph Smith, 67–69

255

translation of Book of Mormon (*continued*)
   sheet used in, 91, 100–101nn34-36
   supported by Whitmer family, 142–45
   thought and study in, 73n25
   through seer stones, 116n22, 124–26, 127–29, 138n37
   through spectacles, 69–71, 99n23, 127–29, 138n37
   use of gold plates in, 87–88, 123
   worthiness for, 129–30
*Translation of the Book of Mormon* (Smith), 243n15
treasure guardian lore, 83–84
treasure seeking, 3–4, 9–10, 22n45, 83–84
Tucker, Pomeroy, 40
Twelve Apostles, 157n22
twelve disciples, 146, 157n22, 210
Urim and Thummim. *See also* seer stone(s); spectacles
   ambiguous use of term, 129
   artists' depictions of, xiii–xiv
   history and description of, 62–65
   Lucy Mack Smith as witness of, 6–7
   and protection of gold plates, 14–15
   revelation received through, 150
   translation of Book of Mormon through, 62
   Wilford Woodruff as witness of, x
*Washington Crossing the Delaware* (Leutze), 230
Weed, Thurlow, 168–71
Whitmer, Christian, 151–55

Whitmer, David
   and Canadian copyright of Book of Mormon, 223n56
   and confusion regarding payment for Book of Mormon printing, 188–89
   interest of, in gold plates, 113
   revelation for, 146
   supports Book of Mormon translation, 142–45
   as witness of gold plates, 149–51, 159n43
Whitmer, Jacob, 151–55
Whitmer, John, 151–55
Whitmer, Mary, 145
Whitmer, Peter Jr., 151–55
Whitmer, Peter Sr., 151–55
Woodruff, Wilford
   and Book of Mormon, ix–x
   conversion of, x–xi
   and seer stone given to Joseph Smith, 68
Young, Brigham, 137n26
Young, Phineas, 137n26